Letters of Roger Ascham

Translated by Maurice Hatch and Alvin Vos

Edited by Alvin Vos

PETER LANG
New York • Bern • Frankfurt am Main • Paris

Library of Congress Cataloging-in-Publication Data

Ascham, Roger, 1515-1568.
    Letters of Roger Ascham / translated by Maurice
Hatch and Alvin Vos ; edited by Alvin Vos.
      p. cm.
    1. Ascham, Roger, 1515-1568 — Correspondence.
2. Authors, Latin (Medieval and modern) — Great
Britain — Correspondence. 3. Humanists — Great
Britain — Correspondence. 4. Scholars — Great
Britain — Correspondence. 5. Great Britain — Court and
courtiers — History — 16th century. I. Vos, Alvin.
II. Title.
PA8460.Z5A4   1989   942.05'2'092 — dc20 [B] 89-2614
ISBN 0-8204-0205-2   CIP

CIP-Titelaufnahme der Deutschen Bibliothek

Ascham, Roger:
Letters of Roger Ascham / transl. by Maurice
Hatch and Alvin Vos. Ed. by Alvin Vos. — New
York; Bern; Frankfurt am Main; Paris: Lang,
1989.
  ISBN 0-8204-0205-2

NE: Vos, Alvin [Hrsg.]; Ascham, Roger: [Samm-
lung]

Printed by Weihert-Druck GmbH, Darmstadt, West Germany

Letters of Roger Ascham

To Joyce,
Miriam and Sarah

Contents

viii

Acknowledgments

My interest in the life and work of Roger Ascham goes back some years, and led me first of all to a series of studies of his Ciceronian rhetoric and style. It was Jay Wilson, long a sharer of this interest in Ascham, who first suggested this edition to me. To him I am especially grateful, both for his enthusiasm for this project and for his confidence in me. Maurice Hatch was a pioneer in work on Ascham's letters; may he delight in his old age to see his work come to fruition in this way. To the dean of Ascham scholars, Lawrence V. Ryan, I am also particularly grateful. His book *Roger Ascham* remains invaluable, and in the course of my work I have to appreciate even more fully his judiciousness and thoroughness. It is also a pleasure to acknowledge his advice concerning the formation of this edition.

The Dean of Harpur College made the completion of this project possible by granting me the freedom of a Research Semester. The immense resources of the British Library have also been of great assistance to me. Finally, I am particularly grateful to my good friend and colleague Al Tricomi, whose generous support and specific advice have sustained me throughout.

His *Toxophilus* is accounted a good book for young men,
his *Schoolmaster* for old men,
his *Epistles* for all men.

Thomas Fuller, *Worthies of England*

Introduction

The letters of Roger Ascham are unrivalled as a record of midcentury Tudor humanism. Sir Richard ("merry") Morison may have been more witty, Sir Thomas Smith more indefatigable, and Bishop Stephen Gardiner more politic, to name but three other Tudor letter-writers of note, but no other set of surviving letters from this period in England so amply documents "the manner of wayfaring men," as Ascham aptly styles his own mode of life.[1] "The record Ascham has left us is unique" in its amplitude, explains James McConica, revealing a university humanist "both attracted and frightened" by the court.[2] His letters are not the dispatches of a secretary or administrator with political power and influence, but the rich chronicle of an educator shuttling between *otium* and *negotium*, forced by the realities of the patronage system to play the role of a courtier as well. Service to Queen and country was, in the words of Lord Burghley to a young gentleman, that "for which you were born, and to which, next God, you are most bound,"[3] and ordinarily such service brought with it wealth, power, and prestige. Ascham's letters, however, often witness as eloquently to his failures as to his successes, and tell the story of a Renaissance scholar-courtier forced to fashion himself out of his inability to be truly self-fashioning.

These letters are particularly valuable as a record of what was already recognized at the time as a Cambridge renaissance. Erasmus' sojourn at Queens' College from 1511 to 1513 may be taken as the first stirring of that renaissance, though his lectures on Greek grammar as the distinguished occupant of the Lady Margaret chair of divinity gen-

---

[1]*The Whole Works of Roger Ascham*, ed. Dr. J.A. Giles, 3 vols. in 4 (London, 1864-65), I, 342; cited hereafter in the text by volume and page number only.

[2]*English Humanists and Reformation Politics* (Oxford: Oxford UP, 1965) 213.

[3]Quoted in Richard Helgerson, *Self-Crowned Laureates: Spenser, Jonson, Milton, and the Literary System* (Berkeley: U of California P, 1983) 56-57.

erally failed to spark his auditors.[4] In the next generation of scholars, however, the "new learning," as they termed it then, according to Ascham (III, 234), kindled an enthusiasm for classical studies that would change the face of education in the schools. In the 1530s Cambridge clearly came to surpass Oxford, and entered upon what may be fairly termed "a new era." In the words of Thomas Fuller, "Ascham came to Cambridge just at the dawn of learning, and stayed therein till the bright day thereof."[5]

Although recent scholarship disallows the more romantic accounts of a humanistic "revolution" and makes us aware of how much intellectual energy continued to be expended in the scholastic analysis of texts and commentaries on Aristotle, the best students of Ascham's day, himself included, were so stimulated and excited by the new learning that they even crowded the private chambers of their favorite teachers to hear Homer and Xenophon, Sophocles and Euripides, Herodotus and Thucydides, Isocrates and Plato read in the original Greek (see Ascham's account in *Toxophilus*, II, 67). Intellectually Cambridge was perhaps the most stimulating place to be in all England. In Ascham and his contemporary humanists one hears new, ringing contempt for Duns Scotus and "all the rabble of barbarous questionists" (III, 237). A generation later the basic ideals of Erasmus were after all being realized.

Ascham proceeded MA and was elected fellow of St. John's College the year before the Royal Injunctions of 1535, injunctions that Mullinger has taken as "the line that in [Cambridge] university history divides the mediaeval from the modern age."[6] With the injunctions came the mandate from the King himself for a new thrust in both ecclesiastical affairs and learning. On June 22, 1535, the sober and saintly chancellor of the University, John Fisher, went to the scaffold, a martyr to the old faith. With his guidance and encouragement the peerless Lady Margaret, Countess of Richmond and mother of the

---

[4]See D.F.S. Thomson and H.C. Porter, *Erasmus and Cambridge* (Toronto: U of Toronto P, 1963).

[5]*The History of the Worthies of England*, ed. P.A. Nuttall (London, 1840) III, 430.

[6]James B. Mullinger, *The University of Cambridge*, 3 vols. (Cambridge, 1873-1911) I, 631.

Henry VII, had been a great benefactress of both learning and piety: they had founded in 1503 the Lady Margaret Professorship of Divinity, in 1505 both the Lady Margaret Preachership and Christ's College, and in 1511 St. John's College. The accession of Thomas Cromwell as chancellor in 1535 portended a clear, if not radical change of emphasis and direction in the arts and in religion at the University. In learning, as in the ecclesiastical matters, Henry VIII's new injunctions mandated a return to sources, and to their purest interpreters. No longer "should any lecture be read upon any of the doctors who had written upon the Master of the Sentences [Peter Lombard], but . . . all divinity lectures should be upon the Scriptures of the Old and New Testament, according to the true sense thereof, and not after the manner of Scotus." All students should be permitted to study the Scriptures in private. Neither should anyone any longer publicly read canon law; degrees in that law should no longer be conferred. In the arts students should read Aristotle himself, and his newer, more humanistic interpreters such as Rudolphus Agricola, Philip Melanchthon, and George of Trebizond, "and not the frivolous questions and obscure glosses of Scotus, Burleus, Anthony Trombet, Bricot, Bruliferius, etc." To implement this new educational policy, each hall and college of the University was to institute, at its own expense, "two daily public lectures, one of Greek the other of Latin."[7]

With such an emphasis Ascham agreed heartily. One of the hallmarks of his humanistic pedagogy was his lifelong campaign to illustrate the precepts of logic and rhetoric with the examples of "the best authors and oldest writers." "I never saw yet any commentary upon Aristotle's Logic, either in Greek or Latin, that ever I liked," he complains in *The Schoolmaster*, "because they be rather spent in declaring school-point rules, than in gathering fit examples for use and utterance. . . . For precepts in all authors, and namely in Aristotle, without applying unto them the imitation of examples, be hard, dry, and cold, and therefore barren, unfruitful, and unpleasant." "At my first coming thither," he continues, Cambridge "committed this fault," but "in my time" the leaders of the new humanism, close friends of Ascham all, reformed the aridities of the old scholarship: "these men of worthy memory, Mr. Redman, Mr. Cheke, Mr. Smith, Mr. Haddon, Mr.

---

[7]Mullinger I, 630.

Watson, put so to their helping hands, as that university, and all students there, as long as learning shall last, shall be bound unto them" (III, 231-32).

These worthy helpmeets of the humanistic learning were so linked by shared interests and united by a sense of intellectual mission that we ought to think of them as a distinct circle of brilliant young scholars, leaders of the general Cambridge renaissance. By about 1535 it is apparent that Ascham belongs to this circle, one Winthrop Hudson has called, for want of a better term, "the Cambridge connection":

A cluster of informal relationships of trust among persons who had been or were to be near the centers of power, quite distinct from a circle of courtiers or a faction and not quite a party, had come into existence. . . . Involved in the interlocking relationships were kinship, marriage ties, congeniality, and friendship--especially friendships dating back to impressionable university days when ties that bind most strongly so often are formed. A common enthusiasm for classical studies, Protestant doctrine, and a reformed pronunciation of Greek had drawn them together.[8]

The group had its center in St. John's College, acknowledged as the leading foundation within the University throughout the time of Ascham's residence. Three of Ascham's "men of worthy memory"-- John Redman, John Cheke, and Thomas Watson--were, with Ascham himself, intellectual leaders at St. John's, and they were joined by an unusually large number of talented students who would go on to distinction in the church, the university, or the service of the commonwealth. Indeed, Ascham boasts in *The Schoolmaster* that "in my time" St. John's "did breed up so many learned man . . . as can scarce be found now in some whole university: which, either for divinity, on the one side or other, or for civil service to their prince and country, have been, and are yet to this day, notable ornaments to this whole realm" (III, 142, 235). Not least of these "notable ornaments" was William Cecil, future chancellor of the University, who was ever wont to style St. John's his "old nurse."[9] Guided by Cecil's legendary discretion and sagacity, these enthusiastic young leaders of Cambridge hu-

---

[8]*The Cambridge Connection and the Elizabethan Settlement of 1559* (Durham: Duke UP, 1980) 35.

[9]James B. Mullinger, *St. John's College* (London, 1901) 57.

manism would during the early years of Elizabeth's reign form, in Wallace MacCaffrey's term, "the new establishment."[10]

In two talented young scholars, John Cheke and Thomas Smith, both Ascham's very good friends, the Cambridge circle found eager and enthusiastic leadership. Members of the society of St. John's and Queens' respectively, Cheke and Smith were during the late 1530s and early 1540s the "two worthy stars" of the University, bringing Plato, Aristotle, Demosthenes, and Cicero "to flourish as notable in Cambridge, as ever they did in Greece and in Italy" (III, 237). Later Gabriel Harvey would term them "the two eyes of this University, and the two hands of two monarchs."[11] Smith was the more brilliant intellect, but Cheke the more popular as teacher and leader. Indeed, in his day Cheke, whose influence on and closeness to Ascham clearly exceeded that of all others, was the cynosure of all Cambridge. "Cheke's effort and example," writes Ascham, "has lit and fed the flame of literary zeal, for without pay he has publicly lectured on all of Homer, all of Sophocles, and that twice, as well as on all of Euripides, and nearly all of Herodotus. He would have done the same for all the Greek poets, historians, orators, and philosophers," concludes Ascham, had he not been called away to court (Letter 2).

As Ascham's tributes to Smith and Cheke suggest, they spurred their Cambridge friends and students into a particular rage for Greek. Ascham's own enthusiasm is representative. In his view, Italian, English, French, Spanish, German, even Latin itself--"Cicero only excepted, and one or two more in Latin"--"be all patched clouts and rags, in comparison of [the] fair woven broad-cloths [of Greek]; and truly, if there be any good in them, it is either learned, borrowed, or stolen from some of those worthy wits of Athens" (III, 134). Along with Smith's and Cheke's decidedly Protestant views, their enthusiasm for Greek was one of the special bonds uniting members of this "Cambridge connection," molding them into an "Athenian tribe."[12]

[10]*The Shaping of the Elizabethan Regime* (Princeton: Princeton UP, 1968) 42. See also Hudson 29-35.

[11]*Ciceronianus*, ed. Harold S. Wilson, trans. Clarence A. Forbes, University of Nebraska Studies in the Humanities 4 (Lincoln: U of Nebraska P, 1945) 81.

[12]The phrase is from the antiquarian John Leland, quoted in Hudson 53.

The intellectual leadership of Smith and Cheke was especially apparent in their campaign for a reformed pronunciation of Greek.[13] Around 1535, when both were scarcely twenty years of age, with minds unusually active and acquisitive, they gradually began to introduce and elaborate their reform in public lectures. In time Ascham, himself publicly reading Isocrates, joined the cause, as did John Ponet, Smith's student at Queens' and the future author of the *Treatise of Politike Power*, and John Redman, their respected senior instructor, educated at Oxford and Paris, and an acknowledged authority in divinity. When in 1542 Stephen Gardiner, a conservative bishop some thirty years their elder and the chancellor of the University, unexpectedly stepped in to forbid the new pronunciation, on pain of grievous and harsh penalties, the issue soon transcended scholarship and became a political and ideological rallying point as well. When the reactionary Gardiner could not be dissuaded (his opposition was still unabated in 1554), the "Athenian tribe" was knitted into even closer relationship by the conviction of the rightness of their humanistic cause and by their ardor to reform learning.

Ascham's relationship to Smith and particularly to Cheke, the "chief glory" of the Athenian tribe,[14] merits close attention, for it not only places him in his rightful context, but also affords us some measure of his stature and his character.[15] In some ways Ascham ranks with them, and his reputation today justly surpasses theirs. Yet in other ways their paths diverged, and Ascham's failure to rise at the time to the same heights and to receive the same honors and preferments supplies, as it were, the frame for these letters, revealing an often poignant portrait of a "wayfaring man."

---

[13]For a brief account of the history of this movement, see Mullinger, *The University of Cambridge* II, 54-63; and Hudson 43-46. Essentially the reform began with Erasmus, who first propounded an improved method of pronouncing Greek in 1528: see Maurice Pope's introduction to Erasmus' *De recta pronuntiatione* in *Collected Works of Erasmus* 26, Literary and Educational Writings 4, ed. J.K. Sowards (Toronto: U of Toronto P, 1985) 352-58.

[14]Hudson 53, citing Leland.

[15]I am indebted to Hudson for the following comparative discussion; but see also Mary Dewar, *Sir Thomas Smith: A Tudor Intellectual in Office* (London: Athlone-U of London, 1964), and John Strype, *The Life of the Learned Sir John Cheke* (Oxford, 1821).

Cheke, Smith, and Ascham were all long-time residents of the University, and clearly found Cambridge an extremely congenial home. Entering the University at early age by today's standards, they found in their colleges a true alma mater, Ascham himself declaring that his election as fellow was "*dies natalis* to me," and "the whole foundation of the poor learning I have, and of all the furtherance that hitherto elsewhere I have obtained" (III, 235). Both Cheke and Smith entered Cambridge at age 12 (in 1526), Ascham four years later at age 14 or 15 (he was thus one or two years their junior). All three advanced regularly. Smith and Cheke proceeded BA in 1530; they were elected fellows of their colleges in the same year, and graduated MA in 1533. Ascham's progress was similar; he received his BA in 1534, with election to a fellowship in the same year; he took his MA in 1537. In 1538 Smith was honored with the position of University Orator; in 1542 Cheke succeeded him. Four years later the position went to Ascham. When Henry VIII in 1540 established five new Regius Professorships at Cambridge, Cheke was appointed to the chair of Greek, Smith to that of Civil Law. Although he received no chair, Ascham did lecture publicly during the late 1530s, and in 1540 took up a position as reader in Greek at St. John's College.

Within a few years, moreover, each found a way to court. All were essentially scholar-educators called into the service of the monarch. After eighteen years at the University, Cheke, as the foremost educator in the land, was called (in 1544) to tutor Prince Edward as part of Queen Catherine Parr's reorganization of the royal nursery. Four years later, also after eighteen years, Ascham too joined the royal nursery as tutor to Princess Elizabeth. Some twenty years after his arrival at Cambridge, Smith too found his way to court when in 1547 he became Protector Somerset's personal secretary. For all three it was a story of a long and fond residence at a place congenial to scholarship and learning, then migration to a court rich with opportunities for service and with potentials for preferment.

These apparent similarities conceal, however, the differences in temperament, attitude, and interest which soon surface at court. While Cheke and Smith were soon to be in a position to further the career of others in the humanistic community, Ascham soon found himself dependent on the favor of those who had been friends and colleagues. In this divergence one begins to see more deeply into Ascham's stature and character. It is a divergence that leaves a lasting impact on his correspondence.

For Smith and Cheke the volatile world of court brought rapid advancement, at least initially. By 1548 Smith had become a Principal Secretary and member of the Privy Council. In 1549 he was knighted. His story is complicated, to be sure, by the "fall" he suffered along with the Protector, but after several embassies in Elizabeth's reign he again regained his position as Principal Secretary. Although he was not, according to his biographer Mary Dewar, a particularly effective or able administrator, he was, as Ascham says in *The Schoolmaster*, one of "my dear friends with full purses" (III, 84).

Similarly Cheke rose quickly from his position as royal tutor, regularly receiving new offices, lands, and financial rewards from the King. In 1551 he was knighted; two years later he became a Privy Councillor, and a Principal Secretary. Like Smith he became entangled in the snares of politics and the quicksands of religion, but his troubles too sprang in large part from his rapid success and his positions of prominence. The best measure of his stature is, ironically, his fate in the Marian revolution. Under Edward he became so prominent that during the Marian period he was obliged to seek safety in exile, and even then he was singled out as the object of an apparent plot by which he was lured to Brussels, kidnapped, bound, shipped to England, and forced to recant.

By contrast Ascham, though no less of an educator, never did advance into the treacherous waters of high affairs of state. Despite Cheke's presence at court, Ascham's pupil William Grindal, not Ascham himself, was chosen as the first tutor for Princess Elizabeth. Only after Grindal's sudden death of the plague was Ascham chosen. From the outset, moreover, he was full of ambivalence, hesitant, as he wrote to Cheke, to "give myself to this new way of life" (Letter 29). The call to court reactivated apprehensions already expressed years earlier when he refused Lord Mountjoy's attractive offer of a position as tutor to his son: "Were I to sail from so calm a harbor [i.e., Cambridge University] into the tempest of the seas, I could not long escape from the sharp bite of sorrow" (Letter 6). Such fears were indeed prophetic, for after only two years, even before he had advanced beyond his position as tutor, he suddenly found himself a victim, to use his own words, of a "disastrous shipwreck" in a violent "court tempest" (Letter 31).

The precise reasons for this embarrassing separation from his position remain obscure. To Cheke Ascham asserts his innocence, blaming "court violence and injustice" (Letter 31). Perhaps he was somehow the victim of the scandal involving Thomas Seymour's indiscretions with Princess Elizabeth. Ascham's biographer suggests, however, that it was more likely "a personal rather than a state matter."[16] In any case, at the outset of the year 1550 Ascham unexpectedly found himself in an "abject and humble condition," totally dependent on others' decisions about his career and his future.

In a further irony, however, the effect of this "shipwreck" was to break down Ascham's earlier resistance to a voyage into service and clientage. He was forced to accomplish that which had stirred in him "every fear of danger and a sense of dread": "to change the nature of his life and somehow to weave himself over again" (Letter 6). For Cheke, who was unable to place himself under the patronage or protection of some official more powerful than himself, such a re-weaving was impossible. His prominence within Edwardian Protestantism essentially cost him his life: less than a year after he was caught in Mary's brutal trap, he was dead. Although Smith did manage under Elizabeth to recoup some positions of responsibility, he too was undone by his attachment to a man of ambition; he was pushed aside, his career in limbo.

In the boisterous turns of midcentury politics, patronage, and power, therefore, it was precisely Ascham's status as a minor figure that afforded him the opportunity to make a new way, to forge a new life. In 1550, ingloriously separated from his post as royal tutor, he learned how to turn absence from the court, which to the ambitious courtier was ruinous, to his profit. For the rest of his life he would have no choice but to follow "the manner of wayfaring men."

At this and other points of transition Ascham invariably talked bravely of charting a course of life, of embarking on "some worthy manner of living," yet always the realities were, as he wrote to Cecil, "the sudden frowning of fortune" or "the former fawning of the same" (I, 342-43). For these necessities he learned an eloquent language of service. Particularly to Cecil, his absolutely reliable friend and patron,

---

[16]Lawrence V. Ryan, *Roger Ascham* (Stanford: Stanford UP; London: Oxford UP, 1963) 112-13.

Ascham's professions of loyalty and dependency were unreserved and exquisitely wrought: "Most glad I am that it pleaseth you I may be yours; and as sure I am I shall cease to be mine own, when I shall leave to labor to be otherwise," he wrote to Cecil in July 1552 as he was anticipating the completion of his service to the Ambassador to the Imperial Court (I, 328). In fact, late 1552 and early 1553 brought forth a whole series of full-throated professions that he was "so bound unto [Cecil], as I shall rather forget myself, and wish God also to forget me, than not labour with all diligence and service to apply myself wholly to your will and purpose" (I, 349-50). In these difficult times of uncertainty and transition the line between the language of service and the language of accommodation was thoroughly blurred.

Nearly all of these professions simultaneously express a strong personal desire to "creep home to Cambridge" (I, 343). Experience at home and abroad, Ascham asserted, had taught him that "there is no such quietness in England, nor pleasure in strange countries, as even in St. John's college, to keep company with the Bible, Plato, Aristotle, Demosthenes, and Tully" (I, 350). Nevertheless, he made it very clear that he understood the regular path to preferment in Tudor England: "I will gladly follow the choice of your wisdom, whatsoever you shall think fit to bestow upon me"; he was "much boldened," he said, "because that kind of learning which sometime was most pleasant for my study in Cambridge, shall now be most necessary for my duty in the court" (I, 342-43).

We scarcely need to be surprised, therefore, to see Ascham quickly adjusting his goals upon the accession of Queen Mary in mid 1553 and transferring his loyalty and dependence to new patrons. Especially in view of the turmoil surrounding "the nine-days' queen," the unfortunate Lady Jane Grey, of whom Ascham was very fond (see Letter 41, for example, and the memorable passage in *The Schoolmaster*, III, 118-19), he was well served by the accidents of timing and distance (he did not return to England until around September 1, 1553), and his years of the wayfaring life had sharpened his ability to work out accommodations with the new regime. The "gentleness" of William Petre, for example, now restored to a position of influence, made Ascham bold, he said, "to venture to live in the court, which life otherwise I should much fear." "Under the hope of your goodness," he concluded, "I shape myself to be a courtier" (I, 393, 396).

Most importantly, Ascham's art of wayfaring taught him the language to use with the old antagonist of the "Cambridge connection," Stephen Gardiner, the conservative Catholic Bishop of Winchester and the Lord Chancellor of the new monarch. The former expressions of unending loyalty to Cecil were simply redirected, with no loss of elegance or force. "You are counted of all men the best friend to every man that this country hath," Ascham wrote to Gardiner in mid 1554; "five sureties I offer unto your lordship for the payment of my debt unto you; that is, my will, word, work, heart, and hand, evermore to wait upon your honour and state as long as I shall live" (I, 418). "The greatest staves were never the surest to stand in this realm," he continued, ironically rationalizing the course of both Gardiner's career and his own; "whether this fault hath been the unjust government of such as did rule, or the unruly nature of those that should obey, I cannot tell; but this I am sure, these many years England would never presently, or could not very long bear a subject which was accounted in men's talk either wisest in counsel or greatest in power" (I, 418-19). Having conjured up this scene of instability and injustice, Ascham readily found sufficient grounds to pledge to Gardiner his total devotion. "No time since I was born so sticketh in my memory as that when I, unfriended and unknown, came first to your lordship with my Book of Shooting, and what since that time you have done for me . . . I never shall forget" (I, 418). In one striking instance, surprising to twentieth-century sensibilities, but altogether consistent with the rules of the discourse of Tudor patronage and clientage, Ascham simply reuses whole passages from a letter to Cecil in a similar letter to Gardiner (see Letter 53).

Two foci, then, control the ellipse of Ascham's letters: scholarly ideals and political realities. Although he retained to his dying day the temperament of an educator, he was obliged, during the last 20 years or so of his life, also to pursue the life of a courtier. Those in power often treated him as an equal, yet he remained on the fringe of influence. Dependent on his patrons, his life was a continual series of petitions for preferment. At the same time, however, he was also a friend to these patrons, and not merely a client clutching at preferment. Though he never became more than Queen Elizabeth's personal Latin secretary, penning some of her correspondence, he was privileged to read Greek and Latin with her each day.

In many ways, then, Ascham was *in* the court, but not really *of* it. He belonged to that interlocking group of friends who made their way from Cambridge to court, yet he never succeeded in making the court a base for establishing himself in land or wealth. Indeed, the story of the last ten years of his life, as Ryan summarizes it, "is largely one of . . . financial predicaments."[17] Unlike such friends as Cheke, Haddon, and Smith, all honored as men of great learning or eloquence, but who also at one point or another occupied positions of power and status in the government, Ascham remained above all the scholar and the educator. In his exhortation that Ascham write a book on education, Sir Richard Sackville cleverly turns the ambiguity within Ascham's career into praise: "God did so bless you, to make you the scholar of the best master [i.e., Cheke], and also the schoolmaster of the best scholar [i.e., Queen Elizabeth], that ever were in our time" (III, 83). More often than not, however, the dualities of these roles were painful and difficult to manage, forcing Ascham to negotiate ways to live as both courtier and scholar, client and friend, leader and follower.

One of the ironies of this collection of letters, then, is that they are the richer because of Ascham's failure to proceed as quickly and to rise as high as his more successful friends. The letters of most value and interest are not those of a man in a position of authority, but those of an avid lover of learning attempting to maintain a way of life in the face of only modest and unplanned success. The letters written during his last 12-14 years, for example, a period of unbroken service as Latin secretary to two successive queens, decline in both number and interest. Were it not for Ascham's earlier periods of intense struggle to accommodate academic ideals to political realities, periods when he developed great skill in promoting himself as the loyal servant of others, obedient to their determinations and their assessments of his usefulness to them, his letters would today remain scattered, unpublished, and few--the fate, ironically, of the letters of Cheke, Smith, and virtually all of the other more illustrious members of the Cambridge circle. If, as Frank Whigham writes in his brilliant study of the dynamics of courtly rhetoric, "the motor of life at court was the pursuit of power and privilege," we must conclude that As-

---

[17]*Roger Ascham* 228.

cham did not have sufficient power to keep up with the leaders at the turns. However, the strain to reach those goals certainly enriched his rhetoric: "life at the margins of power and privilege gave full scope to [the] various modes of rhetorical behavior, and so constitutes an unusually rich object for the study of shifting notions of social being."[18]

More specifically, Ascham's dependency on the patronage of Cecil was to become the key element in the circumstances that make him known today. To Cecil, for instance, the posthumous *The School-master* was dedicated, with a preface by Ascham's widow. The letters constitute an even more important witness to the network of obligations and favors that filled Ascham's life. Their very publication was itself part of the strategy of clientage. Through the agency of Cecil, Ascham's son Giles won the support of the Queen as a student at Westminster school. There Giles recruited his schoolmaster, Edward Grant, to publish these letters. After consulting with Cecil, Grant dedicated them to the Queen as a memorial to her affection for Ascham.[19]

Ironically, then, much of the work by which Ascham's reputation has been secured today--these letters, *The Schoolmaster*, *The Report of Germany*, and Ascham's theological writings: posthumous publications all--appeared in their time as witnesses to his indebtedness to his benefactors. They were all part of the strategies by which Ascham's widow and son continued to draw upon the favor once shown to their husband and father.

Following the manner of wayfaring men, Ascham was obliged to adjust from an older, aristocratic system of patronage to a newer, royal one.[20] Early on he was introduced to the former when his father placed him in the household of Humphrey Wingfield, a Suffolk lawyer and royal commissioner, future knight and speaker of the House of

---

[18]*Ambition and Privilege: The Social Tropes of Elizabethan Courtesy Theory* (Berkeley: U of California P, 1984) 20.

[19]See Grant's account of these matters in the preface to his sixteenth-century editions of Ascham's letters; reprinted conveniently in Giles III, 294-300.

[20]Increasingly during the Tudor era, as Wallace MacCaffrey has argued, "the person of the monarch became the focus of a single, national political world with centripetal force powerful enough to draw into its orbit all rivalries, personal, local, or dynastic": "Place and Patronage in Elizabethan Politics," in *Elizabethan Government and Society*, ed. S.T. Bindoff, J. Hurstfield, and C.H. Williams (London: Athlone-U of London, 1961) 95.

Commons. As a member of one of the leading families of East An-
glia, Wingfield looked after the education of his own and other men's
children, and Ascham had his first experience of the system in which
leading families played the major role within the realm through their
support of the church, education, and perhaps the king's interests in
their area.[21]

During his university days Ascham's first overtures for support
also reflect his appreciation for the old system, with its focus on the
nobility and the learned clergy, for he applied first to two conservative
prelates, Robert Holgate, Bishop of Llandaff, noted for his wealth, and
Edward Lee, Archbishop of York (see Letters 1, 4). Both were linked
to Ascham's native Yorkshire. Lee in particular was hardly the one to
whom one would expect an enthusiastic young Protestant humanist to
apply, for he had attacked Erasmus and opposed Tyndale, the translator of the Bible, but apparently the older style of patronage was the
one Ascham understood best at the time. Indeed, years later it was
the kind of system he continued to understand. In Mary's reign,
when churchman were restored to leading roles, he quickly turned to
Bishop Gardiner and Cardinal Pole.

But Ascham also learned the new system that evolved with the
Tudor centralization of power in the monarchy, when the court increasingly became the focus of men's ambitions and hopes, and when
"new men," talented university-educated laymen often strongly influenced by the revolution in learning, regularly became the central figures in government. Ascham's first and in some ways most signal
success came late in the reign of Henry VIII with *Toxophilus* (1545),
which he dedicated to the King. For this supremely "safe" book, wisely avoiding any of the controversies involving politics or religion, Ascham was received by Henry himself at Greenwich, and rewarded
with a handsome royal pension of £10 a year.

Ascham's management of the shifts in the systems of patronage
formed a significant part of his remarkable ability to accommodate
himself to both Marian and Elizabethan regimes, and in fact to secure
some preferment or office in the reigns of Henry VIII and each of his
three radically different royal offspring. There have been those, of

---

[21]See Ascham's own account in *Toxophilus* of being brought up by Wingfield
"in the book and the bow" (II, 135).

course, who see this durability not as Ascham's accomplishment, but as a measure of his weakness of character. Perhaps this kind of resilience or "flexibility" does constitute one reason why he thrived more in reading Greek and Latin with the Queen after dinner in her privy chamber (see III, 81) than in parlaying for power or wealth within the halls and council chambers of court. However, just as we must reject such anachronistic concepts as "public office" and "public trust" as inappropriate to an understanding of the workings and values of Renaissance patronage, so we should, in reading Ascham's letters, better understand the course of his career if we recall that strong stances and ideological resoluteness were more incumbent on the patron than on the client, on the leading centers of influence rather than on the seekers after preferment, whose role or status did not carry the same obligations or expectations. The letters show Ascham so dependent on the patronage systems and so sensitive to their various requirements and modes of operation that concerns which were paramount to others, better positioned or more interconnected with ideological and religious movements, were to him subordinate.

Recent studies are laying to rest the old notions of a corrupt, flattery-ridden institution, and are enabling us to see the Tudor patronage system as a functional, comprehensive way of managing government, most effective when firmly controlled by the monarchs and their officers.[22] It was a complex social and political system that encompassed financial and political matters even more than it did aesthetic and intellectual enterprises. In Ascham's letters we see some of the mechanisms of that system, and its effect on one who was involved in it with limited and modest success.

Such courtiers as Ralegh, Sidney, Wyatt, and Donne turned their experiences within the patronage system into an occasion for poetry. Petrarchan poets in particular exploited the language of love to explore the economic and social dimensions of the client-patron relationship. But Ascham, with his distress over England's "rude beggarly rhyming"

---

[22]Especially worthy of note here, in addition to MacCaffery's "Place and Patronage in Elizabethan Politics," Whigham's *Ambition and Privilege*, and chapter 3, "Patterns of Patronage," in McConica's *English Humanists and Reformation Politics*, all mentioned above, are *Patronage in the Renaissance*, ed. Guy Fitch Lytle and Stephen Orgel (Princeton: Princeton UP, 1981), and Eleanor Rosenberg, *Leicester, Patron of Letters* (New York: Columbia UP, 1955), particularly chapter 1, "The Nature of Elizabethan Literary Patronage."

(III, 249-55), was no poet, and the sophisticated literary language of in-
direction, in which the poet's personal and cultural roles are encoded
in the romantic fictions of love and service, contrasts with his straight-
forward expression of loyalty and need.   Though his letters certainly
do not lack art, his mode was that of the serious, midcentury humanist.   Eschewing courtly and Petrarchan conventions, his style is learned
and sophisticated in its use of Classical and Biblical expressions of
honor and duty.[23]   Much more congenial to Ascham than the poets'
fancies was the sober manner of the redoubtable William Cecil.   According to Henry Peacham, "Old Burghley to his dying day would
always carry Tully's *Offices* about him either in his bosom or his
pocket."[24]   In discussions of his course of life, Ascham's key concepts
are the Ciceronian ones of *otium* and *negotium*.   His favorite literary
tag on the patron-client relationship is from the exiled Ovid, himself
struggling to learn how to win back his status:

> He who advises you to do what you are already doing,
> Praises you by his exhortation and by his advice
> Shows his approval of your actions.[25]

When he did create elaborate, sophisticated fictions, they involved not the multivalent language of love and service, but the gracious language of epistolary compliment that drew together political
and moral values.[26]   His fictions drew the patron towards a humanistic
ideal in which the benefactor's grace would be a favor to both learning and the state.   The would-be client came not as suitor or lover,
but as one who promoted their mutual honor and worthiness.   In the

---

[23]On the midcentury Protestant literary tradition, see John N. King, *English
Reformation Literature: The Tudor Origins of the Protestant Tradition* (Princeton:
Princeton UP, 1982).

[24]Quoted in Conyers Read, *Mr. Secretary Cecil and Queen Elizabeth* (New York:
Knopf, 1955) 30.

[25]*Tristia* 5.14.45-46.

[26]Two noteworthy examples in English may be mentioned: a letter cleverly
dividing the Queen into "her highness" and "her goodness" (II, 152-161), and one
contrasting "the life of Saul, the image of an ill prince," and "the life of David, the
image of a good prince" (III, 65-75).   The latter functioned as Ascham's dedication
to the Queen of Peter Martyr's commentary on 1 and 2 Samuel, though Giles
erroneously prints it at the head of *The Schoolmaster*.

poets "the cultural myth was that a client served the Queen out of love."[27] In Ascham's letters the motive was not so elaborately encoded. The Queen was not his Petrarchan mistress or goddess of chastity, but the model of benevolence and justice wherein moral and political values, "highness" and "goodness," were conjoined. Such patrons were like David or Josiah, rulers whose policies were conducive not to the fulfillment of the "desire" of the courtier poet's hot blood, but to the refoundation of the state along the lines of Israel and Rome.

Considered as a single achievement, the letters of Ascham form a remarkably complete and rounded articulation of the ideals and strategies of one of England's most representative Tudor humanists. Though by temperament and preference he was an educator, and always the loyal, nostalgic Cantabrigian, his letters also expose his devotion to public service, in the church if necessary, but preferably in teaching, writing, or reporting. Despite his brave talk of "shaping myself to be a courtier," that role, at least as it is ordinarily understood, was hardly congenial to him, and he was in fact actually being fashioned by schoolmates and friends more powerful than he. Never given to the "court-hopes" of the sort we know so well in Sidney or Ralegh or Donne, he took most pride not in the beauty, chastity, or political brilliance of the Queen, but in her learning. She commanded his allegiance above all by the soundness and depth of her doctrine. He never acquired power or influence or status, nor did he seem to desire it. A Sturmian *pietas literata* was his deepest desire; he wants his students, he writes his friend Grindal, "to drink in piety along with learning" (I, 74). In *The Schoolmaster* he tells of his "great rejoicing" in the knowledge that in "the temperate and quiet shade of [William Cecil's] wisdom . . . *religio* for sincerity, *literae* for order and advancement *res publica* for happy and quiet government have . . . specially reposed themselves" (III, 238). Love for the classics, a personal, Reformed religion, devotion to the Prince and the commonweal--these were the elements of his midcentury creed.

---

[27]Leonard Tennenhouse, "Sir Walter Ralegh and the Literature of Clientage," in Lytle and Orgel 244.

The Text

In the history of the collection and publication of Ascham's correspondence, the central figure is Edward Grant, 1540?-1601, the first editor
of the letters. Master of Westminster School, Grant from 1573-1578
numbered Ascham's eldest son Giles among his pupils. As Grant explained in his preface to the first edition (1576), the project began
when Giles proffered copies of letters his deceased father had written
(III, 295).[28] No doubt some of Grant's interest arose from the fact that
he began his university education in Ascham's own St. John's College,
Cambridge (though he took his first degrees from Oxford).

Grant initially published the letters in three "books": the first, he
explained, was comprised of those letters written to Sturm. The second was made up of Ascham's letters to other friends written during
his years at Cambridge and during his tenure as tutor to Princess
Elizabeth; those written subsequent to his departure for Germany constituted the third.

The volume was apparently well received, for two years later
Grant issued a second, enlarged edition, adding a fourth book of
"commendatory and petitionary letters, and others similar in kind,
written on behalf of someone to someone else" (III, 302).[29] Mindful
that Ascham had written many letters, copies of which he had not
been able to locate, Grant had already in 1576 promised that if readers
directed him to other letters, he would publish them in the future
"with other lucubrations I am going to edit" (1576 preface, no page).
Though some may have come forward with copies, it seems more likely that many of these new letters in Book Four had in fact been re-

---

[28]For the sake of convenience, my references are to materials printed in J.A.
Giles' edition, which admittedly is confusing. Here it should be explained that the
dedication to the Queen which Giles prints (III, 294-300) is from Grant's first edition of 1576, a dedication which appeared only in an abridged version in subsequent editions, but the preface to the reader which Giles prints (III, 301-02) is
from Grant's final, 1590 edition; this address was revised each time Grant enlarged
the edition (i.e., in 1578 and 1590). (Giles' note on 294 wrongly terms the 1578
the fourth edition; it was the second.)

[29]He also added about half a dozen letters to the first three books; for example, into the first book he inserted Sturm's first letter to Ascham (Letter 40 in
this volume).

served or had remained disorganized in 1576, and were added in 1578 as additional models of epistolary form.[30]

The 1578 edition was reissued in 1581. Then in 1590, again capitalizing on the success of the volume, Grant enlarged the collection once more, adding a fifth book of letters, none of which, ironically, was written by Ascham himself.[31] The bulk of these new letters were written *to* Ascham: by Sturm in particular, but also by some 14 others (Ramus, Nannius, Osorio, etc.). And Grant even included a few letters written neither to nor by Ascham: Sturm to Queen Elizabeth and to Sir Anthony Cooke, for example.

Grant's principle of organization was decidedly mixed. His editions were a poorly differentiated mixture of five categories of personal and official correspondence: (1) letters written by Ascham to friends, (2) letters written by friends to Ascham, (3) letters written by Ascham as public orator of Cambridge University, and as secretary to Ambassador Morison, to Queen Mary, and to Queen Elizabeth, (4) letters both personal and official written by Ascham as paid scribe for other people, and (5) letters written by others to correspondents other than Ascham. Grant's Books 2 and 3 claimed to be chronological, but the order was rough. Book 4 was ostensibly a collection of models, though ironically in form and style the letters within other books were often more exemplary. Book 5 was obviously a miscellany. Moreover, pride of place (Book 1) went to Ascham's letters to Sturm, his most eminent and esteemed correspondent, "because they excel the other letters in their literary range and their stylistic excellence" (III, 301). Within this group Grant deliberately set Ascham's last (and longest) Latin letter first, correctly recognizing that for Ascham this "little book" on imitation addressed the most important of all issues in humanistic education.

Despite these peculiarities Grant's edition has a special, twofold importance. In the first place, Grant's active collection and publication of a contemporary's correspondence constitutes an almost unique service, for such a publication, nearly contemporaneous with the author's

---

[30]In his 1576 preface Grant spoke of additional "autograph letters hidden somewhere in my office," as though they were buried under some pile of papers, and might turn up.

[31]More precisely, the new fifth book, which is advertised on the title page of the 1590 edition, had its own title page as well, with the date 1589.

own life, was a rare occurrence, particularly in England. There are some exceptions: a selection of Erasmus' letters appeared during his lifetime. And in Italy, to mention but two additional instances, publication of Bembo's and Ficino's letters antedated their deaths. In Ascham's own circle Walter Haddon saw the publication of fifteen of his letters some five years before his death in a miscellany entitled *Lucubrationes* (1567). But for Cheke, Gardiner, Paget, Cecil, Sturm, Wilson, Smith, Parker, Redman, Lever--indeed for virtually every one of the leading figures in religion, government, and learning during Ascham's time--there were no contemporaneous collections, and certainly none based on the author's own papers. Indeed, the letters of almost all of those I have named remain even today scattered and unpublished. Despite its weaknesses and omissions, then, Grant's volume is a rare and valuable resource.

Secondly, Grant's editions have had a lasting influence on subsequent editors of the letters, specifically on William Elstob in his 1703 edition and on Dr. J.A. Giles in his edition of 1864-1865. These editions, the latter of which remains the only collection of Ascham's complete works, do not canvas manuscript sources, as we might expect of a new edition, but simply build on Grant's printed edition of the papers he received from Ascham's son.

Indeed, the most curious and maligned features of Giles' edition of "The Whole Works of Roger Ascham," as he styled it, spring not simply from Victorian methods or principles, but from his (and Elstob's before him) conservativism in following Grant. Two often misinterpreted instances are worthy of mention. Giles' inclusion of only a portion of Ascham's surviving official correspondence springs not from his picking and choosing from surviving letters, but from the fact that his text of the correspondence is essentially from Grant via Elstob.[32] With two exceptions Giles consulted only Elstob/Grant for letters writ-

---

[32]Unpublished official correspondence is preserved in the Public Record Office, and in the following manuscripts in the British Museum: BM Additional MS. 35840 (a file from the Hardwicke papers of letters from Mary's reign, 1554-1558); BM Royal MS. 13. B. I (Ascham's personal register of letters from the reign of Elizabeth, 1558-1568); BM Lansdowne MS. 98 (part of the Burleigh papers: copies apparently made at Cecil's command).

ten in Latin.[33] Secondly, the inclusion of a fair number of letters written by others to Ascham, and even of letters written neither by him
nor to him, results not from Giles' eccentric eclecticism, but again from
his conservativism in retaining within his edition all the letters incorporated by Grant and by Elstob into their editions.

Neither Elstob nor Giles, then, built their editions on sounder
principles than their predecessors, and a new edition of Ascham's
works is desirable, both to collect letters yet unprinted and to establish
the text in the case of those items where there exists some manuscript
authority.   Neither Elstob in the eighteenth century nor Giles in the
nineteenth was a collator or textual critic, but both essentially represented and augmented those editions which had preceded theirs.
Elstob retained Grant's five-book structure.   Essentially the only new
feature of his edition was the inclusion of some 15 additional letters,
none of which, ironically, was by (or to) Ascham.   Giles in turn made
Elstob his basic text.   His innovations were essentially two: he reor-
dered all the letters as best he could into a chronological sequence,
and he included for the first time English letters available from various sources, mostly printed ones.

Despite these innovations Giles' text, like that of any modern edition which might be undertaken, derives essentially from Grant's sixteenth-century collection, and is thus the one on which the translations
in this volume can be based.   With respect to the corpus of Ascham's
Latin letters sufficient groundwork has already been laid to make it
clear, in the first place, that the ones in Grant's editions, transmitted to
us through Elstob and Giles, are the letters of central importance, and
that the uncollected letters, consisting almost entirely of official correspondence, are not of sufficient importance to be included here.   Secondly, manuscripts have already been sufficiently well identified and
reviewed to insure that in the case of the occasional letter included
here which also exists in manuscript (I have discussed each instance in

---

[33]The only Latin manuscripts Giles drew on were BM Lansdowne MS. 3,
which supplied one letter (I, 457-58; here Letter 51B), and BM Lansdowne 98, part
of the Burleigh papers, which supplied some official letters, none of which are
included in this volume. (Giles' own account of his sources, confusing and rather
unhelpful, is found at I, iv-vii, and II, 194-96.) It scarcely needs saying that Giles'
use of these manuscripts is arbitrary.

a headnote to the letter) the minor discrepancies between the manu-script and Giles' text have small bearing on this translation.[34]

Because Giles included Ascham's English letters within his edi-tion, the selection of Latin letters translated in this volume finds its complement in English letters available in Giles. Already in this intro-duction I have cited them, for there were periods when Ascham seems to have been as quick to write in English as in Latin. Particularly during the difficult transition years of 1552-1553, when he wrote some of his most searching letters about how he proposed to shape his ca-reer, the English letters of special interest outnumber his Latin ones.

Whether they were written in English or Latin, Ascham's best letters were immediately recognized as masterpieces of style and ex-pression. Although only the heading of Grant's fourth book presented Ascham's Latin letters as ostensible models of epistolary form, the thought was in fact present throughout, particularly in Grant's accom-panying "Oration on the Life and Death of Roger Ascham, and on the Glories of his Writings, for Young Students of Latin" (III, 302-55). This demonstrative oration, as the title suggests, was not primarily Grant's effort to write Ascham's biography, but to place before his students at Westminster School a model of piety, service, and learning. Both As-cham's life and his epistles were ones to emulate.

There is other evidence as well that Ascham was numbered among the best letter-writers of his day. Copies of his letters appear, for example, in contemporary manuscript collections of model epis-tles.[35] Also, less than a year after Grant's first edition appeared, Abra-ham Fleming quarried from it models of style and form for inclusion in his large *Panoplie of Epistles, or a Looking Glasse for the vnlearned. Conteyning a perfecte plattforme of inditing letters of all sorts, to persons of al estates and degrees . . . vsed of the best and the eloquentest Rhetoricians that haue liued in all ages, and haue beene famous in that facultie* (London, 1576). From ancient Greece Fleming offered his readers model letters by Plato, Isocrates, etc.; from ancient Rome, letters by Cicero, Seneca,

---

[34]For the groundwork see Ryan and two unpublished dissertations: Maurice Hatch, "The Ascham Letters: An Annotated Translation of the Latin Correspon-dence Contained in the Giles Edition of Ascham's Works" (Cornell, 1948), on which more below; and Albert McHarg Hayes, "The English Letters of Roger As-cham" (Princeton, 1934).

[35]For example, British Museum Additional MS. 33271.

Pliny, etc. Amongst Continental humanists of the Renaissance Paolo Manuzio, Erasmus, and others were represented. Lastly he proudly presented letters from two English "gentlemen of late memorie, for their rare learning and knowledge, verie famous" (p. 413): eight letters by Ascham, and five by Walter Haddon, his fellow Cantabrigian and a noted Latinist.

It is, however, not merely as models of form and style that Ascham's epistles deserve to be read. Indeed, by no means all of Ascham's letters are exemplary products of the study, refined and carefully composed. Both the English and the Latin travel letters, for example, are completely casual and unstudied. The letters in this volume, therefore, have not been selected primarily for their stylistic and rhetorical excellence (some of which is inevitably lost in translation), but chiefly for their significance in developing an understanding of an important scholar-courtier of the midsixteenth century. This collection of letters makes readily available for the first time in English materials that supply a unique picture of the dynamic interaction of learning and the court within the life of Ascham.

To put these letters into the context of Ascham's career I have organized these letters into seven parts generally corresponding to what might be termed the important chapters of Ascham's life and work. I have introduced each chapter or part of the book with a brief account of events of Ascham's life in their relationship to his letters. Thanks to Lawrence Ryan's excellent study of Ascham, the shape of Ascham's career is much clearer than it had been, and I have drawn frequently on his work. With Ryan's help even the undated letters can usually be placed into their proper context. For a full and rounded account of Ascham's life and work, readers are urged to consult Ryan, whose thorough and reliable book I consider an indispensable companion to this volume.

The Translation

This translation is a revision of one completed by Maurice Hatch as a dissertation at Cornell University in 1948.[36] Essentially I have revised for the sake of readability and accuracy, and have generally followed Hatch when neither was being jeopardized. Whenever his rendering compromises the sense of the passage, or his structure grows too convoluted or wooden in an effort to adhere rigidly to the Latin, I have offered a smoother, more idiomatic rendering of syntax and structure. As translations go, Hatch's tends to be literal and formal, generally retaining much of the complexity of syntactic structure characteristic of Ascham's Latin. I have tried to retain enough of this formality to convey favorably Ascham's own rhetorical formality. Such formality is indeed characteristic of Ascham. In this context one thinks of Ascham's own letters in English, which have been singled out by Morris Croll, the dean of modern students of Renaissance prose styles, as the most successful examples he has ever seen of a truly Ciceronian style in English.[37]

This translation silently expands the various abbreviations appearing now and then in the text, especially in superscriptions and subscriptions. In the case of the official correspondence, for example, one frequently finds such formulations as this: "Elizabeth, etc. to Frederick, etc." In personal letters a closing line may be abbreviated thus: "The Lord Jesus etc." Sometimes names too have been abbreviated, or "N." appears (for *nomen*, "name").[38] Although Grant's printer retained these abbreviations, Ascham would have filled them out in penning the fair copy, and supplied the correct names. Thus where such ab-

---

[36]Hatch's translation was published in the obscure Kentucky University Press Microcards, Series A, No. 19.

[37]"The Sources of the Euphuistic Rhetoric," rpt. in *Style, Rhetoric, and Rhythm*, ed. J. Max Patrick et al. (Princeton: Princeton UP, 1966) 276. Croll specifically cites a letter of Ascham to Cecil (I, 349-55); two masterful letters to Queen Elizabeth might also be mentioned: II, 152-61 and III, 65-75.

[38]Such abbreviations are one of the clearest indications that the existing text of a letter derives from a copy Ascham kept. See also my introduction to Letters 49, 50, and 51 for additional indications about the textual history and the status of the text as it is printed in Giles. There are a variety of still other pieces of evidence, too technical to be recounted here, about this complex question.

breviations appear in Giles' text, this translation fills in the names (if possible) and supplies Ascham's customary words from the printed letters in which they do appear in full.

Throughout his correspondence Ascham sprinkled his text with Greek words and phrases. Here they have been translated into English, and italicized. An exception is Letter 38, where the issue is the pronunciation of the Greek symbols themselves.

With respect to dating, I have in the first instance followed the dates of the original editions. The undated letters pose more of a problem. Giles suggested dates for many of them, but he made mistakes. Sometimes he misconstrued events or lacked information now available. He also failed to note that in Ascham's dating of his personal correspondence, January 1 ordinarily marked the beginning of the new year. In matters of dating, therefore, I have followed the authority of Hatch and Ryan in corroborating or correcting Giles. It remains the case that some letters can be dated only approximately.

Notes on dating as well as other annotations have been generally kept brief. Often I am indebted to Hatch's notes, which are extremely uneven, but nevertheless helpful in many instances. To cut down on repetition in notes, I have supplied a Biographical Register of those who figure most prominently in this collection.[39] Briefer identifications of those who are not on this roster of correspondents have been supplied in notes.

Large as this edition is, including 60 letters, I have been obliged to omit many others, some of which have claims for inclusion and which are not without significance in a full account of Ascham's career. References to those letters, as well as to ones translated here, are supplied in this style: I.x, where the large Roman indicates the vol-

---

[39]In preparing the Register I have naturally made use of the basic universal and national biographies, most notably, of course, *The Dictionary of National Biography*, as well as such other standard guides as Charles Henry Cooper and Thompson Cooper, *Athenae Cantabrigienses*, vol. I (1500-1585) (Cambridge, 1858); John Venn and J.A. Venn, *Alumni Cantabrigienses*, 4 vols. (to 1751) (Cambridge, 1922-1927); Christina Garrett, *The Marian Exiles* (Cambridge: Cambridge UP, 1938); and Peter G. Bietenholz, *Contemporaries of Erasmus*, 3 vols. (Toronto: U of Toronto P, 1985-1987). I have also consulted a wide variety of historical and biographical studies to supplement and sometimes to correct them. Since this Register essentially presents only sketches and basic information, I have not included bibliographical citations.

ume number of Giles' edition, and the small Roman indicates his number for the letter. (Compare I, 35, where the Roman again indicates volume number, and the Arabic number indicates page number.)

Giles' edition has a large number of typographical errors. In this translation they have been silently corrected.

PART ONE: 1541-1544

"the whole foundation of the poor learning I have"

In 1530, around the age of 15, Ascham entered St. John's College, Cambridge. Proceeding regularly, he was admitted BA in February 1534; one month later he was elected a fellow of St. John's. Very quickly St. John's became for him a nurturing alma mater. In "a sweet remembrance of my time spent there," Ascham much later declared that the day of his election as a fellow was "*dies natalis* to me, for the whole foundation of the poor learning I have, and of all the furtherance that hitherto elsewhere I have obtained." St. John's was then, he continued, "such a company of fellows and scholars . . . as can scarce be found now in some whole university: which . . . have been, and are yet to this day, notable ornaments to this whole realm" (III, 232-35).

When he received his MA in 1537, Ascham was not at all ready to leave Cambridge. He first lectured in the University for a time; after 1540 he read Greek within his own college. Never would he lose his emotional attachment to Cambridge. Indeed, not until 14 years after his "birth" at St. John's (and thus 18 years after he first arrived) would he venture forth from her shelter.

Already in the letters written during these years in Cambridge the dilemma of Ascham's whole career becomes clearly visible. To augment his meager salary, Ascham made parallel overtures, both awkward and mildly surprising, coming as they do from one wholeheartedly committed to the "new learning," to two learned, but conservative clergymen, Robert Holgate, Bishop of Llandaff, and Edward Lee, Archbishop of York (Letter 1 and I.ix). In a pattern that became increasingly familiar, he felt compelled to lay out before his prospective patrons "the petitions and plans of [his] life" (I.ix) as he sought, sometimes deftly, sometimes desperately, to reconcile the desires of his heart to pursue learning in Cambridge with the necessity of pledging his whole devotion to the service of those on whom he was dependent for support.

Notwithstanding his professed readiness to "forsake Egypt" (i.e., classical learning) and to journey toward "the sacred land of promise" (see Letter 1), the letters of this period make it clear that in fact Ascham had little interest in a career within the church. In particular his letters to his friend Richard Brandisby and to his mentor John Redman (Letters 2, 6) convey his fondness for Cambridge, and his unwillingness to leave its *otium* and security. Even Lord Mountjoy's unsolicited offer of a position as tutor of his son--an attractive offer which would have put Ascham directly in the tradition of Erasmus--struck him, he said, as sailing "from so calm a harbor into the tempest of the seas"; he would be forced to "change the nature of his life, and somehow weave himself over again" (see Letters 5, 6). His embarrassment over his faux pas in the translation offered to Archbishop Lee (see Letter 4) further reinforced his determination to persevere in the "leisure and tranquillity" of Cambridge, proposing to direct the rest of his life to "the examination of God's word, attended by the reading of Plato, Aristotle, and Cicero, which is, as it were, its attendant and handmaid" (Letter 6). To this basic humanistic program he would be committed for life.

1 / To Bishop Robert Holgate   (Giles I.x)
[Yorkshire, 1541?]

> Beset in 1540-1542 by the "huge beasts" (I, 18) of serious illness and a stu-
> dent's poverty, Ascham appealed to two conservative prelates with connec-
> tions to his native Yorkshire: Edward Lee (see I.ix, which closely parallels
> this letter, and Letter 4 below) and Robert Holgate, president of the York-
> centered Council of the North.   At this time Holgate was also Bishop of
> Llandaff, and one of the wealthiest prelates in England.   Ascham writes
> from his family home, where he was forced by sickness to remain for near-
> ly two years (see Letter 2); the reference in this letter to eleven years of
> study at Cambridge suggests a date of 1541.

Since you are burdened with so much important business, most esteemed Bishop and worthy President, I would appear to convey a
great injury to others and a great trouble to you if I were to take a
minute of the time you devote to the causes and affairs of others or
add anything to the immense number of your daily cares.   I would
also appear to have acted improperly and unfairly should I dare intrude with my letter upon your thoughts, for you are so well surrounded by all the defenses of character and wisdom that when men
observe your supreme intelligence in making decisions, your justice in
administration, your authority in accomplishing things, they judge you
by virtually universal agreement and acclaim as the one man born as
it were to hold this office.

But whenever learned men, who are always considered the most
sound judges of things, exercise counsels full of moderation and prudence, they know and acknowledge that your mind is rich with an
extraordinary abundance of all learning.   The vote of all men having
been tallied, with one voice they proclaim you a leader such as Jethro
defined in Exodus,[1] and a bishop such as Paul represented in Timothy.[2]   Is it not proper for us to respect you and admire you when by
the kindness and providence of God, the most righteous dispenser of
every gift, you have become a most vigilant bishop, and by his Majesty's most wise judgment, you have been made a high magistrate?
What is this if it be not, "Well done, thou good and faithful servant.   I

[1]See Exodus 18:17ff.
[2]See I Timothy 3:1-7.

shall set thee over ten cities,"[3] and, "Behold, I have found a man after my own heart"?[4]

Therefore, most esteemed father, since you are not so much the most upright judge as the most learned bishop and high-priest of learning, my muses, rather animated despite their filthy garb of mourning, having fallen prostrate at your Lordship's feet, lift suppliant hands and turn confused countenances toward your generosity, praying and entreating you in the name of all literature and the muses to take them up in your patronage and embrace their cause against the most hostile enemy and antagonist of all learning.

That cause I shall set forth briefly. Although for eleven whole years I was engaged in the study of language and literature at Cambridge University with such enthusiasm that in my study I long ago resolved to forsake Egypt and to take the road to the sacred land of promise, about six months ago I was driven by an attack of quartan fever into such straitened circumstances, and the course of my studies was so precluded, that not only was any opportunity of advancing unhampered in my work cut off, but I was almost deprived of the possibility of returning to the University once more. And so if your Lordship would deign in some measure to supplement my means, so broken and weakened, on behalf of literature, not only will I make public proclamation before all learned men that my studies were maintained and preserved by your help and munificence, but you also will by this kindness so exceptional and so earnestly desired have put me under obligation to you for as long I live for everything I have--my devotion, duty, assistance, diligence, and regard, all most ready to obey your Lordship. In my daily prayers I will also importune our good and great Christ, who allows not even a cup of cold water given to one who asks in his name to lose its reward,[5] that he himself may repay you with abundant interest for anything you bestow on me at this time. As Paul said, he is able to make every gift abound to himself. May our Heavenly Father prosper and direct your most holy Lordship's concerns and interests eternally. Farewell.

---

[3]See Matthew 25:14ff. and Luke 19:11ff.
[4]See I Samuel 13:14 and Acts 13:22.
[5]See Mark 9:41.

2 / To Richard Brandisby (Giles I.xii)
[Cambridge, after October 2, 1542]

Brandisby, once Ascham's fellow student, left Cambridge in 1538 for the University of Louvain, apparently for religious reasons. Ascham himself returned to the University in 1542 after a two-year illness. The *terminus a quo* for this letter is given by date of the last of a series of letters Ascham mentions passing between Cheke, Thomas Smith, and the conservative chancellor of the University, Stephen Gardiner, Bishop of Winchester. The chancellor's interdiction of these young scholars' reformed system of pronunciation of Greek threatened to destroy the burgeoning zeal at Cambridge for Greek learning. The controversy focused on a question which had exercised philologists since the early years of the Renaissance. Byzantine scholars pronounced the language as it was spoken in Greece in their day. Erasmus was the most prominent Renaissance scholar, though not the first, to urge the recovery of the alternative, ancient pronunciation.[1]

Ascham's memorable account of the glory of Cambridge learning should be compared with his tribute to Cheke in *Toxophilus* (II, 67-68).

Most excellent Brandisby, our friend Tennand[2] was here with us last marketday, and I was glad to seek from him some news of you and your affairs; I did it the more gladly because for two whole years I have heard nothing about you. His conversation about you was very delightful; even as a boy I always enjoyed his special and extraordinary good will towards me. Since he claimed he could stay with us hardly more than an hour or two, I could not forbear writing something about what goes on here to you, who, though separated from us by so many miles, are yet close to us in our daily recollections. In practice and experience even I have already learned how true that passage is in Caelius' letter to Cicero, "Nothing can be more pleasant to a traveler than to be informed of even the insignificant incidents which occur at home."[3] The past two years have clearly shown me that this is so, as I have received letters from friends. During almost that whole time I had to drop my more serious studies, and I was

---

[1]See the introduction by Maurice Pope to *De recta Latini Graecique sermonis pronuntiatione dialogus* (1528), in *Collected Works of Erasmus* 26, Literary and Educational Writings 4, ed. J. K. Sowards (Toronto: U of Toronto P, 1985) 348-56.

[2]Stephen Tennand, like Brandisby, had left Cambridge for Louvain, where he matriculated in September 1541.

[3]Cicero, *Epistolae ad fam.* 8.1, with slight changes.

kept away from all the muses, being laid up at my parents' home in York by an attack of quartan fever. I would complain strongly of your never writing to me, were I not guilty of the same failing. I think it better that we redeem ourselves by writing faithfully since we are equally sinners.

If you want to hear about Cambridge, here is something which will seem almost new to you: our best Prince in his liberality has enriched the University with divine and immortal resources and ornaments of learning.[4]   Wiggin for Theology, Smith for Civil Law, Cheke for the Greek language, Wakefield for Hebrew, and Blythe, who married Mr. Cheke's sister, for Medicine have been appointed public professors.   They will have a yearly salary of 40 pounds.   Aristotle and Plato are now being read in their own language by the boys, something we had been doing amongst us for five years.   Sophocles and Euripides are now better known here than Plautus was when you were here.   Herodotus, Thucydides, and Xenophon are more on our lips and in our hands than Titus Livy was then.   What you once heard about Cicero, you would now hear about Demosthenes.   The boys have more copies of Isocrates in their hands than they had of Terence then.   Yet we do not reject the Latin writers, but cherish the best of those who flourished in the golden age.   Our Cheke's effort and example has lit and fed this flame of literary zeal, for without pay he has publicly lectured on all of Homer, all of Sophocles, and that twice, as well as all of Euripides, and nearly all of Herodotus.   He would have done the same for all the Greek poets, historians, orators, and philosophers, if bad fortune had not cast her evil eye on our happy advancement in literature.

For just when Cheke had applied his great resources to the correct, ancient pronunciation of Greek and his great energy to teaching it, behold, the very reverend Bishop of Winchester, yielding to the entreaties of some spiteful men, issued a very severe edict forbidding the use of that system of pronunciation,[5] and despite the protests of

---

[4]In 1540 Henry VIII created five Regius Professorships; Ascham's list of appointees follows: Eudo Wiggin (Wigan), Thomas Smith, John Cheke, Thomas Wakefield (Wakefeld), and John Blythe (Blyth).

[5]In an edict of May 15, 1542, Chancellor Stephen Gardiner upheld the modern system of pronunciation upon pain of severe reprisals appropriate to the status of the offender: expulsion, denial of degree, forfeiture of scholarship, or public

almost the whole University, not only forcibly deprived us of that pro-nunciation, which was, you might say, the salve of learning, but also utterly extinguished practically all the fire we had for learning the Greek language.   Do you think that an insignificant barrier to our study of Greek has been cast in our way when everyone knows that all our knowledge of things is transferred into our minds with the aid of the senses?   I repeat: when we are deprived in this way of the resource of our ears, and are driven and reduced to such difficulties, can we even detect a slight shade of difference in the letters of the alphabet unless our eyes are constantly glued to the letters?   For all the Greek letters now sound the same, so weak and subdued and thin, and so enslaved to the domination of a single letter, the *iota*, that all you can hear is the idle chirping of sparrows and the offensive hissing of snakes.

We are more bitter about this near death and destruction of the Greek tongue because it has to some extent been brought upon us by one who, except for this one matter, is adorned with all the resources of learning, wisdom, counsel, and authority, and is the most generous patron of learning and our University.   Between my lord of Winches-ter and Cheke some letters nearly as large as books have been ex-changed concerning this matter.   No one is more learned than my lord of Winchester to defend a pronunciation so barbarous, one introduced by the barbarians themselves.   I will say this much: he has the stronger, we the better side of the argument.   Unless by chance you have read the letters which Cheke wrote, you will not easily believe how strongly he has defended his opinions, and what sturdy troops of literary passages, reasons, and authorities he has mustered.

Farewell.   Cheke, Madew, Seton, Tongue, Langdall, and Bill greet you.[6]   I have always believed a long letter the best; such I await from you.

---

birching. The letters and treatises exchanged by Cheke and Gardiner in 1542 were later published without Cheke's knowledge by Caelius Secundus Curio: *De pro-nunciatione Graecae* . . .(Basel, 1555); Thomas Smith's contribution was published as *De recta & emendata linguae Graecae pronunciatione*. . . (Paris, 1568).

[6]John Cheke, John Madew, John Seton, Roger Tongue (Tonge), Alban Lang-dall (Langdale), William Bill: all fellows at St. John's.

3 / To John Seton   (Giles I.xi)
                    Cambridge, January 1, 1543[1]

Ascham's New Year's gift to his friend John Seton was a handwritten Latin
translation of excerpts taken by Oecumenius, a tenth-century bishop, from
Greek patristic writers on Paul's epistle to Philemon: *Expositiones quaedam
antiquae in Epistolam Divi Pauli ad Philemonem ex diversis Sanctorum Patrum
graece scriptis commentariis opera et diligentia Oecumenii collectae et nunc primum
latine versae.* The beautiful autograph manuscript, including this dedicatory
letter, is now in the library of St. John's College, Cambridge (MS. L 3). It
was not printed until Ascham's editor, Edward Grant, included it in his
posthumous edition of Ascham's theological writings: *Apologia pro caena
dominica, etc.* (London, 1577). There are only minor verbal differences between the manuscript and Giles' text of this letter, which is based on
Grant's 1578 edition, which in turn goes back to drafts or copies Ascham
kept of his own letters (see my Introduction). For the sake of consistency,
Giles is followed here.

Most moderate sir, the good poet and grave philosopher Empedocles
of Agrigentum concluded, wisely in my opinion, that the world is
founded upon friendship and encircles itself with a certain mutual and
harmonious love.[2] Many centuries ago even the untutored and ignorant masses discovered this truth through frequent experience and
practice, a truth which has been handed down to us by divine providence and infused into our minds. Hence it is that as we enter each
new year and receive a world completely reborn, as it were, we reckon that nothing should be done with greater care or worked out with
more eagerness than to strive at a moment auspicious especially to
ourselves to appease the supreme god of friendship, who guards and
preserves the entire universe, by pledging our services to each other
and exchanging small gifts, as though pouring out a sacred libation.
       That holy vessel of God, Paul, was of the same opinion. If you
were to except Christ, you would have nothing greater or more sublime than when he said that the fulfillment of the whole law was a

---

[1]Here I follow Ryan (301) in believing that Ascham's date is old style, and
thus correct Giles to read 1543. Incidentally, Giles' reference to a printed edition
of 1542 is also in error: see Ryan 301.

[2]According to the poetic fragments of Empedocles, Greek philosopher from
Sicily (5th century B.C.), the composition of the world through the association of
the four immutable elements results from the action of Love.

certain mutual, shared love.[3] Those men, therefore, who are distracted in mind and will and who every day are eager to brawl and fight, not only shatter and violate the universal laws of God, but also as much as they can, they rend and destroy the whole glorious fabric of things. Thus we who live together in the same devotion to virtue and integrity, who are united by our very close companionship, and who are marked with a certain civilized stamp of humanity, will not allow this excellent yearly custom of strengthening friendships to lapse, a custom originating in ancient times, always venerated and confirmed by the remarkable humanity of men, and finally brought into our own times and perpetuated in us, the husbandmen of all humanity.

Therefore as I was thinking a good deal about sending a small gift to my very distinguished friend at this time, I decided nothing would be better than to prepare the kind of gift which would not involve the slightest diminution of our little capacity for friendship, but which rather would somehow effect an additional increase, and from which you would obtain and store away not some common pleasure, but a substantial one, one not merely appealing to the eye for a while, but one giving much delight to the mind for a long time. I do not want you to imagine that I have done this with the intention or the idea that I was trying in this way to keep a tight hold on our friendship, which is already very solid, or to make larger and greater that which is already very full and very complete, and toward the increase of which there is apparently no place at all where anything can be added. Rather, I have done it partly in keeping with the custom at this time of year, and partly, as much as I am able, to make the indications of my affection for you more explicit and more public. So much for this.

When it comes to this little book, or pamphlet if you wish, the Oecumenius who complied these commentaries, whoever he was,[4] seems, if I am any judge, to have had the same idea that Theophylac-

---

[3]Romans 13:8-10.

[4]Oecumenius is usually identified now as a tenth-century Bishop of Tricca in Thessaly. Ascham undoubtedly translated Donatus' *editio princeps* (Verona, 1532). Oecumenius' commentary is essentially a catena of excerpts from Greek patristic writers whom Ascham names below.

tus did.[5]   That is, he abridged all those things which in St. John
Chrysostom, that vast and endless river of Christianity, had sprawled
expansively and freely, and crammed them into a narrower framework, as though he was forcing them into a single channel.   And he
did not pick these flowers from the garden of Chrysostom alone, but
he took many from Cyril, Gennadius, Theodoret, Gregory, Basil, Sever-
ian, Photius, all men of the better sort, outstanding for their erudition,
endowed with the utmost integrity of life.   The ravages of time have
for the most part destroyed the monuments of their work on the epistles of St. Paul, or else they have not been handed down to us because of man's carelessness.   Meanwhile we owe much to Oecumenius,
who has, as it were, snatched these holy relics from a fire or from the
voracious jaws of time, committed them to writing, and taken pains to
transmit them to us and to all posterity.

I have also translated commentaries on the Epistle to Titus,
which I have resolved to send to the most Reverend Father and my
Lord Edward of York,[6] provided they seem worthy, in your judgment,
to be offered to so great a bishop.   I shall go on to greater things,
God willing, if I learn that these are not displeasing, and if you wish
to be, if not someone who instigates and pushes me, at least my silent
approver as I progress further.   But if not, I shall easily retreat.

In the translation of this Epistle I have followed Erasmus in everything, except that I translate *deprecor* for *rogo*, having the great M. T.
Cicero for my authority,[7] who said that when we *deprecamur* we do
not deny our deed, but ask forgiveness for our transgression, which
this whole letter to Philemon concerns.   But if in the case of such a
sublime and momentous matter, this seems to have been too daring, I
shall confess my sin and not despair of easily deprecating my *deprecor*
and winning your indulgence.   Farewell, and love your Ascham as
you usually do.   January 1, 1542 [i.e., 1543].

[5]Eleventh-century Byzantine commentator on Scripture.

[6]Edward Lee, Archbishop of York: see Letter 4.

[7]In his Latin translation of the Greek New Testament Erasmus employed the
Latin verb *rogo* to render Paul's plea in verses 9 and 10 ("I *beseech* thee for my son
Onesimus . . . ," in the Geneva Bible).   The Vulgate has *obsecro;* Ascham argues
for *deprecor,* citing Cicero.   The reference is not to a specific passage, but to Cicero's general usage (see also Aulus Gellius, *Noctes Atticae* 11.8, conforming to Cicero's usage).

4 / To Bishop Edward Lee   (Giles I.xvi)
[Cambridge, 1543?]

About the time he appealed for the patronage of Bishop Holgate (see Letter
1), Ascham also made a bid (I.ix), this time successful (see Letters 5, 6), to
Edward Lee, Archbishop of York.   In 1543 he offered his new patron the
gift of a Latin translation of Oecumenius' collection of Greek commentaries
on Paul's epistle to Titus (I.xiii), much as he gave his friend John Seton a
translation of Oecumenius on Philemon (see Letter 3).   (The translation was
first printed by Edward Grant in his posthumous edition of Ascham's theological writings: *Apologia pro caena dominica, etc.*, London, 1577.)   The present elegant letter of apology, along with one other (I.xviii), represents Ascham's efforts to redeem himself for offending his conservative episcopal
patron with the inclusion of commentary on Titus 1:6 (concerning married
clergy):   see Letter 6.

Last year, most Reverend Father in Christ, when a consideration of the
service by which you have bound me to yourself persuaded me to go
to London for the sake of visiting you, the journey itself plunged me
into bitter grief and a three-fold distress of mind.   Missing the enjoyment of seeing you and talking with you, which I was looking forward to, was very painful.   It was much more painful, however, to
have my misfortune, which affected me alone, linked to such a great
crisis in your health, which quite properly troubled many.   But adding
a third misfortune to these two, whereby the very road which I was
attempting to make passable in order to obtain your greater favor led
me to give some slight offense, was by far the most painful of all,
filling me with a sense of grief.   For I never thought that those commentaries which Oecumenius compiled from Basil, Gregory, and in
large measure from Chrysostom, just as from a garden wholly unde-
filed and free of all hemlock and noxious herbs, would have been able
to hold more poison leading to an immediate death from plague than
wholesome and healthful sap for the preservation of health.

After I returned home, the matter drew me into various thoughts
and anxieties and cares, and burdened me the more heavily because I
did not share any part of it with even my close friends, but kept it all
to myself, buried in my heart.   After this anxiety had tormented me a
long time, and I had not been able to take my mind off it for any
length of time, finally I thought of what would free me from all this
mental anguish and show me a clear and evident indication that there

is no change in your good will.   For in this situation I have readily seen wise and serious men, sometimes with a mere nod and with veiled signals, correct the errors of inexperienced and presumptuous men.

Your wisdom was of the opinion that I had taken up my project foolishly, and that before I attempted the task of translating such weighty matters, I should have tested my skill on other things of lesser weight or lesser danger.   Since therefore your Lordship, if I understand anything, has not so much rebuked any deed of mine as shown me how I must do it, I am accommodating all my future plans for study to this sober advice and your wise warning.

In fact, I immediately took Sophocles' *Philoctetes* in hand.   This tragedy, translated as much as possible in imitation of Seneca, with the same iambic lines and nearly all the choric meters which Sophocles used, will be published in your name unless your Lordship is plainly averse to this proposition of mine.[1]   When this is done, both my duty and the regard by which you have obligated me will have been made clear to you, and the affection and good will of your Lordship, by which you are most favorably inclined to sustain the study of literature from day to day, will in some measure have been made evident.

It remains therefore to pray your Lordship that just as I have reserved and directed all my respect toward the wish and will of your Lordship, so the favor and kindness of your Lordship toward me may not diminish in any way.   The Lord Jesus Christ preserve your Lordship.

5 / To Lord Mountjoy   (Giles I.xix)
[Cambridge, late March 1544]

In this and the following letter to Redman Ascham offers somewhat different reasons for declining the patronage of Charles Blount, fifth Lord Mountjoy and one of England's leading courtiers.   Mountjoy was himself well-educated; his equally distinguished father William was once a pupil, and then a patron of Erasmus.

[1]The translation was never published, and may not have been completed.

The date for this letter can be fixed from references in other letters: Ascham's spring stipend from Archbishop Lee was due on Lady Day (see I.xxiv and Letter 6); this letter was written near that date (see Letter 7).

The last time Mr. John Redman was at Cambridge he urged in conversation, and only recently he strongly argued in a letter, that I would be putting myself and all the plans of my life in a truly honorable position if I were to serve you at court or teach your son at home. I have considered the matter thoroughly and have realized that I, who had been for some years devoted to the leisure of learning, am somewhat frightened by the business of the court and the tumult of affairs, and that because of the sweetness of the liberty I have long enjoyed I wish to avoid going into servitude, and that for teaching your son I can not offer as much as your wisdom would expect of me, the kindness of others would predict of me, and the acceptance of so important an office would demand of me. Despite all these considerations, I have nevertheless been much moved by the encouragement of so prominent a man and I have been very much attracted by the name and the renown of the very learned Mountjoy family. As a matter of fact, I have been thinking that I was not being summoned from leisure into business, from learning into the court, from the sweet fruit of liberty into the burdensome and vexatious experience of servitude, but that I was being called to the dwelling and company of the Muses. Except for the Medici in Italy you cannot find another similar or equal in history, even in antiquity.

In this the more your glory exceeds other men's, the more they have wished that their families had been founded on the pursuit of learning and made famous through the splendor of erudition, as your father was. But there are very few who have cultivated what might be called this legacy of learning, maintained and preserved by many vigils and hard study, or enlarged it by that great increase of learning which is common to you, but not to many others. Truly, those who have been eager that learning should be maintained so scrupulously and completely, enlarged and increased in every way, have preserved it for their children and thus for all posterity. But hardly a man has been born after them--and I doubt there will be many to come--whom you can consider deserving associates and consorts of a glory so splendid as yours.

This matter, most illustrious sir, would have drawn all my devotion and the plans of my life into following your will if the most Reverend Father, my Lord of York,[1] had not two years ago bound my whole allegiance and regard to himself through his most generous benefactions. Therefore if there is any other way in which my slender capacities can be of use to you, you will find no one more willing or more ready than I to bring it to fulfillment. Consequently I pray you, most distinguished sir, in the name of the literature which you daily adorn that the good will toward me which you harbor on the basis of the recommendations of others will forever be preserved unchanged through your kindness to me. The Lord Jesus have you ever in his keeping.

6 / To John Redman   (Giles I.xx)
[Cambridge, late March 1544]

> The absence from Cambridge of John Redman, Ascham's senior friend and distinguished colleague, prompts this major apologia for his chosen mode of living, as well as further efforts to mend relationships with his patrons and supporters. The bitterness which Ascham tries to allay in the opening pages of this letter apparently goes back to 1540, when he and Redman backed rival candidates for a vacant fellowship (see Ryan 31-32).
> The date for this letter can be fixed from Ascham's indication that his spring stipend is now due (it was to be paid on Lady Day: see I.xxiv), and from a reference in Letter 7 indicating that the year is 1544.

The letter, most distinguished sir, which G. Hodgeson[2] recently brought to me from you affected me with a kind of wonderful pleasure. For besides renewing the very pleasant memory of the time when we were very closely associated with each other through daily contact, it also gave me an excellent and especially weighty testimony that the singular good will and kindness with which you always cherished me since boyhood are not altered by the evil of time nor dimin-

---

[1]Edward Lee, Archbishop of York. See Letter 4.

[2]Probably William (*Gulielmus*) Hodgeson or Gavin Hodson, both fellows of St. John's at this time.

ished by physical separation, but are maintained and most lovingly preserved in your memory. I have always felt that to lose your devotion and kindness toward me became more grievous and painful to the extent that I have understood that you took an interest in me in the name of learning and virtue, and that your interest arose out of your good judgment and good will rather than out of any compulsion.

Indeed, when I think back over the last three years, during which time, as some have supposed, there has been some separation of outward wishes between us, but, as we know, no division of inward feelings, and when I look carefully at the reasons why people thought so, I see that they are all greater in opinion than in reality. For the chief and only issue was that I differed from you and your wish in the elections of our fellows,[3] yet even in that I was inclined toward the same thing, with the same motive, though perhaps with a divergent interest. Both of us had been moved by the same interest in helping our own students, and we were competing to bring about the same conclusion. Wherefore if I seem to be somewhat at fault in this--in the name of our love for one another and your own good sense, I shall speak freely--you yourself are not wholly free from blame or far removed from it, unless perhaps it seems fair that you should have toiled to the utmost for your friends, but that I should have abandoned all my care and guidance and loyalty to mine. I rather think I had the obligation to show the greater devotion at that time by seizing the opportunity of helping my students, since you had a far greater opportunity each day of advancing yours. Indeed, after that occasion I would never have a better chance of laying hold of this opportunity.

As for J. G.,[4] whatever you asked me to do in that matter, either at Cambridge or when I was with you in London, I did with all my strength, diligence, and good faith. For you told me yourself that you wanted him elected into our college, not so that he might then live more affluently, but that he might there have a better chance to study. I took care of the matter as soon as I could. I was never of the opinion of those--on the contrary, I want to distance myself from them-- who think that what you do on behalf of one person is to be consid-

[3]Ascham's candidate, John Thomson, was chosen: see I.v and vii.
[4]Unidentified.

ered as nothing unless you show yourself a formidable adversary to
the other poor, honest fellow.

I am certainly unwilling, excellent sir, to renew any recollection
of those times, or to reopen the wound of my bitter grief, which is
now healed over.   Nevertheless, I feel more free to discuss this with
you because I know you well enough that if you had been present
during these quarrels, under your guidance I would have been less
hurt by others, and I would much more easily have taken care of the
wounds I received with the help of the seasoned remedy of your native wisdom.   For to pass over my personal troubles and my very
sharp feelings of rejection, which lately have just about destroyed me,
to use very mild language about such an important matter, the hardest
thing I have to endure is that the drive of some to injure others ever
breaks out with such passion that they believe it is not enough to reduce my slender resources and virtually push me to desperation unless they also attempt to destroy my whole reputation with many eminent men.   In this matter some have applied themselves busily and
worked so hard that no one of my age, place, and condition has experienced an injury as painfully calamitous or as seriously damaging
to reputation as the things that have been done to me.   Truly, best
Redman, I speak from my heart when I say that if in the same way
that time has tempered my memory of the injustice heaped upon me
and has even made me forget the whole thing, time would have also
redeemed the distorted affections of others and wholly restored my
violated reputation, I would hardly have renewed this memory or sad-
dled you with such complaints at this time.

But I am extremely joyful to have this opportunity to write to
you, and I do so willingly because I hope to have your love toward
me more like the old vigorous love, and I know that your sense of
moderation even with respect to the most serious injuries is too gentle
to allow any serious and special grievance to abide within you, since
in this whole affair my offense was surely not the chief one.
Therefore I pray, most excellent sir, in the name of our long-standing
love, in the name of all the devout and deepest relationships which
have ever existed between us, that you will wish the course of your
old opinion of me, shaped not by my deserts but by your own good
will, to run more free and without impediment rather than the course
of any grievance, newly invented not through any fault of mine, but
through the ill will of others.   I want to obtain this old esteem from

you as well as from that distinguished gentleman Mr. ___,[5] whom I
have always determined to cultivate and respect.

But if you wish, we will have a better opportunity to discuss
this matter in person. Now I come to your letter, in which you called
on me to serve Lord Mountjoy at court and teach his son, which is
surely not the worst proposition. To answer briefly each point, I am
happier to be asked this of you now, even if the stipend should be
small, than I would have been to be summoned to a post that might
pay very well. But when I consider myself and my whole way of life
and see what difficulties the acceptance of the position would entail,
to me it seems to be not so much an invitation put forth to attract me,
but a diversion thrown up to frighten me. For changing the nature of
your life and somehow weaving yourself over again, as it were, is an
order so large and arduous that it can only be accompanied by every
fear of danger and a sense of dread. Thus since for some years I
have betaken myself to the study of literature, if not with very great
profit, yet with no small pleasure, were I now to sail from so calm a
harbor into the tempest of the seas, I could not for long escape either
from the sharp bite of sorrow on account of my recollection of my
former leisure and tranquillity, or from a considerable fear and risk of
danger because of my immoderate ignorance of such important matters. Moreover, since I have not yet come to consider my youthfulness even moderately settled down into a quiet and "even" way of
living, as I call it, how, I ask, could I stand firm on the slippery floors
of the bustling court and escape from a serious and perilous fall?
Thus whether I am allured by the fruits which a life of leisurely study
might not yield, or diverted by a fear of some rather serious fate
which might overtake me, certainly at this time and in my present
circumstances I am somewhat frightened by the court.

Lord Mountjoy, although not, I suppose, hostile to learning, encouraged a good deal by the splendid example of his father, yet may,
I fear, prove disposed to other things, enticed in his youthful fervor
by the traps and snares of the court like a silly bird. It has not escaped me that all courtiers are liberal and effusive in promising something, but tight and niggardly in discharging their promise. Why is it

[5]Edward Lee? Lord Mountjoy? The text gives only "N." (the abbreviation
for "name"; Ascham would have filled it in when making the fair copy).

that ornaments of mind and character, which in my case are very plain, are not esteemed, while strength of body and military capacity, of which I have absolutely none, are at certain times greatly desired? You advise me to try out for a few months the position to which Lord Mountjoy invites me, and to keep it if I like it, but if I do not, to return to the college, where in the interim my position might be kept open for me.   Your advice is certainly kind, but I hardly think I should follow it, for if I did, I would bring upon myself a certain severe reproach and serious criticism from those not well enough acquainted with your advice, either for rashly undertaking something I could not live up to, or for abandoning faithlessly, as the story would be, something I set myself to do, or for having so insecure and inconstant a way of life that I changed it from day to day.   As for teaching the boys grammar, I have scarcely enough of it on the tip of my tongue for my own use; I have not learned it so fully and perfectly that I could teach others the whole subject.   I am not capable or suited for it, and in one part of my mind I am extremely afraid of the task.

I do not disdain the salary, however small, for experience has long hardened me to the buffeting of any fortune, however meager.   I am not the kind of person (I don't want this to sound presumptuous) who is fired up by a very strong desire for things, or driven to covet affluence or some special fortune.   Therefore, since the approach to court is scarcely safe for a man of my age and station, and since there will be no honor at all in returning home with this idea in mind, and since I myself am in no way capable or suitable for such an important position and easily rest content with my rather modest circumstances, I hope that Lord Mountjoy will not be upset if I cannot satisfy his wish in this respect.

As a matter of fact, to settle these issues conclusively, I am barred from taking this job by something else far bigger than all these considerations.   For a long time I have been offering all my learning, respect, and plans of service to the most Reverend Archbishop of York.[6]   I do not think I could look for anyone who is more generous in providing for my material wants and who offers a better opportunity to pursue the leisure of learning.   And I pray you earnestly, excel-

[6]See Letter 4 to Edward Lee, Archbishop of York.

lent sir, to give him the letter I am writing to him.[7]   The more earnestly I plead with you for this, the more I am afraid that some evil
perversity of others, in this evil time, will have taken something away
from the good will he bore me most willingly of his own accord.   For
there is no place so distant that perversity does not reach it (for *injuries are swift-footed,* as Sophocles says in *Antigone*[8]), nor is any heart so
saintly and pure that it does not take note of it.   I do not say this as
though I were consciously aware of having done something or perpe-
trated anything on account of which he should in any way be estranged from me.   Unless Seton and Watson have given an honorable
testimony of my studies and my way of life, if such are demanded, I
shall ask no more of you than one word from your mouth on my
behalf.

But I shall not hide this from you.   Last year, as you know, I
translated the Greek commentaries on the epistle to Titus, which I
thought proper to give to the most Reverend Archbishop of York as a
token of my respect.[9]   When I went to his home, but could not see
him because a serious illness had confined him to bed, I gave the
book to his brother, Geoffrey Lee, who was to give it to the Archbishop. He gave it.   The Archbishop read it, and found something in
it which offended him.   He returned the book, with a gift, so that I
could examine the passage.   This is the passage: *"let the husband of
one wife know, he [Paul] says, that she is his only lawful wife.   Those who
abhor marriage he stigmatizes as heretics, since they are capable of making
provision for the office of marriage."*[10]   When I got home I looked at my
Chrysostom, from whom Oecumenius in large part took his commentaries.   I quickly knew which passage he had quoted.   But I did not
have in hand a copy of Chrysostom in Greek, and I am asking you to

[7]Probably I.xviii, a second letter of apology for the offense within Ascham's
translation of Oecumenius.

[8]Line 1104.

[9]See Letter 4 on Ascham's troubles with Edward Lee, Archbishop of York, to
whom he offered a Latin translation of Oecumenius' collection of Greek commentaries on the Biblical book of Titus.

[10]A strong conservative in learning and religion, Lee was offended by this
passage from Oecumenius' commentary on Titus 1:6, which speaks of bishop's
having one wife.

look over the passage. I think that when the church was being born, many things were allowed out of necessity which, when it matured and reached its nobler age, so to speak, were rescinded in the councils of its wise rulers. And this is all that I preferred not to conceal from you. Thus I certainly do not see how this matter can arouse distrust of me in the most Reverend Father, or what it can stir you to think about the whole business. This I do know: when I was translating the book, I was thinking about what was unsound and unorthodox about as much as I was thinking about what was happening at the same moment in Utopia.

Therefore, in order that there be some proof of my loyalty and respect, all of which I have devoted to him for a long time and which I have hitherto reserved solely for his service and good pleasure, and in order that he know how disturbed I should be to give up and forgo his favor in the hope of some gain or the acclaim of men, I entreat you on the basis of all the bonds of our sacred friendship to restore me wholly to his favor by your testimony, if I have lost it through any offense beyond this one evident mistake. For your testimony would have so much weight with him that without a doubt your casual commendation of me would secure a new and singular addition of favor to that which I formerly enjoyed. If you will do this, you cannot devise anything more welcome and useful for me and my way of life, nor anything more proper and fitting for yourself and our old acquaintance and lasting friendship.

Since you will do this, see how much I promise myself from your goodness to me: I must pray you to do something else for me too, namely, that you will ask Geoffrey Lee, or whoever manages the most Reverend Father's household, to send me through you the money which the most Reverend Father supplies me each year for the support of my studies. The sum is forty shillings; twenty were due me last Michaelmas and I should receive as much now, for that is the schedule my Lord of York decided upon. But truly, if this annual stipend could be changed through your urging and his generosity into some prebend, as it is called, of even the least value or worth (although my Greek Readership allows me to hold even the very best along with my other college revenues), I cannot think of a greater favor for you to do for my sake, and an easier one for him to grant at your request, or a more desirable one for me to ask from you or hope from him. So much for this matter.

Now, indeed, most honorable sir, if you were to ask me (I wish that speaking with you in a letter were not as troublesome to you as it is pleasant for me) how I have planned my way of life and the conclusion of my studies, to which in particular all my cares and nightly meditations have been devoted, I should frankly respond: the study of God's word, attended by the reading of Plato, Aristotle, and Cicero, which is, as it were, its attendant and handmaid. This is the end to which I have proposed, God willing, to direct and guide the rest of my life. But if the option were given to me, and the Lord of York gave me the opportunity, and my slender resources allowed it, I should like nothing better than for a few years to accompany some distinguished man who was serving abroad as His Majesty's ambassador. For I trust that I would not be incapable at all of handling work of this sort, whether it be in *studying literature together*,[11] or, when needed, in sending letters home to lighten the load to some extent when the ambassador was being overwhelmed by the magnitude of his responsibilities. I certainly believe that pursuing such a way of life for a time would not be contrary to what I was saying earlier. Perhaps you will think these are vain and idle thoughts, like a youthful dream of mine. But however it is, since my thinking is connected to the work I've done and the danger I feel, two conditions which customarily excuse all offenses, and since I have never more strongly desired anything, I earnestly entreat you, unless it displease you very strongly, to do what you are able to do for me when an opportunity of attending to it presents itself.

I heard, and later learned for certain, that my help last year in transcribing the book which you took to His Majesty[12] was very welcome. I certainly am sorry, not so much that my chance to help you turned out so badly, but that you think that because my service to you was not very pleasant for me to perform I was somehow looking for a favor. Therefore, if you want me to know that you love me, when you have some work for me which will not take too long, ask

[11]Ascham's Greek phrase is adapted from Cicero, *Ad Fam.* 16.21.8.

[12]As a prominent and learned divine, Redman was collaborating at that time with bishops and other doctors on several projects; perhaps Ascham alludes to *The Necessary Doctrine and Erudition of a Christian Man*, or *The King's Book*, to which Redman contributed, and which was presented to the King and the nobility of England in May 1543.

me to do as much as you promise yourself concerning me, for if my ability to do it were as great as my willingness to do it, you certainly would not find anyone who would take up the task more eagerly or finish it more skillfully.   There is nothing which I would do more gladly than spend a few days with you, for such a visit would not be so much a useful opportunity for you to profit somehow as it would be for me to carry away the pleasant fruit of renewing your old acquaintance.

You see how I have repaid your letter with a troublesome epistle.   I would write you more often if I knew it was not too displeasing.   You would do me the greatest kindness if you would write three words in answer to this letter, either through our friend Christopherson[13] or anyone else, for nothing is more pleasant than the conversation of your letters.   Farewell.

---

[13]John Christopherson, fellow of St. John's at this time, was particularly fond of Redman.

PART TWO: 1544-1548

"here then is the target"

The letters of this period show Ascham's increasing ambivalence about a desirable course of life. He had habitually thought of Cambridge as a "calm harbor" and the court as "the tempest of the seas" (Letter 6), but around 1544 the University began no longer to seem an unambiguous and sure refuge. At roughly the same time (early 1544) that he was declining Lord Mountjoy's attractive patronage out of a professed devotion to "the leisurely occupation of letters" (Letter 5), Ascham was being shaken by his father's deathbed abjuration that he "leave Cambridge as soon as [he] could and turn to some worthy manner of living." His father's sharp accusation, he cried to Cheke, was that "by our contentions we were provoking God's most severe wrath and indignation against ourselves" (Letter 7). The death in September 1544 of Archbishop Lee, Ascham's first patron, spurred him to explore new avenues of preferment. Tempering his positive aversion to "the slippery floors of the bustling court" was the discovery of a new set of potential patrons, and an increasing awareness of the worthiness of a career in the service of the state.

A few months after his mentor John Cheke was called to court to tutor Prince Edward (July 1544), Ascham's favorite pupil, William Grindal, also migrated there, having been named tutor to Princess Elizabeth. With both his master and his pupil present to guide him, Ascham cautiously sailed his light pinnace into court for visits. Soon he was self-consciously cultivating his new acquaintances: the Astleys, the Parr family, even Prince Edward and Princess Elizabeth (see Letters 13-16). Ascham's first and perhaps greatest triumph, *Toxophilus* (1545), won him both an audience with King Henry at Greenwich and the reward of a handsome royal pension of £10 a year. In presentation letters to many of the leading men of the realm he eagerly promoted his new book, and thereby his own cause generally (see Letters

11, 12). In yet another brave effort, a showy and clever supplication to the Archbishop of Canterbury, Thomas Cranmer, he successfully won permission to eat meat during Lent--as well, of course, as the opportunity to make himself known to this godfather of young Prince Edward (Letter 10).

From one point of view, then, we have in these letters, as James McConica has argued, an unsurpassed record of the course of English humanism in the 1540s.[1] In his deft, organized strategies to improve his fortunes, Ascham points to the remarkable range of those capable of being enlisted in support of the new humanism. The roster of his correspondents is impressive indeed, and he covered many bases, preparing himself even better than he knew for the twists and turns of the future. The list included leading conservative clergymen (Bishops Gardiner and Day), principal ministers and Councilors under Henry VIII (William Paget and Anthony Denny), members of royalty (Queen Catherine Parr and members of her circle, Prince Edward and his uncle, the Lord Protector), as well as others, both Protestant and Catholic, who already were, or would soon be, in positions of authority and influence.

At the same time, this impressive roster of correspondents represents Ascham's frank concession to his own predicament and that of the University. Engendered by political stresses, these letters are unrivalled as vivid, detailed accounts of the turmoil constantly threatening the University's welfare, and the distress suffered by one of her most loyal members. They are suffused with Ascham's uneasiness and his uncertainty about how to let fly the arrow of his life so that it would hit the center of the target (Letter 11). To Cheke Ascham speaks bitterly of betrayal and of the treachery of members of his own college (Letter 9). In another letter he rationalizes his imprudent involvement in University debates over the Lord's supper, which seemed to the authorities to have gotten altogether out of hand (Letter 27).

Particularly in the letters he wrote in his capacity as paid scribe or as University Orator (Letters 17-26 constitute a representative sample) Ascham exposes the reasons for his deepening distress over the fortunes of the University, and his continued insecurity about his own course of life. Relations between town and gown were never worse

---

[1]*English Humanists and Reformation Politics* 206ff.

(see Letters 19, 21, 22). The realm's economic crises (e.g., the Price Revolution, the Great Debasement of coinage) and the revolution in religion (e.g., the first Chantries Act) seemed profound threats, forcing Ascham on behalf of the University into anxious appeals to friends in the highest places (e.g., Letters 18, 19, 26). The impressive roster of his well-placed correspondents is, from this perspective, not so much an enthusiastic campaign for self-promotion and the cause of the new humanism as it is a measure of the University's political distress and of Ascham's own struggle to learn whether "the road would lead . . . to some splendor of life and reputation" within the court or to "some quiet and pleasant means for the life of a studious man" within the University (Letter 11).

7 / To John Cheke (Giles I.xxi)
[Cambridge, late March-early April 1544]

Cheke's absence from Cambridge at this time anticipates his more permanent departure in July 1544, when he began to tutor the young Prince Edward at court. The letter may be dated more specifically from Ascham's indication that "last week" he wrote to Archbishop Lee and to John Redman (i.e., Letters 5 and 6).

Most accomplished Cheke, I would have written to you last week by Wilson or John Christopherson[1] if I had not at that same time been writing letters to his Lordship of York, to Lord Mountjoy, and to John Redman,[2] who had previously written to me that I should enter Lord Mountjoy's service. You will remember that I once communicated with you about a journey I intended to make to London before Easter. I cannot possibly make it unless I have the book which I undertook to translate from the Greek Chrysostom. Therefore I entreat you in the name of our friendship to send back the Greek book as soon as you can, either by Christopherson or by someone else who is going to return shortly.

Your Ascham writes this letter, most accomplished Cheke, overwhelmed by sighs and tears. A short time before I began to write I heard, with far more certainty than my weakness can bear, that my father, a very wise man, departed this earth to Christ. Although this alone would have made for very bitter grief, to it was added another load which was by far the heaviest of all, for all my friends despair of the health of my dearest mother, at least as far as it pertains to this life.[3] Oh harsh fate! First I lost my brother,[4] such a one as not only

---

[1]Wilson is probably Thomas Wilson, now known especially for his *Arte of Rhetorique* (1553). Having graduated from Eton, he was in 1544 a young student at King's College; Christopherson was a fellow of St. John's.

[2]Letters 4, 5, and 6 above.

[3]Ascham's father, John, was steward to Henry, seventh Baron Scrope of Bolton; his mother, Margaret, may have belonged to the Conyers family: see Ryan 8-13. Margaret and John died on the same day, having been married for 47 years (see Letter 42).

[4]Thomas. He preceded his younger brother Roger at Cambridge, and was associated with St. John's College from about 1516 to 1527 (Ryan 9).

our family, but England scarcely ever bore, and now I have lost both
my parents at the same time, as if I were not already overwhelmed by
calamity and a sea of tears. How grievous my sorrow is you yourself
will understand, especially as you know that I am a man thoroughly
broken and humbled in matters of lesser importance. But what could
be more grievous, more sorrowful, than to be bereft of both father and
mother at once? How unhappy I am, now deprived of your conversation and discussion, the solace I desire most. I wish you were here,
my Cheke, so that I could pour out my tears to you and give my
groans and sighs over to your very wise and comforting advice. But
truly I am not so much overcome that I forget who I am, and how
much of God's goodness my parents have had, and how he guided
them through a long and vigorous old age, for I know this is the way
of all flesh. I know also--it consoles me particularly--that our departure from this life is our entry into a better one, and this hope of
mine is fixed in my bosom.

I think that you remember, my Cheke, that I had a letter from
my father shortly before Christmas day--alas, the last one I received--in
which he warned me, while he also bound me by a kind of oath of
benediction, as it were, to leave Cambridge as soon as I could and
turn to some worthy manner of living, because by our contentions we
were provoking the severe wrath and indignation of God against ourselves. If I am not mistaken, I told you at the time how much this
shook me. Now it is again fresh in my mind; night and day it so
continually occupies my thoughts that no dictum of Isaiah, John, or
Paul sticks with me more firmly or has more weight of authority with
me. Is anything more important than heeding a father's warning? *A
father's consolation is best*, sang that most wise Gregory Nazianzen.[5] Is
there anything to be observed more religiously than a father's last will
and testament? That was his last letter to me, his last words. Was
this something he commanded me lightly? Was not this his wisdom
for me about Christ and the things pertaining to Christ at the very
moment when his soul would shortly ascend to Christ?

Since, then, I have such a solemn obligation to honor my father's
warning, there is nothing more important to me, most accomplished

---

[5]Many of the orations, poems, and letters of St. Gregory Nazianzen (c. 329-
389), one of the great Eastern Doctors of the church, reflect his close attachment to
his father and mother.

Cheke, than entreating you by the bowels of Jesus Christ that just as you were always, as I can abundantly testify, the leader in following all honorable pursuits, and just as since we were first acquainted with each other, you never stirred up even the smallest contention, so you will now offer yourself as the principal leader in establishing peace among us, even among those who have been your bitterest enemies. For just as it served as a glorious mark of your renowned sense of fairness, so it will also serve as a testimony to your prudence, and a lasting, timeless monument of your service to us all.   Although the heathens preferred an honorable war to a dishonorable peace, Cicero's disagreement notwithstanding,[6] nevertheless I am afraid that we Christians--who under one roof have devoted ourselves to the study of the same literature, virtue, and honor, who have been united by some rather close relationships, who have been brought up with such a great knowledge of literature and the will of God--nevertheless we, I say, are able to rationalize why we sometimes burn with irritation, as well as why we always are drawn into opposing camps.

And in our trouble I believe that every single one of us ought to take this verse of Psalms to heart, "Incline not my heart to any evil thing, to practice wicked works with men that work iniquity."[7]   If peace and unanimity can be wholly restored to us, I shall then think that I have virtually left Cambridge according to my father's warning, that is, I shall have been freed from such great confusion and dissension.   But if peace is not restored, which God forbid, than I shall entrust myself wholly to your friendship and attempt to get along with everyone in very deed while displeasing no one by so much as a word.   If my course fail, I shall leave the University as soon as I can.

Groaning between my tears, I have expressed myself, as you see, in a mournful, almost tearful letter, devoid of all feeling except sorrow.   Nothing can be more desirable than word from you for my solace and the lightening of my sorrow.   I pray you, greet most dutifully our friend Henry Cumberford.[8]   Jesus Christ have you ever in his keeping.

---

[6]See *Ad fam.* 6.6.5-6.

[7]Psalm 141:4 (Vulgate 140:4), AV.

[8]Student and fellow at St. John's, contemporary with Ascham and Cheke.

8 / To Sir William Paget   (Giles I.xxii)

[London?, June-July 1544]

> "Even by Renaissance standards," observes Ryan (41), this letter is "a master-
> piece of commendation and supplication." Ascham's appeal for the Regius
> Professorship of Greek to Paget, a Cambridge man who had become a Prin-
> cipal Secretary in 1543, anticipated Cheke's departure from Cambridge
> (Cheke's appointment as tutor to Prince Edward was confirmed in July
> 1544). As it turns out, neither Ascham nor his unnamed and unidentified
> rivals were nominated for the position, for Cheke maintained the chair of
> Greek *in absentia* and did not resign until 1547, when Nicholas Carr was
> chosen. The *terminus a quo* for this letter is June 12, the date of Paget's re-
> turn from the Continent; the *terminus ad quem* is July 14, the date of Henry
> VIII's departure for the siege of Boulogne.

Your goodness, most accomplished and good sir, is the common refuge of all men who have devoted themselves to learning; that is the
common opinion and the public cry of nearly all good men. For this
reason, therefore, I have for the moment no regard for the magnitude
of those affairs which our wise king has entrusted to you because of
your extraordinary wisdom, nor am I reminding myself of the lowly
condition to which my fate subjects me. I shall apply myself to pull
you toward this cause of mine, away from the great burden of affairs
which surround you every hour during these very burdensome times.
It may not be a cause of the greatest urgency, but it is nevertheless
not least with respect to what you can honorably support and I desire
to obtain.

The nature of my cause is this. For the professorship of Greek
which our most munificent king established three years ago in the
public schools at Cambridge[1] two young men are campaigning, both
well-founded in the fine points of the literature and both aided by the
very powerful support of very powerful friends. Since I could not in
any way match the resources and influence of their friends, I abandoned not only all hope, but even any thought of this thing, until a
certain rumor was spread abroad among us at the University to the
effect that the king was going to give the office to the one who was
most skilled in the Greek language. When this became known, many

---

[1]In 1540 Henry VIII established five Regius Professorships, with the handsome salary of £40 per year. See Letter 2.

of our learned men, who were thinking highly of me (how correctly I know not), not so much with a hope of my obtaining the position, but more with a desire that I listen to them and make an attempt, urged me to go to London to make trial whether God, who is always able to work wonders, and very often does so, and who is the helper of all orphans and paupers like me, wished to promote my cause also.

While I was casting about at court, the most obscure of the obscure, I never dared, destitute as I was of all support of friends, to enter my scanty erudition into competition with those two, nor if I had been especially daring did I know any way to do it. At that moment, lo, you suddenly returned to England to the hearty applause of everyone of high and low degree, the mission, as everyone was saying, having been very skillfully executed.[2] By chance I was present, and I readily saw this in the joyous faces turned toward you, and I heard it in the way everyone was continually talking about you in conversations very full indeed of your praises. Then it came to me that you, like a *deus ex machina*, were being sent by Almighty God not only for the welfare of the state, but also for the support of my cause. For I was hoping even then that that great probity of yours, by which you have gained the high favor of the King's Majesty, focussed the good will and devotion of all men on you, especially embraced learning and its cultivators, and very skillfully handled every cause, would bring something to my cause as well.

For this reason, most accomplished sir, if the King's Majesty by your efforts and influence should grant me this position of professor of Greek--provided that my learning is not found utterly inadequate, of course--I must tell you that I cannot give you any remuneration, yet you will obtain all the favor and receive an abundant enough reward from him who said, "Whatsoever ye have done unto one of the least of these, ye have done it unto me."[3] You yourself know very well that a dictum from such an author has never been vain or fruitless.

If you ask whether there are any circumstances which can support my cause, there are some, and not the most insignificant. For before his Majesty established his professorship at the University, I

[2]From May 18 to June 12, 1544, Paget travelled to the Imperial court in order to coordinate plans for a joint attack by Charles V and Henry VIII on France.

[3]Matthew 25:40.

was appointed by the vote of the entire University to the public readership of the Greek language at a handsome stipend, and since that
time I have read Greek daily at the College of St. John, where I am a
fellow. The letters, moreover, which were sent from the University to
his Majesty or to any other men in positions of honor during the past
twelve years were always written by me.[4]

I have also written a book for his Majesty, *On the Art of Shooting,*
now in press;[5] in it I have set forth how useful bowmanship may be
to Englishmen at home and in wartime, and how the true art can be
taught in such a way that every Englishman may learn it fully and
completely. This small volume, when published (which shall be, God
willing, before the King's departure), will, I hope, be neither an obscure sign of my love for my country nor an insignificant testimony of
my inconsiderable learning.

My character is well-known to my Lord of Chichester,[6] to Redman, to Ridley,[7] but best of all to John Cheke, if he should be present,
with whom I have been associated in the study of Greek literature for
several years. I report all this to you truly, not so that I may appear
boastful and ingratiating, but wholly without presumption, from which
I want to remain as far away as possible, with the intention, most
accomplished sir, of helping my own cause with you as much as I

[4]On Ascham's roles within the University, see Ryan 23-27. His work as
scribe for University letters anticipates his election in 1546 as Public Orator (see
Letter 20).

[5]Ascham describes a preliminary version of *Toxophilus.* When Henry VIII left
England for the siege of Boulogne on July 14, 1544, Ascham apparently recalled
the book for revision. It did not appear until 1545 (see Letters 11-13).

[6]Dr. George Day, who was named Bishop of Chichester in 1543, knew Ascham from their days at Cambridge together. Once a fellow of St. John's, he was
Master of the college for a year (1537-1538) while Ascham was there, and then
became Provost of King's. He was the University's Public Orator from 1528-1537,
and received his doctorate in divinity in 1537. He was about 15 years older than
Ascham, and more conservative in religion. At one time he was chaplain to John
Fisher, the Catholic martyr. Bishop Day died a Catholic under Mary.

[7]Dr. Nicholas Ridley received his BA, MA, and DD degrees from Cambridge,
although he also studied at Paris and Louvain. He was associated with Pembroke
rather than St. John's, but Ascham admired him for his strongly Protestant views.
In 1540 he was named Master of Pembroke; later he became Bishop of Rochester,
then Bishop of London. He was burned at the stake with Hugh Latimer in Oxford in 1555.

can. If this letter too sorely wastes your time and impedes your work, you must ascribe it to your own highly esteemed generosity, which is so superior that it provokes all men to put their best hopes in it. Finally, anything you can do in this matter, you will do not for me alone, but for all of learning and for Jesus Christ, who inspired me to write to you and whom I pray every day to keep you forever well-disposed toward learning and healthy in the service of the state.

9 / To John Cheke (Giles I.xxiii)

[Cambridge, September 1544]

In July 1544 Cheke's appointment as tutor to Prince Edward was confirmed. Ascham lost a dear friend and mentor; after Cheke's departure the Athenian circle lost its dominance, and strife increased. The bitter struggle recounted in this letter to Cheke swirled around William Grindal, Ascham's favorite pupil. For almost seven years they had shared a room. In scholarship, character, and talent Ascham had scarcely seen his equal in England (see Letter 42). The last-minute addition to this letter (see penultimate paragraph) anticipates Grindal's imminent appointment as tutor to Princess Elizabeth, a departure that would deepen the distress and sense of alienation Ascham displays in both this letter and his subsequent letters to his absent pupil (I.xxvi and xxx).

The letter can be dated from Ascham's awareness of Bishop Lee's imminent death, which occurred on September 13, 1544.

The more pleasure I always took when we were together and you in your ready wisdom settled our domestic squabbles and excited us to the diligent pursuit of learning, most accomplished sir, the more bitterly and seriously do I now feel the necessity, such a change having followed your departure, to write a letter telling you that I feel a special grief arising from the loss of your counsel, which we need, rather than any joy arising from the fruits of that counsel, which not all of us have enjoyed. For we are now at such a point that I do not know whether the consent of good men may any longer be expected, as it was once believed, to advance learning and to check the unruly intolerance of some men. Although much has always depended upon the worthiness of the cause, mostly we have hitherto been sustained by your wise guidance. Thus some have tried with all their might to prevent me, through whom they have made themselves of some account, from ever again looking forward to any source from which I may bring honor to my friends, who are also, if anyone's, yours, or to prevent me from even supporting myself in my present humble lot.

For lately, if I may tell you the whole story, when we were choosing our readers, I wanted very badly to help my Grindal because of his poverty. To that end I was hoping to make use not of every means in my power, but only of such as I thought you would approve of as the most honorable. I put my case only to M__, B__, and A__ [1] and other men of that kind, and not until one or two days before the matter was to be decided. Then suddenly F__ and your friend B__, whether prompted by their own treacherous plan or by H__, or by both, having joined forces with S__ and his friends, upset all the authority that M__, P__, and all of us had so long possessed, and though they might have accomplished the same through us as has now been accomplished, they have so utterly scorned M__, A__, me, and M__, as he himself admits, that they boasted openly that they could and would name whomsoever they pleased without our help. If this behavior is to be approved or tolerated, those who can look out for their own interests on all sides are the prudent and successful men, and the fools are the ones who did not abandon an honorable cause and subject themselves to ridicule, and their friends to extreme danger.

At that point I boldly despised those unruly fellows in the interest of achieving my objectives and of defending my friend Grindal, and now I rejoice and am proud that I stood by my decision and handled everything in the way I did. If from this tempest any adversity should come hereafter to the general administration of our college, whose properties have hitherto been kept safe only the guidance of your counsel, you, whose love and approval of all my actions I have

---

[1] The use of initials rather than names at several points within this letter reflects Ascham's practice in some of his draft copies; he would have filled in these abbreviations in penning the fair copy: see my Introduction. I am unable to identify those whom Ascham has in mind here; without explanation Giles fills in M__ and B__ with (John) Madew and (William) Bill, each at this time a fellow of St. John's pursuing a doctoral degree in divinity.

wished to have, will clearly understand from which storm it came about.

Perhaps you will say that I have taken too much offense from a slight cause. Is it a slight cause when the authority of our president and our seniors has been despised and curtailed? Could I let my hopes be shattered at the very time when I had the best opportunity of defending my friends and striking those who bore me malice? Did either my kindness in being lenient with them or my power to do them harm have the slightest impact in restraining their hatred? How could I ever forget my friend Grindal, who I know for certain was so learned in Greek that he was second to none in the University, now that you and Smith[2] are gone? Oppressed by poverty, he had neither heart for study nor sufficiency for life. He has so much good will for me that his joys and troubles are also mine. Could I then forget that my Grindal would forever be separated from the learning in which he excelled, from the studies to which he wholly devoted himself, from me, with whom he had lived so intimately?

In short, even if all the offenses and painful wounds which afflict me and our community were passed over lightly, yet I can in no way endure such fraud, faithlessness, backbiting, bickering, and intolerance, which no longer rest quietly, exhausted and sleepy, but rather burst into the flames of a more serious conflagration, as though they had gathered new fuel or strength from the shameful behavior which is always occasioned by evil. Most accomplished sir, I would surely blot out the memory of all events, however calamitous, for the sake of our general harmony, except that I deeply fear that the faithless counsel of these men portends more bitterness to us and to learning. When profit, not law, the belly, not the books, shady treachery, not open counsel, *officiousness, not propriety,* ignoble fury and dishonor, not authority and the guidance of the wise predominate, I do not know what more may be expected from any consensus of virtuous men or from anyone open, frank, and unassuming.

So much about this public matter. If you have time, now a little about me. Since your departure, most accomplished sir, I have begun

---

[2]After his appointment in January 1544 as Vice-chancellor Thomas Smith was increasingly occupied with University affairs at London and the court. Not until February 1547, however, did he formally leave Cambridge to enter government service.

nothing of which I wished you not to be the silent approver as well as the present spectator, so to speak. To perfect it, I have given myself completely, much more attentively than ever before, to learning, to keeping impetuous agreements under control, and to maintaining peace. To what extent I have achieved my objective in this newest project and in everything else, M__ and B__,[3] with whom I never disagree, can testify. I would have had the ripest and most valuable fruit of their quiet counsel, which to my great sorrow those malevolent ones have misused in accordance with their own remarkable willfulness, if during these times I had not lacked the guidance of your wisdom.

For this reason, think always of your Ascham as a man who would set aside all injuries, enmity, and abuse before he would renounce the least part of your friendship. Thus I entrust myself and all this business to you, so that according to your inclination you may regulate it, though it is not my own wish to make changes, but rather to recount in this letter the incredible perversity of faithless scoundrels. They have alienated me from themselves (unless you see it differently), although they could have kept me a most firm supporter. Still, they have not in the least changed my mind about defending our general interests. Command me whatever you wish, but I hope that through your salutary admonition M__'s authority, which we all ought to obey, may not be further disdained, that the seniors may be respected, and that *officiousness* and insolent boasting may be checked as rank and order demand, so that from now on men will not seize the rewards of honor and learning by intruding into everyone else's business, but that these rewards will be bestowed on those who diligently withdraw themselves to study. For unless we heed our wiser men, enforce our own rules, and rouse ourselves to the study of literature, there can be no firm peace among us. Think this over, most prudent sir, and spell out what you think about us and our affairs.

So much about my public life; now about my private. As you know, my Lord of York is dying, which will significantly diminish my

---

[3]Here Giles again fills in the blanks with the names of John Madew and William Bill.

little fortune.[4] But that is the least of my problems. I am looking for another master, and I hope for much from the one, whoever he may be, who will succeed Lee. I wish more than anything else that the good Bishop of Winchester[5] would succeed him. Give me over to anyone you wish. But if you keep me yourself, it would fit my hopes to perfection. If you think of anything later on, make me happy with just a little indication of it.

As I was about to seal this letter, Madew and Bill came to me to speak about sending Grindal to you. I was somewhat upset because of my close relationship with him, but poured forth my huge joy because it would be a useful move for him. I commend him to you as a man "of the best stamp," as our friend Cicero would say,[6] pledging and promising that he will be very diligent about building a friendship, very adaptable to your teaching and interests, very virtuous in his taciturnity, faithfulness, and temperance, very unassuming in doing whatever you need done. Therefore if this letter results in a new measure of good will being added to the benevolence which you formerly conveyed to me through your kindness and recently through words of commendation delivered by B__ and M__,[7] I shall think it a kindness bestowed not on him, but altogether on me.

May the Lord Jesus defend that most illustrious rising sun,[8] the great hope of his father and his fatherland, and protect him from all harm, yoked to the chariot of your guardian care, tutelage, and counsel. Farewell in Jesus Christ.

[4]Ascham's patron Edward Lee, Archbishop of York, died September 13, 1544; from Lee Ascham received a very modest pension of 40 shillings per year. See Letter 4.

[5]Here I diverge from all editions, including Giles, emending "Westminster" to "Winchester." A letter to John Seton around this time (I.xxv) confirms that shortly after Lee's death Ascham was seeking the patronage of Stephen Gardiner, the powerful Bishop of Winchester.

[6]*Ad fam.* 7.29.1, adapted.

[7]Here Giles also supplies the names of Madew and Bill.

[8]Prince Edward, whom Cheke was tutoring.

10 / To Archbishop Thomas Cranmer (Giles I.xxvii)
[Cambridge, early 1545]

> The death of his patron, Bishop Edward Lee, in September 1544 prompted Ascham to a series of efforts to win new supporters; these efforts would be crowned in 1545 with the King's favorable reception of *Toxophilus* (see Letter 11). Even before the book on shooting was complete, however, Ascham set his sights on the highest possible sources of patronage, composing Latin poems in honor of Prince Edward and King Henry (see Ryan 43-45). He also began to reach out to Stephen Gardiner, Bishop of Winchester (see Letter 9, as well as a letter to John Seton [I.xxv]). The present letter to Cranmer, a Cambridge graduate well-known for his engagement with Protestantism during his university days and now the Archbishop of Canterbury and the godfather to the Prince of Wales, is one of Ascham's most elaborated and eloquent appeals, providing an occasion for him to display the full range of his rhetorical skills, to disclose his Protestant sympathies, and to advance the interests of the University. Evidently the appeal was a successful one, for in another letter (I.xxix) Ascham thanks the Archbishop not only for the dispensation requested here, but also for the financial relief of his poverty. The letter can be dated from an allusion to it in a communication to William Grindal dated February 13, 1545 (I.xxx).

Receiving letters from obscure and unknown men will not be a new experience for you, most accomplished bishop, but neither can the readiness to write to so prominent a man be considered presumptuous or strange in a person of my position. For as long as your great generosity stands out and shines out to challenge everyone, and so many reminders are at hand to arouse those of us who have given ourselves to learning, and as long as one is driven by poverty, another is hurried along by his eagerness to promote himself, and some--virtually all, at some point, certainly--are compelled by necessity while still others are drawn in voluntarily, certainly there can never fail to be an occasion for you to receive letters nor for us to write them.

Thus, most learned bishop, though I am asking for nothing new to your experience of receiving, as a new man I am perhaps offering something new in the way I write. Nevertheless, it is with all your old familiar kindness, not with some new style, that I earnestly entreat you to accept this. Moreover, I am not requesting your money or anything of that sort, but your great assistance and some measure of your favor and authority, something which will be easy and quick for you to give and very desirable and delightful for me to receive.

Who am I, and what do I request? Well, I am one whom fortune has made poor and obscure. I live in Cambridge. I have been brought up to be an eternal lover of learning. I have a weak stomach, and I am melancholic.

What's the point, you say. Let me tell you. When God's providence above all, the solicitude of my friends to some degree, and something of my own wish had aroused me to devote my life to the study of letters and I had not unhappily entered upon that way of life, lo, partly this leisurely study of letters and the kind of life I lead, partly the location and the intemperate weather of the place in which I dwell, and partly my natural weakness and the ravages of a quartan fever with which I was gravely ill for some months set upon all aspects of my health, and together or separately these conditions attacked the soundness of my mind and body so that for a long while I was able to be neither steady nor diligent in holding to the course I had determined to follow in my literary studies, and I acquired neither excellence nor profit from them.

Since, therefore, my fortune will not allow me to change this situation by moving to another place, and since I do not want and am not inclined to relinquish this way of life, and since no corrective measures can remedy my natural weakness, and since thus far time has not been willing to restore my lost strength or rid me of the effluent and the dregs of my melancholy and the effects of the quartan fever, and since in part the regulations of mankind, against which I consider an attack to be sinful, and in part the over-scrupulous consciences of a few men, for which I know it would be wrong to have no respect, exclude me from the best remedy and from a way of nourishing myself--since, I repeat, the restrictions of fortune, the intemperate weather of this place, the considerations of my studies, the natural weakness of my body, the tenacity of my melancholy, the harsh law and the over-scrupulosity or the ignorance of men have made a serious attack on the soundness of my body and immensely hinder the course of my studies, I pray your Lordship on account of the position at the University which I occupy, on account of the plan of life and of studies which I follow, and on account of the natural weakness of health which gravely burdens me that you will authorize me to be no longer restricted by that tradition which enjoins a certain selection of foods at certain times.

This petition of mine has not been fashioned out of a concupis-
cent desire for meat nor suborned by any license for insolence; rather,
it has been devised only by a consideration of my health, in order to
expedite the progress of my studies.   If I should obtain my request, I
shall not give offense by spreading the word around in casual conversation, but I will employ my dispensation silently, considerately, calm-
ly, and moderately, with a giving of thanks.   Those who grant this
liberty to no one unless he is struggling with a desperate illness are
much the same as men who never repair their buildings until they are
rotten with age and on the verge of collapse.   Thrifty masters of estates do otherwise; so do skillful physicians, who do not administer
medicine late, but always check illness at its outset.   Thus those who
never grant the use of this divine favor to men unless their health is
in desperate straits, by which time it has very little usefulness or none
at all, do not know what prudent foresight does in all public matters,
and arrogantly abuse the good divinely given to us--even though this
kind of good, because it is external, is not good except to the extent
that some benefit follows it.   Therefore we ought not to allow the misuse of food to make our illnesses desperate, but accommodate the use
of food to preserving our health, as Paul himself commands, saying,
"Wherefore I pray you to take some meat; for this is for your health."[1]

But this is not the place, and a letter is not the means, most
learned bishop, to press my case, nor does a consideration of your
time or any obscurity within the case itself require it.   Yet I can by no
means pass silently over one point which Herodotus recorded in Euterpe[2] about Egyptian priests.   Since all the arts and all kinds of sciences flowed forth from these men as though from very fountains, as
Homer, Pythagoras, and Plato knew, being three men of genius and
masters of the whole of learning who roved about Egypt for that very
reason, these priests, always engaged in the study of literature, con-
suming their minds and their whole lives in the contemplation of nature and virtue, abstained perpetually from all eating of fish, bound by
a certain scruple, doubtless for this one reason alone: so that the
glowing force and excellence of their wits would not be extinguished
by some frigid humor, which the eating of fish engenders.

[1]Acts 27:34, AV.
[2]Histories 2.37.

On this issue it is unjustly appointed, most accomplished bishop, that many kinds of scrupulosity which flowed from the Egyptians first to the Greeks and then to the Romans (a fact very easy to prove) have in our times spread throughout that papist bilgewater, so that the excellent counsel of the wisest men and their prescription for increasing learning have thus been stolen away from us by unlearned men in their ignorance, or by weak ones in their superstition, to the great disadvantage of great wits. Since, therefore, no one knows better than your lordship whence this regulation has arisen, by whom it was cherished and elevated, through whom it was introduced and applied especially to us, and since any consumption of fish in the springtime is useless, unprofitable in this swampy place, unhealthy for our plans of study, pestiferous to our state of melancholy, and always hateful to my stomach, I pray you in this letter, to which you are accustomed to give every consideration, most accomplished bishop, that in as much as I have decided never to rush into possession of that liberty, you will authorize me to enter quietly into it. If you do not allow me to recover that liberty completely and establish my seat and residence in it, at least permit me to set foot in it, and give me some inn in which to tarry, if not a home in which to dwell.

I have no money to purchase this for myself except for a small special sum left to me by my father, now in heaven, all of which I shall expend according to your Lordship's wish and will in order to regain some possession of my old liberty, either by translating Greek into Latin, or by using my slender ability in lecturing publicly at the University or privately in this college in either Greek or Latin. Under the wide umbrella of your great influence and authority I hope to obtain something from you in this matter, since I am certain that the very name of learning regularly secures as much from your Lordship as the great power of money can wring from other men by force. And you know yourself that a dispensation of this sort may be more justly conferred to students devoted to learning in order to preserve their health than any license may be given to I know not what sort of men in order to satisfy their passion. You understand the whole matter and will give to it as much as you want. I know that you will be willing to do as much as a worthy petitioner ought to hope for from a most equitable authority, and as much as a lover of learning ought to expect from a true priest and a great patron of letters.

And because I have long been aware that the lengthy discourse of my letter has shamelessly taken advantage of your good nature and transgressed all the bounds of modesty, I am certainly at liberty to avail myself of Cicero's counsel to be thoroughly and completely impudent.[3] Therefore if you would like to know how the University flourishes and what harvest of learning we reap, I shall give my opinion in a few words.

Many pursue the road to a knowledge of sacred learning, but different men have different ideas and are attracted by differing methods of study, and they open up sometimes one, sometimes another approach to it. Some--and however many they are, they are mad--ascribe a tremendous value to Pighius.[4] Following his footsteps in the controversy over original sin and God's predestination, they prefer to be swept precipitantly into error than to follow the right way with St. Augustine, who by reason of his industry and the superior excellence of his intellect and erudition and his greater opportunity for elucidating it very fully, has surpassed all the rest who either preceded or followed his time.

In connection with the daily reading of God's word, others follow Augustine's thinking above all, and go as far as they can in bringing to it the full range of their knowledge of languages, as though calling in the reserves. Everywhere languages are taught by those who are considered the best teachers of both knowledge and understanding, so that no thought is silent for want of speech and no language swells loquaciously for want of wisdom. We bring in Plato and Aristotle, from whose fountains among the Greeks articulate wis-

---

[3]*Ad fam.* 5.12.3.

[4]Albert Pighius (Pigge), c. 1490-1542, a Dutch theologian called to service in Rome, was a forceful defender of papal supremacy and the traditions of the Church of Rome; among his works were attacks on the English king's divorce from Katherine (*Hierarchiae ecclesiasticae assertio* [Cologne, 1538]), and on the views of English reformers William Tyndale and John Frith concerning the Lord's Supper. In his opposition to Luther and Calvin he emphasized free will to such an extent as to imperil the doctrine of original sin, and some of his teachings on sin and justification were rejected by the Council of Trent, where his work was much discussed. Ascham's defense of the Lord's Supper (*Apologia . . . pro caena Dominica*, posthumously published in 1577) scornfully attacks Pighius as "the head of the papists" (see Ryan 310), while *The Schoolmaster* (III, 162-63) terms him and Machiavelli the "two indifferent patriarchs" of papistry and atheism.

dom can best be drawn; from the throng of Latins Cicero is almost the only one we add to them. Herodotus, Thucydides, and Xenophon, the three lights of history, truth, and Greek eloquence, bring a great splendor to the rest of our studies. Homer, Sophocles, and Euripides, one the source, the other two the rivers of all elegant and learned poetry, water and irrigate the rest of our studies more abundantly now than Terence and Virgil did just a few years ago.

Many have given themselves to this best way of studying, helped along especially by John Cheke's might and power or spurred on by his counsel and example. He has led us on our way into an easy and ready course of study, and we tolerate his departure from us more cheerfully as we grow more certain that our own disadvantage is joined to and involved in the advantage and welfare of the entire realm.[5] Henceforth one can easily understand the truth of Plato's statement that the existence of one outstanding and excellent man, whose virtue others may imitate, building and adapting themselves totally and resolutely with will, industry, devotion, and hope, is of the greatest value to the state.[6]

These ways of conducting our studies, made free enough in this manner for their distinguished voyage, are being hindered by two very serious impediments. First, I know not by what fate or rather by whose action it happens that very few older students, by whose example the study of letters could very properly have been stimulated, and by whose influence the mores of youth could have been molded and shaped, linger in the University. Second, almost all those who converge here on Cambridge are mere boys and rich men's sons, or those who never get it into their heads to acquire a polished and complete education. Instead, they use their thin and superficial knowledge to get themselves more easily into some government position.

This unique double injury has reached into the University either because all hope of full and complete learning is cut off long before harvest time, as though in the greenness of its growing, or because every expectation of the poor and needy, whose whole life is consumed with an interest in literature, is mockingly stolen away from them by these drones usurping their places. For inborn ability, learn-

[5]In July 1544 Cheke was appointed tutor to Prince Edward at court.
[6]See *The Republic*, Book 6.

ing, poverty, and good judgment are worth nothing in a home where influence, favor, letters from great men, and other extraordinary and illegitimate considerations exert their pressure from without.   Hence the misfortune befalls us that certain wise men take it ill that a portion of the royal funds is given to the fellows of the colleges, as though they were not especially needy, or as though some hope of perfect learning could reside in anyone other than in those who have pitched the tent of their lives eternally in the eternal study of letters.

About this matter I could well discourse longer than the format of a letter demands, but I wanted to touch on it briefly so that we can never in any way lack either your joy in congratulating us when our studies are progressing, or you counsel in helping us out when they are being impeded.   For you are someone who, because of your singular good will, is accustomed to rejoice very much in the progress of learning, and who, because of your great influence, is uniquely able to help out in the struggles of learning.   Farewell, glory and pride of learning.

11 / To Bishop Stephen Gardiner   (Giles I.xxxiv)
[Cambridge, 1545]

Ascham thanks Gardiner, the Bishop of Winchester and the King's powerful minister, for securing the Privy Council's approval of *Toxophilus*, which appeared sometime in 1545.   A letter in English to Gardiner some eight or nine years later shows an undiminished gratitude: "No time since I was born so sticketh in my memory as that when I, unfriended and unknown, came first to your lordship with my Book of Shooting, and what since you have done for me . . . I never shall forget" (I, 418).   Ascham's appeal at the end of this letter for Gardiner's support of his cause before the King bore much fruit: Henry VIII received Ascham at Greenwich, and awarded him an annuity of £10 (see I, 412).

Most accomplished father, I am filled with a most wonderful joy at knowing how, with such a general consensus of everyone, my book has been approved by the King's Council.   And to be honored with a matchless commendation from you, so honorable a man, has left me anointed with an incredible abundance of almost infinite joy.   For since you surpass each individual on the Council by your engagement in all kinds of business, and surpass the whole group in decisions about how things are to be written, I submit this my design for approval to you, the leader, much before everyone else.

In writing my book I studied a course varying widely from that taken by almost every English author, not because I am ill-disposed toward anything written in English, but because I understand that mostly unlearned and thoughtless men have undertaken this sort of study. Moreover, they pursue inane material or something unequal to their abilities; they forsake appropriate and plain words, and are ignorant of metaphor and of words suited to the true splendor of the subject. And then they are unskilled and ignorant of how to organize it correctly. Dialectic for reasoning and rhetoric for adornment have not even touched their lips, and so in our vernacular they study to be not native and appropriate, but rather outlandish and bizarre. I know this for a fact. I am terribly upset that Englishmen are empty and barren of ability to write English, yet rush into it heedlessly. For some years only the more audacious, not the more skilled, have given themselves to this matter, which fact has introduced great confusion into our language and filled our realm with all kinds of crazy books. I have pursued a topic neither unsuitable to my ability nor useless and harmful to anyone. Wherefore if in your judgment I have to some degree given satisfaction, I know that I shall satisfy much of my own longing and, certainly, the expectation of my betters.

Indeed there are many reasons why I wrote this book. First, I wanted certain well-known men who thought I was distracted too much from more serious matters by my interest in archery to have some knowledge that not all of my time *has been shot away*, to use Aristophanes' words.[1] I wanted archery, something well-known and used in many a way, to be brought to people's notice and attention, elaborated in one manner or another in my work, if not to perfection, at least with my modest efforts. Another reason is that I am accustomed to a poor and meager style of life and spend long periods indoors, like students generally, and have recently been cast into great anxiety by the migration to a more splendid light of our most Reverend Father and liberal patron, Lord Edward of York,[2] and I wanted at

---

[1] *Plutus* 34.

[2] Ascham's patron, Edward Lee, Archbishop of York, died in September 1544.

least to set foot upon the road which might at some point lead me if not to some splendor of life and reputation, which I do not want, at least to some quiet and pleasant means for the life of a studious man, of which means I most certainly have a need.

And a happy outcome will follow this plan of mine if in accord with the love with which you particularly have embraced learning and the lovers of learning you would support me and my cause with his Royal Majesty with some testimonial of your opinion of me when occasion shall warrant it. From his Royal Majesty I look for nothing with greater eagerness than that he make it possible for me to study for a few years in Italy and across the sea.

Here then is the target which my *Toxophilus* tries to hit. If I have hit it, I shall believe that I have aimed most correctly and honorably. I have the greater hope for my petition to the extent that I certainly know that his Majesty is accustomed to offer excellent positions for life to outstanding archers (and I am not altogether unskilled in the thing myself), even to those completely rough in learning.

Therefore for the accomplishment of this matter I promise myself from your Lordship as much as a most honorable cause can look for from the highest authority, as much as my study of literature can look for from an unsurpassed patron of the same, and as much as an alumnus of Cambridge can look for from his most worthy chancellor.[3] The Lord Jesus have you ever in his keeping.

12 / To William Parr, Earl of Essex (Giles I.xxxii)
[Cambridge, 1545]

William Parr, Earl of Essex and future Marquis of Northampton, to whom this dedication of *Toxophilus* was addressed, was brother to Queen Catherine and to Anne Herbert (see Letter 14), and a prominent member of the court. Ascham also presented copies of *Toxophilus* to a number of other influential people at court, including the Prince of Wales, the Lord Chancellor, and the Bishop of Worcester (see I.xxxiii-xxxvi). A variant of this letter, differing

[3]Gardiner, himself a Cambridge man, succeeded Thomas Cromwell as Chancellor of the University in 1540.

slightly from that printed by Giles, is found on flyleaves of the copy of *Toxophilus* presented to Essex, a copy now in the Folger Shakespeare Library in Washington, D.C.

Of all the leading men in the realm, most noble sir, you are the first and principal one, in whose hands this book longs especially to be carried about.   For it knows that it is more obligated to you alone than to anyone else, since assuredly you were the first to whom it dared entrust itself in the beginning and by whose help it dared appear in the light of day and the sight of men.   I regard with earnest admiration and esteem your most temperate discretion in acknowledging it and your ready goodwill in praising it.

I shall cherish forever in my memory what you declared about it when it was presented to the most honorable King's Council and most recently when it was carried very modestly and fearfully to his Royal Majesty.   For I still seem to see, as though gazing with admiration, how you extolled this book to her Majesty Queen Catherine when she asked by chance what book it was, and how you commended it with an agreeable countenance, indicating your divine pleasure in it and prophesying extraordinary fame for it.

Therefore, since these individual favors clearly declare your singular kindness, and collectively attest very obviously to your heroic and godlike nature, born to promote learning and archery, the two highest honors and distinctions of England, I must therefore take pains so that although despite all my application I am unworthy of the least part of your great goodness toward me, I am always ready and willing to serve, and you will consider me to have shown myself forever as the man on whom these efforts were not unworthily bestowed. Continue then, most noble sir, to support learning more and more, so that she will in turn distinguish you; strive to surpass all others in capturing that glory which normally gives rise to a noble and genuine and everlasting renown.   The Lord Jesus have you ever in his keeping.

13 / To Barnaby Fitzpatrick   (Giles I.xxxviii)
[Cambridge, 1545]

> Through the offices of Cheke and Grindal, tutors of the royal children at
> court, Ascham was introduced to a number of prominent people, whom he
> greeted in the following series of graceful, if slight letters.   This salute to
> Prince Edward's favorite schoolmate, for example, was considered a model
> of epistolary form: Abraham Fleming included a translation in *A Panoplie of
> Epistles, . . . Conteyning a Perfecte Plattforme of Inditing Letters of All Sorts*
> (London, 1576).

I know of your glowing enthusiasm for the study of literature, most
excellent Barnaby, yet I have resolved to encourage you somewhat by
writing to you, for you requested me to write, and in your presence I
agreed to do so promptly.   There are many considerations which can
encourage you a good deal in the pursuit of learning: your great natural talent, your opportunity as a young person, the bright hope for
what hard work brings, the place which you have above others with
his Majesty, and the excellent learning of your teachers.   Individually
these qualities certainly offer much, and together they ought to incite
you the more as you daily observe how much the splendor of intellect, of study, of virtue, and of learning stands out and shines forth in
our most illustrious Prince Edward.   You cannot set before yourself
greater diligence, a more perfect example, or a brighter hope of glory.
      I have said enough.   I have spoken of everything which you can
define for yourself to value or which I can define for you to imitate.
You promised that you will write to me, which you will do either to
discharge your promise or to declare how well you write and how
diligently you study.   You cannot ask for a more suitable courier than
the one who carries this letter.[1]   I have sent copies [of *Toxophilus*] to
his Majesty and the rest of that very noble company.   May Christ
grant that our royal Edward surpass his father in honor, his teachers
in learning, and the prayers of his Englishmen in years and happiness.
And Christ increase you each day with a new accumulation of virtue,
learning, and nobility.

---

[1]Probably William Ireland, Ascham's pupil at St. John's. See I.xxxvii.

14 / To Anne Parr Herbert[1]   (Giles I.xlii)
[Cambridge, 1545]

> Anne Parr was sister to Queen Catherine, and brother to the Earl of Essex
> (see Letter 12). She was married to Sir William Herbert, whose fortunes
> rose dramatically when Henry VIII married Catherine in 1543. Herbert
> would be created Earl of Pembroke by King Edward VI.

At last I send you your Cicero, most noble lady. Since you enjoy his
book so much, you are acting wisely in studying it. In this volume
Cicero surpasses all the rest. You could not ask for more intelligent
discourse, or more eloquent intelligence. The splendor of the Christian
religion dims the rest of his philosophy; our modern forums do not
admit his ancient orations. His book *De officiis* embraces no small part
of human life. A genuine model of honor is expressed in his books,
and anyone who has given himself to imitate them cannot be very far
from the finest tradition in civic life.

I do not write this so that I appear to have undertaken the job
of encouraging, but to have shown the office of congratulating. For
you study most diligently, and do not need any exhortation, nor do I
have anything to propose to you to imitate, unless you wish to imitate
yourself and compete with yourself daily. Having obtained this victory, as I wrote to you at another time, you can add nothing more
illustrious to ennoble your position or more constant to perpetuate true
honor. The Lord Jesus increase your stature each day with a new
accumulation of virtue and learning.

15 / To Princess Elizabeth   (Giles I.xxxi)
[Cambridge, 1545?]

> Doubtless Ascham made his acquaintance with Princess Elizabeth through
> his friendship with Grindal, Elizabeth's tutor. He cultivated her friendship
> in a variety of ways. For example, through her governess he sent the Prin-
> cess a pen, an Italian book, and a book of prayers, and he offered to have

[1]Giles erroneously heads this "To Ann Countess of Pembroke." Her husband
was not created Earl of Pembroke until 1551.

another broken pen mended, which he then quickly returned with a brief
salute (I, 86-87). Like Letter 13, the present commendatory epistle was
translated and included in Abraham Fleming's *Panoplie of Epistles.*

For a long while I have been much in doubt, most illustrious Elizabeth, whether your greatness has prevented me from writing more
than your kindness has invited me to write to you. But after reflect-
ing upon how much you have honored me with your remembrance
when I am absent and with your gentleness when I am present, I
have definitely decided to risk your reproach of me for importunity in
writing rather than your conviction of me for some silent ingratitude
in not writing. I can more easily suffer you to reproach my excessive
duty than to accuse me of the silence of ingratitude, since I know for
certain than my letter cannot be a trouble to your highness.

And although I have an infinite number of arguments for writing
to you, I can do nothing more gladly than congratulate you, because
you more and more give luster daily to the great resources of your
fortune and natural talents with such great reinforcements of your
learning. It is difficult to determine whether the increase of your true
glory is greater than the commendation in every man's mouth of your
talent and industry. And although I know for sure that your education, in which distinguished teaching is linked up with your own great
worthiness, has its source in Plato's discipline, I do not hesitate to
affirm that your own volition and fine judgment have sustained you
most, Mistress Champernowne's[1] excellent counsel has advanced you
much, and the best instructions of my William Grindal have helped
and assisted somewhat.

Moreover, in both genuine histories and fictional poems we read
that even before the time of Plato the best prince was wont to sum-
mon some wise philosopher for advice about the whole course of life.

---

[1]Katherine Champernowne (Queen Elizabeth called her "Kat") came to court
in the 1530s, and became Elizabeth's affectionate and loyal governess. Kate's
strong personal influence upon her charge virtually made her Elizabeth's surrogate
mother. Her sister Joan was married to Anthony Denny. In 1545 or 1546 she
married John Astley (Ashley), also a member of Elizabeth's household, and the
Princess' cousin. See Letter 16 below. She welcomed Ascham during his visits to
his friends at court. "Your favor to Mr. Grindal and gentleness towards me,"
Ascham wrote to her, "are matters sufficient to deserve more good will than my
little power is able to requite" (I, 86). Despite some brushes with scandal and
intrigue, Kate remained high in Elizabeth's service until her death in 1565.

Thus the poets imagined that Jove made use of Prometheus, Agamemnon of Nestor; thus the historians teach that Hiero took to himself Simonides, Pericles Anaxagoras.[2] From them, whether it be from the glorious deeds of most glorious princes or the wisest counsels of the wisest philosophers, we learn that nothing ought to be more valuable to us than that supreme power always be joined with supreme learning.

But I do not mention these so that my letter seem to scold you for loitering, but rather to arouse you to hasten on, as though at the very end of the race you hear my congratulatory applause. In this very famous race for glory there is no one with whom you ought to compete more or from whom you can carry away a more famous victory than yourself. Therefore, most noble Elizabeth, do what you are doing every day, so that in the future you will make yourself and the fame of your family even more illustrious by the splendor of learning. If you do this, nothing greater can be added to your good fortune, nothing more desirable can befall your hopes, nothing more laudable can be proposed to the present judgment of men, nothing more admirable can be bequeathed to an expectant posterity. May our Lord Jesus Christ daily increase your Highness with an addition of virtue and of learning.

16 / To John Astley   (Giles I.xlv)
                            [Cambridge, 1545?]

> Like others whom Ascham cultivated at this time, Astley (Ashley) was part
> of an inner circle at court; he held a confidential position in the household
> of Princess Elizabeth. In another letter apparently written after Astley's
> marriage to Kate Champernowne, Elizabeth's governess (see Letter 15, note
> 1), Ascham declares that he considers Astley's friendship to be "amongst my
> chief gains gotten in the court" (I.xxxix); Ascham's *Report of Germany* would
> be addressed to him (see III, 4). Like Anne Parr, Astley is the recipient of

---

[2]Ascham probably had the stories of Pericles and Anaxagoras, and of Hiero of Syracuse and Simonides not simply from Thucydides and Xenophon respectively, but from such passages in Cicero as *De oratore* 3.34 and *Brutus* 44 (for Pericles/Anaxagoras) and *De natura deorum* 1.22.60 (for Hiero/Simonides).

a copy of Cicero's *De officiis* (see Letter 14); the presentation provides an occasion for Ascham to display his Christian humanism.

From a conversation with my friend William Grindal, most accomplished Astley, I readily learned that the idea Cicero borrowed from Plato is altogether true: if the form of virtue were to be discerned by the eyes, she would arouse in men a wonderful love of herself.[1] You would scarcely believe how much the extraordinary strength of your virtue stimulated me toward loving you forever.   Your virtue was marvelously reflected, just as in a mirror, in Grindal's conversation and in his constant mention of you.   This fire of love for you, first kindled in this way, inflamed me wondrously, and as though I were a man too wise who had voluntarily hidden himself away in the nooks of his obscurity, I was roused to send you this little book, which I myself enjoy immensely, as a sure testimony of my devotion and good will toward you.

I have done so, not so much to ingratiate myself with you shamelessly as to indicate lovingly by this pledge that I should like some part of your friendship to be shared with me.   I send this volume because I hear you would take great delight in reading it.   Truly, your thinking is very wise and very well suited to the attainment of all the greatness of an honorable life, which you seek to the great credit of your constancy.   In these books no shadowy simulacrum is sketched in, but the true and faithful image of virtue is expressed.   It is so connected and bound up with the religion of Jesus Christ himself that even if eternal salvation is not to be sought herein, at least that whole course of life on which we have set ourselves will not be hindered by reading these books, but will be completed more easily and readily.   Who feels otherwise, let him go to Christ, who says, "Whosoever is not against me is with me."[2]

Read therefore, most learned Astley, and may your ears so resound with the noble precepts of the book that you will never mingle with the common crowd of courtiers in the pernicious charms of the court, which catch the inexperienced sooner than any songs of the Sirens.

[1]*De officiis* 1.5.15, adapted.
[2]Matthew 12:30, adapted.

I do not write these words as though they would not come into your mind without my exhortation or as if you had any need of my warning, but rather so that you may understand what the elegant poet has expressed in his most elegant poem:

> He who advises you to do what you are already doing
> Praises you by his exhortation and by his advice
> Shows his approval of your actions.[3]

I rejoice to hear that my friend Grindal, with whom I lived for so many years in very close friendship and who has been stolen from me by I know not what harsh fate, has been received into your fellowship. Indeed, I hope that it will be a lasting one. Nonetheless, in loving him I shall concede nothing to you. Whether you surpass me or I you in this competition, I certainly do not care. But in leaving the possession of my old friendship and so auspiciously immigrating into yours, Grindal will understand that he has made an excellent and useful change. I shall write more later if I learn that this has not displeased you. Farewell.

17 / To John Cheke:[1] For the University   (Giles I.lvii)
[Cambridge, early 1546]

The allusions in this letter to threats against the University and the impassioned appeal to Cheke to act on behalf of her privileges and resources were most likely prompted by developments in late 1545 and early 1546. (On unspecified grounds Giles gives a date of 1547.) To finance the ruinously expensive wars with France and to spur Henry to reward his court favorites, Parliament in late 1545 passed the first Chantries Act, which allowed the King to take control of a whole range of intercessory institutions, including not only chantry colleges, but all colleges within the universities.

To counter this severe threat, Ascham anxiously rushed this letter to Cheke, along with another to Thomas Smith (I.lvi), also now an influential spokesman at court for University interests. Thanks to their influence, when

---

[3]Ovid, *Tristia* 5.14.45-46, one of Ascham's favorite tags.

[1]Giles erroneously heads this letter "To Sir John Cheke"; Cheke was not knighted until 1551.

a commission was appointed in January 1546 to investigate the revenues of Cambridge colleges, those appointed were themselves "insiders," eminent men of the University: Matthew Parker, the Vice-chancellor; John Redman, later Master of Trinity; and William May, President of Queens'.   In the event the act was not systematically implemented.[2]

Abraham Fleming also chose this letter for his *Panoplie of Epistles* (cf. Letters 13, 15).

From that whole multitude of very eminent men who have left this University and entered into the service of the state, most eminent Cheke, you beyond all others are the one whom the University has always esteemed while present and admired while absent.   You in turn, more than all others, distinguished the University when you were present and help her now when you are absent.   For when you were among us, you furnished her with those precepts of learning which support all of education, and proposed for imitation those models of talent which all have followed to the greatest advantage, but in which no one has achieved perfection.   Certainly there is no one among us either so ignorant as not to know, or so spiteful as to deny that these most felicitous fountains of our studies, to which so many have applied themselves with much diligence, devotion, and hope, have flowed from the glory, the assistance, the example, and the advice of your unique genius.   And these monuments of your humanity, ability, and learning have been immortalized in all our minds as a lasting record in memory of you.

However, while you are absent, you are furnishing a greater support and a more certain defense for the eternal protection of the honor of the University than either the remaining friends could have imagined or we ourselves could ever have expected.   For although the King, established in learning by your teaching and counsel, has a great love of learning, we are not ignorant of what the rest are willing or ought to do for our University.   We have drawn this our hope and discipline out of your Plato's teaching of that bad King Dionysius; but recently we have experienced through your assistance the fruit and its enjoyment in our good Prince Edward.

---

[2]See Alan Krieder, *English Chantries: The Road to Dissolution* (Cambridge: Harvard UP, 1979) 165-85, and Ryan 85-86.

Thus so many mutual responsibilities, so many sacred relationships and ties exist between you and the University that in recalling your progress from the very cradle of your infancy to the glory of the honor which you now enjoy, we can discover no benefit of nature, no fruit of diligence, no glory of genius, no assistance of fortune, no distinction of honor in which the University did not aid you to your benefit or share with you to its own glory; we do not doubt but that the University now can hope and seek once more from you the fruit of her distinctions conferred upon you so that there will be no faculty of your greatness which is not willing to exercise all its powers in preserving the greatness of the University. We entrust to you not one, but all the interests of the University, on which we hope you will exert yourself as much as you ought to bestow on us or we ought to expect from you. The Lord Jesus have you ever in his keeping.

18 / To Sir Anthony Denny: For the University   (Giles I.lxv)
[Cambridge, early 1546?]

The second sentence in this alarm about the future of learning appears to allude to threats in late 1545 and early 1546 against the universities' sources of revenue (see Letter 17). Ascham's own St. John's College was particularly fearful of those men who "creep into our farms," for the master, a few fellows, and some of the undergraduates were supported by income from lands attached to a grammar school at Sedbergh in Yorkshire, a school entrusted to the College's control under terms originating with its founder, Roger Lupton (see I.xv). Between 1543 and 1550 Ascham wrote some ten or more letters concerning the Sedbergh matter. Anthony Denny, one of the King's special favorites, would render great service to St. John's in this struggle, managing to have the school repaired and its lost lands recovered (see I.lxxxix and Ryan 86-87).

Since no one, most accomplished sir, has more authority and influence with the King, or a more ready devotion and good will toward learning than yourself, we are encouraged by the sure hope that with you as our special patron, learning itself, which you love so much, will be allowed to petition something from the King, with whom you are so influential. As you know, all our properties and resources have been placed wholly under the King's control. Wise men, who know that the King's wisdom is wonderfully ardent to cherish learning, also know that therefore no danger menaces learning, but they clearly envision that learning is become eternally secure, and they openly give assurance of it.   Yet a number of men (for there are such men) are strongly concerned about this change in affairs, and in their alarm they are afraid that some, enticed by the pleasantness of our farms, will become more interested in their own profit than in working for the advancement of learning.

We earnestly desire that every avenue for such men to creep into our farms be precluded. Even if such men are prevented from interfering in the administrative aspects of education, the whole matter ought to be referred to those men who have a good understanding of the great value of learning for the entire country with respect to the ordering and direction of society. For if these little acreages of ours, which are in reality the sinews of our studies, are for any reason taken away, you yourself, most prudent Denny, clearly understand that the immediate destruction of learning would follow.

For you know that the first movements toward learning begin with ignorant parents.   When they send their sons to school, they are not influenced by the excellence of knowledge, but are allured by the hope of making a fortune. If you remove the profit, the parents' hope is defeated, and thus every road toward progress in education is blocked.   Therefore, unless definite rewards for learning stimulate the feeble hope of parents, the country will lack all the fruit usually received from knowledge. We hope for a timely and speedy remedy for this situation, which envelops many in fear.   The situation is so bad that scarcely any possess the hope of coming to the University and few have the desire of abiding long within it.

Therefore we petition you to use your influence and resources to see to it that first of all we and our properties are not handed over to anyone, and then that some haste is applied to resolving these matters. Having done this, you will win the commitments of parents with higher expectations, whet the talents of young men to a keen edge, awaken learning to new distinctions, and furnish yourself lasting glory in the memory of all men. The Lord have you even in his keeping.

19 / To Bishop Stephen Gardiner: For the University (Giles I.xlvii)
[Cambridge, Spring 1546]

With minimal protestations of lofty motives the University boldly solicits the
assistance of its Chancellor, Stephen Gardiner, Bishop of Winchester, newly
returned on March 21, 1546, from an embassy to the Imperial court (see the
opening of this letter). The first of Ascham's three concerns, the threat from
the Chantries Act of 1545 to college properties, was being addressed on
several fronts, including letters to John Cheke and Thomas Smith (see Letter
17). The second, the comical "Maxwell affair," also prompted a letter (I.
xlix) to the Lord Chancellor of England, Thomas Wriothesley, in which Ascham grows even more indignant than he does here about this wretch's
affront to the University's ancient rights and privileges. The affair even
came before the Privy Council on May 14, 1546, a date which supplies the
terminus ad quem for this letter.

The anxious regret into which our entire University fell because of
your absence at this time cannot be as clearly indicated in our letter as
it can be truly and expressly comprehended by your imagination, most
accomplished bishop. In accordance with everyone's general congratulation of you at your return, we would rather recollect with thankful-
ness your former good service for us than so suddenly impose upon
you any new business. Nevertheless, we are now engaged in three
matters which, though not inherently difficult, are complicated by circumstances, and we urgently need your advice, assistance, and service.

Your Lordship cannot but know that the King's visitors have
assessed the manors of all our colleges with their annual incomes, and
recorded them in certain registers.[1] However, the rumor has reached
us that some new visitors are also being dispatched by his Majesty to
all the colleges in Cambridgeshire. We are very much afraid they will
exercise the royal might against the University, for we hear we are not

---

[1] The King's visitors or commissioners were Matthew Parker, John Redman,
and William May (see Letter 17); their report, undated, is noted in *Letters and
Papers of the Reign of Henry VIII* 21, i, 299; a translation of a summary of the sur-
veys is found in Charles H. Cooper, *Annals of Cambridge* (Cambridge, 1842), I, 431-
38. Parker's "memorandum" concerning the commissioners' successful meeting
with the King is printed in his *Correspondence*, ed. John Bruce and Thomas Per-
owne for the Parker Society (Cambridge, 1853) 34-36. See also Kreider 180-82.
There is no record to support the rumor Ascham reports in the next sentence.

specifically exempted.[2]   This news has plunged us into shifting and distressed states of mind.   For although we enjoy the certain, explicit, and eternal favor of his Majesty, and his undying zeal for the protection of honorable learning, and in addition have in hand a letter of our most serene Queen, in which she has confirmed this very matter absolutely and with certainty,[3] yet we are somewhat in fear that the very obvious unsuitability of certain men will bring us confusion and trouble.   Unless their insolence is checked and contained by prudent direction and distinguished authority, no one can doubt what further hope there is for learning.   And therefore, since this one cause contains within its limits not only the honor of learning but its life and hopes also, you will understand better and better in your great wisdom what sedulity must be employed and what authority imposed.

We bring to the attention of your Lordship another cause which, though not tending to the destruction of the University, yet will cause a very troublesome situation for all students unless some specific remedy and timely precautions are employed.   There is a poor and base man here, by the name of Maxwell, a townsman most violent by nature and a jailer or keeper of bears by trade.   It turns out that he has been employed to cart the King's fish.   In the name of this cartage business, this fellow, posted here, capriciously pressed a horse into service without general recruiting.   A few days later, after his wagon had already set out on its journey, by an unprecedented new usage, unknown in the history of many centuries, he took a horse belonging

[2]The 1545 Chantries Act, unlike some earlier acts of Parliament which exempted university colleges from various financial obligations, did not distinguish them from chantry colleges and other intercessory institutions marked for royal takeover. See Kreider 180.

[3]This letter from Queen Catherine Parr, which begins with an acknowledgment of the University's letters to her, "presented on all your behalfs by Mr Doctor [Thomas] Smith, your discreet and learned advocate," is further indication of the University's panic over the Chantries Act. The Queen reports, "I (according to your desires) have attempted my lord the King's Majesty, for the stablishment of your livelihood and possessions; . . . his highness being such a patron to good learning, doth tender you so much, that he will rather advance learning and erect new occasion thereof, than to confound those your ancient and godly institutions" (Matthew Parker, *Correspondence* 36-37).

to the master of Peterhouse,[4] not making the least agreement with its owner.   An agreement should have been previously arranged, so that we need not invoke our privileges, which guarantee that we shall not be troubled by these men to the extent of going to court.

Your wisdom can easily fathom this whole matter: the total unacceptability of such a man, the disgrace of the affair, and everything else which usually accompanies such insolent opportunism.   You will also see where this audacity flows, and what confusion is created by this incident among those who want to maintain a horse here for their own use if the flagrant dishonesty of that man is not stopped by some penalty.

Then there is another man, extremely litigious by his very nature, who has summoned to London Mr. Edward Bucknam, a quiet man and a fellow of your college,[5] for a trial over a debt before the Lord Chancellor of England.   If you can arrange matters in this case through your authority so that this innocent man may not experience harm, and our privileges suffer no violence, we shall be convinced that a great tranquillity is furnished for our studies and that all hope for the evildoer's success is cut off.

These three very important causes we have touched upon lightly in this letter, since could not pursue each one individually to its fullest.   Therefore we earnestly entreat your Lordship to put your confidence in this our representative, G. Sh.,[6] a prudent and grave man, who will explain in full each matter which pertains to these causes. The Lord Jesus have you ever in his keeping.

---

[4]Ralph Ainsworth.   Cooper prints several documents from this period concerning disputes over the King's purveyors' right to take horses belonging to members of the University (*Annals of Cambridge* II, 7-17).

[5]Trinity Hall.

[6]Cambridge bedell William (*Guilielmus*) Sherwood?

20 / To Sir William Paget   (Giles I.xlvi)
[Cambridge, June 1546]

Ascham's posture as well as some of his language is reminiscent of Letter 8, an earlier commendation of Secretary Paget as his *deus ex machina*. The present letter alludes to Paget's leading role in negotiations with France concerning Boulogne, culminating in the Peace of Ardres, signed June 7, 1546.

Ascham's election as Public Orator, replacing John Cheke, serving as Prince Edward's tutor at court at this point, testifies to his standing at Cambridge. The office conferred precedence over other members of the university senate in academic processions and ceremonies. The Orator's duties included writing letters in the name of the university and delivering formal welcomes to eminent visitors. It is true that Ascham had already been writing university dispatches for some years, but only as a paid scribe (see Letter 8, note 4).

I do not want you to think, most accomplished sir, that because I have not seen you or written to you for so long a time, I have forgotten my duty owed to you or your very great kindness to me.[1] During a great part of last year I was beset by a serious illness and did not live at Cambridge, and you, because of your great wisdom, were chosen by the universal vote and will of all England to carry on very important negotiations with the French. It thus follows that my duty toward you seems to have been interrupted by the vicissitudes of these times and not to have been neglected through a fault of my own.

But now that you have returned to England, bringing peace to the country to the great delight of everyone, and arousing praise for yourself which will be remembered beyond our time, I cannot but at least show by a letter that I myself have followed with great respect and joy the propitious course of the public welfare which was born through your efforts, with great praise showered on you by everyone. Yet I cannot show in words my delight, which is mingled with and enfolded in the advantage of the state, and united and commingled with your glory. I want to leave it to you how you ought to value it, not by the modesty of my humble station, but by the magnitude of the kindness by which you have most securely bound me to you.

[1]Paget had been instrumental in gaining Ascham an annuity for *Toxophilus* (see I, 398).

If you have time now to hear something about me, whom you have of your volition undertaken to protect and assist, recently the full senate of our University named me Orator of the University in place of John Cheke. I do not tell you this in order to boast of myself, in whom everything is insignificant, but to show that this part of my joy cannot be taken away from me, because the testimony of the University, where I am to some extent well known, has confirmed your wise judgment in having supported me as an unknown man. For nothing is more desirable to me than that which can by some new addition increase your old esteem for me; to preserve that esteem forever all my respect of every kind will forever be devoted to you. Farewell.

21 / To Lord Chancellor Wriothesley: For the University (Giles I.liii) [Cambridge, October 1546]

Records going back to the reign of Henry III chronicle the endemic border warfare between town and gown, the fiercest crises being those of the sixteenth century.[1] During the 1540s Ascham wrote well over ten official letters concerning the "impudence" of the townsmen of Cambridge. This letter to Sir Thomas Wriothesley, Lord Chancellor of England, exposes some of the bitterness of the conflict; the Privy Council itself was forced to step into the dispute recounted here (see *Letters and Papers of the Reign of Henry VIII* 21, ii, 333, 334). The date of their meeting (November 1, 1546) and the date of the townspeople's refusal to swear to keep the peace (October 22, 1546; see Giles' note to I.li) help to date this letter.

Reluctantly, most honorable Lord, do we impose any new burden upon you, who almost alone bear so much responsibility for the kingdom. But those old abusers of our peace, the townsmen of Cambridge, drive us to the point that we are now forced to consume just a little of your time. Moreover, we are forced to do this by reason of their unjust actions, which are the more unjust because hitherto we

[1] See Helen Cam, "Town and Gown" 76-86 in *The City and University of Cambridge*, vol. III of *A History of the County of Cambridge and the Isle of Ely*, ed. J.P.C. Roach (1959; London: Dawsons, 1967); George Dyer, *History of the University and Colleges of Cambridge* (London, 1814) I, 54-66; Mullinger II, 3ff.; C.H. Cooper, *Annals of Cambridge* II, 1-21.

have never challenged them more to claim their rightful place in civic life, so that we may keep inviolate the King's peace among us.

The facts are as follows. We have a charter, drawn up in the time of Henry III, guaranteed in perpetuity thereafter by the decrees of successive kings, and for centuries deposited with us for annual employment. It decrees that each year our Vice-chancellor and the mayor of the city shall meet at a stated time and place to administer an oath to certain scholars and townspeople for the keeping of the public peace and order.[2] Of these townspeople, two alderman and two others from each parish are required. This year no aldermen and scarcely anyone else from the roster of citizens could be persuaded to take the oath, notwithstanding the Vice-chancellor's repeated requests in the name of the King that they take it. We believe that "the name of the King" should be included in all oath-takings, just as though it were a kind of sacred obligation, so that the public authority will not be scorned. We cannot include the whole affair, which been drawn out into a long and wordy debate, within the limits of a short letter; with that in view, we entreat you to put your confidence in our representative, an eminent man.

However, this one word we earnestly desire you to fix in mind, or rather recall to memory: there was a time when our townspeople contained themselves in virtuous behavior out of their great respect for the scholars. Now, however, we and the University have come to the point that we cannot command any respect, and their ferocity extends even beyond nocturnal rioting. They are so puffed up that what once they never dreamed of they now dare to do openly, and to stir everything up into lawlessness.

In our domestic resources we have established no protection against them, but have long entrusted ourselves wholly to the equity of your keeping, that is, to your wisdom. This decision has led us into the hope that there never can be such boastful insolence within the townspeople but what your authority can repress it; neither can the welfare of the University fall to such disrepair that your assistance cannot easily raise it up. May our Lord keep you eternally the high-

---

[2]See Cam, "Town and Gown" 77-78; for an index of the University's charters, see George Dyer, *The Privileges of the University of Cambridge* (London, 1824) I, 4ff.

est of our Prince's counselors, the chancellor of our realm, and the patron of learning.

22 / To Sir William Paget: For the University   (Giles I.lxi)
[Cambridge, September 1547[1]]

The University took the small-town high jinks recounted in this letter with utter seriousness. On behest of the Senate Ascham also detailed the mayor's defiance and his son's jail-house raid to the King (I.lxii) and the Archbishop of Canterbury (I.lix). On October 2, 1547, both "malefactors," as the minutes term the offenders, were brought before the Privy Council, where they "confessed their faults." To promote the "increasse of frendship between the Toune and Universite," the Council decided "there shuld not be any extremite of punishement," and instructed the guilty to make public apology to both townsfolk and the University.[2]

The Privy Council's record confirms that the episode involves the famous and ancient Sturbridge Fair. In town-gown affairs "the most persistent source of dissension," according to Roach, "was the rights of the University in the markets and at Sturbridge Fair, involving questions such as the assize of bread and ale and the courts leet which the University claimed to hold."[3] Repeatedly, and sometimes violently, the town challenged the University's right not only to police the Fair grounds, but also to control the retail trade in victuals at the Fair and within the town generally.

If our townsmen, most prudent sir, had had any consideration for their oath, for a peaceful University's gentleness which they now en-

---

[1]Giles dates this letter September 17 from evidence not explained. The record of the Privy Council (see below) does provide a firm, if not precise indication of the date.

[2]*Acts of the Privy Council of England,* ed. John R. Dasent, II (London, 1890) 133-35; the Council's orders and the text of Mayor James Fletcher's apology are also found in Dyer I, 111-13, and Cooper II, 3-4.

[3]"The University of Cambridge," in *The History of the County of Cambridge* III, 175; see also Helen Cam on trade policies and privileges at the Fair in "Town and Gown," Roach 82-84.

joy, for the circumstances of our country,[4] or for your dignity and that of the other members of his Majesty's Council, we would not at this time have written this letter to you, or would have written another kind of letter. But since there never was a time when our townsmen enjoyed a more mellow University, since no harm from us threatens them, since no nocturnal raids or youthful savagery engenders any disturbance among them, and since our gentleness does not restrain them, but instead they have found it to be a favorable occasion for rioting willfully and insolently, we are forced--indeed forced, since for these many years we have set up no means of protection from our own resources--to entrust and commend the welfare of the University to your wisdom, inasmuch as we have determined to heed your authority and advice alone.

During the recent market days our proctors, aroused by the complaints of many good men, were on a certain evening patrolling the outlying districts and other alleys and lurking places of the market, where usually a great off-scouring of nefarious persons who at market time always flock here in droves hide themselves. Having discovered them in a great tumult committing actions which are too evil to be mentioned, the proctors came to the mayor of the town to get the key to the common jail.[5] The mayor, however, with new insolence, beyond all custom and precedent, contrary to all our privileges, although he has by a special agreement bound himself to maintain them, denied them the key. We do not know his reasons, unless he was irritated at having to restrain by law the desperate insolence of the wicked.

Our proctors, refused the jail, betook themselves to the castle (our privileges permit us to use either place at our discretion) and locked up the offenders whom they had arrested. Suddenly, an hour or so later, the mayor's son, definitely more agitated and insolent than his father, abducted them from the castle and set them scot-free to recommit their former crimes with new hope, with new courage, the

---

[4]Here and elsewhere in this letter Ascham alludes to the concern about possible instabilities within a country now ruled by the boy King Edward VI, who had succeeded to the throne upon the death of his father January 28, 1547.

[5]The University was entitled to use this jail, called the Tollbooth, and also controlled the ancient Norman castle standing outside of town; concerning the oft-disputed powers of police and the control of the jails see Cam, "Town and Gown," in Roach 77-78.

laws broken, the magistrates disdained, and the good men whose complaints led to their arrest mocked.

We are neither willing nor able to wax eloquent about the unseemly behavior of this action, most prudent sir. But simply and straightforwardly we say this: in view of our gentleness under your authority during these times in our country when all domestic matters ought to be very quiet, if this youthful licentiousness, if such great impunity in the wicked, contrary to the welfare of our country and contrary to so many royal privileges and laws of Parliament, can be covered up without censure, or be defended and thus breed new license, we cannot tell whither insolence will spread, where violence will break out, what evil men will dare, what the wicked will not dare, or what good and law-abiding men will expect in the future.

Acknowledge our cause therefore, most noble sir, and through your authority make these men know what it is to violate the laws, to commit the crime of breaking an oath, to support impunity, and to be unafraid of constituted authority. From this service of yours, all men will know that because of you lawbreakers cannot expect to vex others, and good men will not lack resources to defend themselves.

We would explain this matter more fully as well as other affairs of the University, but the eminent bearers of this letter will have a better opportunity to do so in person. We pray you to trust them. The Lord Jesus have you ever in his keeping.

23 / To Archbishop Thomas Cranmer: For the University (Giles I.lxvii) [Cambridge, Autumn 1547]

In anticipation of the November 4 opening of the first session of Parliament under Edward VI, Ascham wrote official letters to the Dowager Queen (I.lviii) and to no fewer than eight of the most prominent Privy Councillors,[1] each time appealing for support in the upcoming deliberations of Parliament

---

[1]Besides this letter to Cranmer, Ascham also wrote in his official capacity to the Earl of Warwick (I.lxviii), the Marquis of Northampton (I.lxix), the Earl of Arundel (I.lxx), Lord Chancellor Rich (I.lxxi), Protector Somerset (I.lxxii), Sir Anthony Denny (I.lxxiii [Letter 24 below]), and Sir William Paget (I.lxxiv). He also wrote a personal letter to his friend John Astley, who was going to be a member of the new Parliament (I.lv).

and for a reauthorization of the University's privileges. In this letter to Cranmer, the Privy Councillor who would play the central role in the decisive movement toward Reformed Protestantism during Edward's reign, Ascham unleashed his most colorful rhetoric, attacking the Pope and the Church of Rome in coded language that obviously betrayed strong partisanship and that anticipated the measures of radical Reform that would be enacted under the leadership of Protector Somerset (see also Letter 25 for the rhetoric of Edwardian Protestantism).

Humbly to petition you for something when you willingly give us everything, most learned bishop, is not, we are persuaded, a ridiculous and superfluous business, but rather a duty owed to an affectionate goodwill. Therefore we beseech you that our privileges be confirmed in this your senate. Nearly everyone understands how much it concerns the state that the objectives of learning be considered, but you alone beyond all others observe how much it concerns the true faith. For you know that for 500 years or more learning began to withdraw itself from the sight of man and slip back again into darkness because of the failure of kings by whom it should have been nurtured. During those times so blinded by fogs and entangled in ignorance, that extraordinary boar of the woods[2] laid waste beyond measure the vineyard of Jesus Christ, not only trampling the kings of the earth and gathering to himself the kingdoms of the world, but assailing and bursting into the holy precincts and the temple of conscience so that today there are no morals of men, no purpose of life, no ceremonial rites, no sacraments of the church, no footprint of Christ which has not been subverted by his destructive powers or made foul by his stinking breath--nothing which has not, to speak more gently, but more graphically with St. Paul, been most foully corrupted and defiled by the wisdom of human *will-worship.*[3]

This darkness of knowledge, this ignorance has taken from us the word of God, and carried the control of humane learning into such lawlessness that hypocrisy, idolatry, and adultery have been very craftily put around the necks of men in place of the true worship of God, the right use of the most divine things, and the conduct of a

---

[2]Ascham's term for the Pope and papistry comes from Psalm 80:13 (79:14 in the Vulgate). See also *The Schoolmaster* (III, 205, 236).

[3]The Greek word is from Colossians 2:23.

sound and pure life. We recall the more willingly this pestilence of ignorance because now we derive great hope of establishing anew the honor of learning, especially during these days when everything has been made wonderfully ready for elucidating the true faith, which certainly cannot be far from distinguished learning.

And since your wisdom by divine providence has long been saved up and has now been aroused for the restoration of the word of God, we do not doubt but that you will devote all your effort and power to the preservation of the welfare of learning also, and that you will be encouraged somewhat by the sense that certainly at this time no unexpected misfortune, no expected advantage can befall learning of which you will not be either the author, to your great commendation, or the participant on behalf of some correction, stirred up by the speech and conversation of all men. The Lord Jesus have you ever in his keeping.

24 / To Sir Anthony Denny: For the University   (Giles I.lxxiii)
[Cambridge, Autumn 1547[1]]

This is another from the series of eight similar letters to leading Privy Councillors in anticipation of the first session of Parliament under Edward VI (see Letter 23). This letter to one of the most faithful friends of the University has an ironic relationship to the extravagant Protestantism of the preceding letter to Cranmer, for here--and only here--Ascham appears to caution that sweeping action against papism might injure the cause of learning by its effect on conservative scholars still holding to the old religion.

Whether you are more distinguished, most noble sir, by wisdom, judgment, influence, and authority than by your good will, kindness, most refined manners, and humanity is surely an undecided question in the minds of all men. All these qualities are the distinctions of fortune, the gifts of nature, or the fruit of your industry and labor; nevertheless, however great these advantages are, your greatest glory does not

---

[1]For unspecified reasons Giles dates this letter November 8, 1547. Parliament convened November 4.

blossom in them.   The voice of the general consensus of all men spreads around another commendation of you, namely that you have set yourself, not under the auspices of fortune but under the guidance of the Holy Spirit, to restore the true faith, to care for the welfare of the state, and to guard the honor of learning.   These three things are your studies;   their glory in you will be the admiration of all ages, their fruit will redound to the use of many men, and your example will endure forever to be imitated by the most excellent men of the state.

And while religion, learning, and the state so occupy all your efforts that you have no time to devote to other pursuits, we nonetheless find it necessary at this time not to attempt to take anything from you, but to recall to your mind and to pray you to give us your aid in the coming assembly of the realm in the matter of confirming the privileges of the University by a new authorization of the King and new ratification of Parliament.

This cause, as you will wisely discern, does not concern the welfare of the studious ones who are now enclosed within the walls of Cambridge; it concerns the welfare of absent ones who are ignorant because of lack of knowledge or excluded because of youthfulness and cannot comprehend what is useful or petition for what is right and just.   It concerns the hope of those fathers who are accustomed to send their sons here for study; it concerns also the welfare of posterity; it concerns the distinctions of a flourishing state; it concerns the defense of the true faith.

We can reasonably press this case, but are reluctant to do so with you.   Yet one matter we earnestly desire to bring to your careful attention, and not to yours alone but to the attention of all who have been ordained by God at this time to guide the nation.   It is this: that there be no plan which might justly punish the ignorance of an evil priesthood but which would also sweep away the hope of excellent and talented men from their devotion to learning.   Such a remedy would not bring evil men to sanity, but drive good men to desperation.

These matters can better be encompassed by your wisdom than we can explain them in writing.   Therefore, wherever the defense of the faith, the welfare of the state, and the utility of learning leads you, lean towards your own interests, ability, influence, and authority.   The Lord Jesus have you ever in his keeping.

25 / To the Duke of Somerset: For the University   (Giles I.lxxv)
[Cambridge, November 14, 1547[1]]

To check the stubborn resistance of Stephen Gardiner, the conservative and formidable Bishop of Winchester, the Privy Council imprisoned him in the Fleet from September 25, 1547, to January 7, 1548, and ousted him from the Chancellorship of Cambridge. Here the University formally offers the position to Edward Seymour, Duke of Somerset and Protector of the King. (Giles also prints his acceptance letter, dated December 9, 1547 [I.lxxvii].) Like Letter 23, this one displays the flourishes of Edwardian Protestant rhetoric. It should also be compared to a remarkable letter in English (III, 65-75)[2] which Ascham wrote nearly 19 years later to Queen Elizabeth. In both instances the Biblical story of David, Saul, and Samuel supplies the tropes and themes, including the "word from God's own mouth" with which the present letter opens.

"I have found a man after my own heart" is the word of our eternal Father[3] and a most noble testament for David, right honorable Duke. But why such great praise of so great a man? Peace, prosperity, and justice, along with fear of God, true religion, highmindedness, and a divine skill in crushing the enemy--these attributes individually pleased God and collectively commended David to him. Despite their great fear of God the family of Jesse did not flourish with the greatest honor among the people, and from small beginnings the wonderful providence of God carried David, not a great man, into the highest position.[4]

As we observe God's singular grace and extraordinary favor toward the Seymour family, and as we follow you and your whole course of life from the cradle to this day, we certainly see, and have seen these many years, that you, right honorable Duke, have been cho-

---

[1]Giles' date is that cited by M. R. James, *Catalogue of Western Manuscripts in Corpus Christi College* I, 214 (MS. 106, art. 172).

[2]Giles erroneously construes the letter as Ascham's dedication of *The Schoolmaster* to Elizabeth, whereas it apparently served as his presentation to the Queen of Peter Martyr's commentaries on the two biblical books of Samuel (see III, 74).

[3]Acts 13:22, which in turn refers to 1 Samuel 13:14. The Vulgate text of the two passages differs slightly; Ascham employs the language of Acts.

[4]David, a shepherd, was the youngest son of Jesse, and an unlikely prospect for the kingship of Israel (see 1 Samuel 16:1-18).

sen from all men in the world not by Mercury's wand, but by the
new spirit of Samuel and the finger of God.[5]   To you alone God has
entrusted four things in this world.   The peace and welfare of the
realm, the management and conduct of war, the pursuit of a purer
religion, and the custody of our sacred virgin King Edward have been
imposed upon you alone.   Give heed to what we say, understand the
gravity of your undertaking, and acknowledge how much you owe to
God in all these matters.

Through you such great peace and pleasantness of life in England has now been established that what people's opinion of you is,
how high the favor of each man is, and how all men eagerly speak of
you as the father of the country, you may more agreeably recognize
than we declare in our letter.   In war God has entrusted to you the
sword of Gideon.[6]   He gives you not a common victory, such as the
princes of this world enjoy, but one such as Joshua gained over the
kings of Madon and Hazor,[7] such as Judas once gained over great
Antioch and Nicanor.[8]

In religion God has aroused in you the same spirit as Gideon's
for demolishing Baal's altar,[9] whose every abomination we all beseech
you to eradicate.   In the sacred custody of our Josiah[10] you undertake
the holy responsibility that this virgin King (for in the history of our
kings he is the first to deserve that title) live a pure and irreproach-
able life, free not only from any defilement, but even from any suspicion of fornication with the Babylonian whore.[11]   Accordingly, since
God has constituted you alone as the author of peace at home, the

[5]See 1 Samuel 16.

[6]Judges 7:20.   Gideon was a judge, and victor over the Midianites.

[7]See Joshua 11:1-15.

[8]For Judas Maccabeus' victory over Nicanor, general of the forces of Antiochus Epiphanes, see the apocryphal book 1 Maccabees 7:26-50; for the inglorious
end of Antiochus, see 2 Maccabees 9.

[9]See Judges 6:25-32.

[10]The story of the reformation wrought by the boy King Josiah is told in 2
Kings 22-23, and 2 Chronicles 34-35.   Concerning the image of Edward VI as a
new Josiah, see King, *English Reformation Literature*, chap. 4.

[11]I.e., the Pope and the Church of Rome; see also Letter 23.

defender of our country abroad, the strongest protector of religion, the most holy guardian of his sacred royal Majesty, God's voice and the people's voice say of you, "I have found a man after my own heart."

Whereas your dignity is adorned with these four very great titles, in order that there will seem to be no place left for increasing it, behold, God, since you acknowledge, lay hold on, and reverence him and his providence with a holy fear in your duties, has resolved to enlarge you more and more with a new supply of honor and a new addition of glory.   Behold, learning and the pursuit of learning at the University of Cambridge offer themselves to you.   They are eager that you occupy a fifth place of honor.   They entrust and commend themselves to your good will, support, advice, favor, and authority.   With one mind and will, with one voice and prayer they acknowledge you as leader and protector, as their High Chancellor.   The public peace prays, military glory requests, true religion entreats, and his royal Majesty commands by his example that you receive into your trust the honor of learning, for these four petitioners, great as they may be, certainly cannot defend their distinctions and splendors without the resources of learning.   You can now hope for no greater glory, we can seek no greater.   Now only this remains: that the voice of God, King, country, religion, and learning proclaim in unison, "We have found a man after our own heart."

We recently wrote to you about the preservation of the honor of learning in this Parliament.[12]   Now the entire matter is yours. Therefore incline towards whatever the welfare of religion and the country, as well as whatever his Majesty's and your own will call you to do in the matter.   If you seek to do a service, hear us, O most prudent sir; we speak freely and truly, and are bound by our word to you.   Upon no person, upon no thing have you ever bestowed a kindness which can keep it in memory for a longer time and pass it on to all posterity more fittingly than upon learning.   What we desire you to do, we have hitherto written, and you know it well.   We add only this much, desiring you to lay it next your heart: that you be willing to labor not so much to furnish rewards to those who now flourish in learning as to arouse to a new liveliness the hope of youth, of talent, and of parents who want to send their sons to study.   We have

---

[12]I.lxxii, which is one of the series to which Letters 23 and 24 belong.

wrapped up a most important matter in a few words.   If this one thing goes well, the country can expect the course of the best education will largely be unimpeded, a situation which, since it generally involves the greatest profit to mankind, will certainly be your greatest distinction.

We fear that we have been troublesome to your Lordship.   We therefore all pray to God that with the same foresight by which he has preserved you these many years for this multiple honor, he will ever have you in his keeping as the steadfast author of peace, the strongest defender of the republic, the purifier of true religion, the most trusty guardian of his royal Majesty, and the High Chancellor of the University of Cambridge.

26 / To the Duke of Somerset: For St. John's College   (Giles I.lxxvi) [Cambridge, November 21, 1547][1]

> This letter to the Lord Protector witnesses to what historians regularly term the "price revolution" of the sixteenth century and the "great debasement" of coinage during the last years of Henry VIII and during the reign of Edward VI.[2]   Ascham, writing this time on behalf of his college rather than the whole University, is not simply complaining about inflation, however, but he also exposes the college's hopes to share in the spoils of the ecclesiastical institutions which would be expropriated in the new wave of Reform.

We men set in this humble condition would not write to you, elevated to the highest office of the state, most honorable Duke, if our cause were not great and if your kindness were not of the greatest.   And although God has touched you with his singular grace, and although you, inspired by God, devote yourself wholly to caring for the public

[1]Giles' date for the letter is confirmed by Thomas Baker's report of a copy in the archives of St. John's: *History of the College of St. John the Evangelist, Cambridge* (Cambridge, 1869) I, 368-69.

[2]See J. D. Gould, *The Great Debasement: Currency and the Economy in Mid-Tudor England* (Oxford: Clarendon, 1970); C. E. Challis, *The Tudor Coinage* (Manchester: Manchester UP, 1978); R. B. Outhwaite, *Inflation in Tudor and Early Stuart England*, 2nd ed. (London: Macmillan, 1982); and Peter H. Ramsey, ed. *The Price Revolution in Sixteenth-Century England* (London: Methuen, 1971).

welfare, defending the country against enemies, or restoring true religion, yet from God you have something else of which the usefulness for the nation is equal to your singular virtues, and of which the glory surpasses your general commendations: you take up the cause of the poor and give heed to the cry of the needy. This is not a human wisdom, but a divine benediction; there certainly exists in these very remarkable times a most remarkable felicity. Acknowledge this your true glory and ever guard it, most prudent lord; this one glory surpasses all your other good fortunes.

Encouraged by this confident judgment of you, we bring you our cause. If you want to know who we are, we answer, the whole body of students of the College of St. John the Evangelist at Cambridge. Where do we come from? From all parts of England we come together in this college. For what reason? To study. What is our chief goal? First to spread the gospel to God's people. Then as much as possible to abolish human doctrine, that is, papistry, with its hypocrisy, superstition, and idolatry. What laws govern us? Those most difficult for labor, and carefully framed for the harvest of studies. What support and enrichment of the nation do we offer? First, we nurture the best talents with the best teaching and manners. Second, those who staff and make famous almost every one of the colleges go forth from our fellowship.[3] Finally, we have sent many laborers into the vineyard of the Lord, and into the rest of the state, men fit and well-trained. What number do we sustain? In that point we exceed every college in this kingdom. By what farms and incomes do we accomplish this? Indeed here we are exceeded by almost every college. What fixed expenses do we have? For victuals, each week, from three to seven pence, at the most twelve. For the clothing of students, nothing; for fellows, one mark.[4] For the remaining essentials of life, for household supplies, and for the repair of books, they receive another mark. But do good men help out? They are no longer living. But what about the fathers? They cannot help today.

What remaining hope is there for us? That we suppliants come to you, most noble Duke. What are we going to ask? Partly that we

---

[3]See also *The Schoolmaster* (III, 235) for Ascham's pride in St. John's as the "metropolis" of which other colleges are but "colonies."

[4]During the Tudor period the mark as a unit of account was equal to 13s 4d.

may petition for what is fair and what is ours, partly that we may arouse your sense of duty. It is lawful to ask for what is justly one's own. Today it is surely lawful, and blessed are these times in which it is permitted; most blessed are you, through whom it is permitted. Let flatterers contrive whatever they will; that nation is most blessed where each man is at liberty to ask freely for his own, and it is the general will of all Englishmen that England may long enjoy through you this blessedness, the greatest for your glory and the most useful for the prosperity of the nation. But what petition do we bring forward? In this matter we petition justice, certainly useful to us, but most useful to the nation and very glorious for your own reputation. Give heed with good will to what we say and grant with liberality what we petition.

Lady Margaret, great-grandmother of our King Edward, founded this college; she provided it with the best statutes for the promotion of learning and with most suitable estates for support.[5] Since her day three very hard times have afflicted this college. First, certain ministers of the King, who count the King's wealth in heaps of money, even though the good will of the people, the welfare of the nation, true religion, and the best learning exist as the most certain wealth of a good king, took a large part of Lady Margaret's gift away from us.[6] Four hundred pounds per year were cut off and taken away from our estates. Many years later, John Fisher, Bishop of Rochester, while defending false doctrine with too much perversity, stripped the best learning in this college for his own adornment and wealth. This man ruled the college at his own pleasure, and later the most celebrated adornments which Lady Margaret had bestowed on this college were placed in his hands.[7] We prefer not to be specific, and we have cov-

[5]On the benefactions to St. John's and to the University generally of Lady Margaret Beaufort, Countess of Richmond and mother of Henry VII, see Mullinger I, 434-52, 461ff., and Baker I, 55ff.

[6]Lady Margaret died in 1509, while the college was still in embryo. In the contest in court over the validity of Lady Margaret's bequest, St. John's interests were defeated by the King's claims, and by the predations of courtiers. See Mullinger I, 468-69, and Baker I, 72-73.

[7]Ascham's highly negative opinion of the saintly Fisher, beloved in his time as the father of St. John's and its great benefactor, reflects the charged atmosphere and the vigorous anti-Catholicism of the Protectorate. When Fisher in 1535 refused to support Henry VIII's divorce, his goods, including his books, which he

ered the entire matter in a word. His whole collection of books was ours. When we speak of his books, we are talking about a rich treasure. Surely it was a worthy treasure, which had fallen to good and learned men. What more shall we say? His perverse doctrine deprived him of life and us of our greatest riches.

Our college, reduced to great penury in these two ways, has suffered a third calamity, which has long burdened us, confined us in amazing poverty, and brought to a desperate situation at this time not only us, but all other students. It is the very burdensome expensiveness of all retail items. The price of everything increases, but our money does not increase. Where once one could live on twelve pence, one now cannot live on twenty. Whence this misery? From God? There is a better answer. God has never blessed this earth more. From single individuals? We easily believe this, because single individuals sin singularly. Where is the fault? There is much to blame in many; the greatest fault lies in certain men.

And since we have come thus far in our speech, and you are the one whom God has given both the power and the obligation to correct such matters, let us openly declare what constitutes the nation's greatest disaster. There is no clothes dealer, no butcher, no shoemaker so unskilled in business that he has not learned to rob the public. In every craft there are individuals very skilled in raising the normal price of things, that is, in stealing from the entire society and throwing the whole nation into very deep misery. Does the fault therefore reside wholly in these common craftsmen? Surely some of it, but minimally, because they do this not so much encouraged by their own volition or ill-will as driven by extreme necessity and the evil of others.

Who are the authors of such great misery? Let us explain, and explain it in the words of God's warning and declaration. They are those who join house to house, who gather their plunder from the needy, who very seldom eat the fruit of their own labors.[8] Thus says the Lord through the prophet Isaiah. Let us speak more openly. Everywhere today there are those in England who enrich the estates expropriated from the monasteries with very heavy annual returns.

---

had bequeathed to St. John's, were seized by the King. See Baker I, 103.

[8]Isaiah 5:8, 3:14, 3:10.

Hence the exceedingly high prices of everything; these men are plundering the entire country. Stewards and farmers all toil, starve, and scrape to satisfy these men.   Hence individuals are forced to cheat each other, and the entire country is most grievously burdened. Hence so many families are broken up, so many homes broken down, so many common tables either of no account now or confined to nooks and crannies. Hence, which is worst of all, that noble splendor and strength of England, I mean the name of the *Yeomen of England*, is battered and beaten.

This misery redounds most of all to its own authors.   For there are very few London merchants (these men have marvelously stirred up this misery) who today do not live more poorly, more meanly, more tenuously than when they allowed others to live.   For the life which many live today is not life, but misery.   Then everything was readily available and for sale; the price of things was reasonable. Now the only concern of many people is somehow scraping together some money to satisfy a few merchants.

It would be too much to review how this thing has crushed the vigor of the nation, how it has taken away all courage and power to sustain war, and how it has introduced new thievery and unheard-of insolence. All men have learned that the misery of everything is endless.   Those Babylonian owls who hate the evangelical light ascribe this entire misfortune to true doctrine shining forth again.   But the cry of these men is not new.   In their fashion they scream that the church under the law is against the prophets, and the church under grace now being born is against the apostles.   How much more sane that insane Ajax in Sophocles, who thought that the gifts and spoils of his enemies were damned.[9]   These spoils of Egypt, to use the words of the scripture, and these gifts of the monasteries--once it was their masters, now it is the goods themselves, through the fault of certain men-- deeply disturb the nation.   Our discourse is excessively long, but it is very true.

You see, most prudent Duke, how the entire nation is convulsed and confined in the most wretched poverty, and by which means and by the dishonesty of which men it has been brought about.   This calamity is surely the more calamitous, because those men who can

[9]*Ajax* 665: "The gifts of enemies are no gifts, and bring no good."

bring the most effective remedy for such a great evil think it of little account. Abject men and men suddenly knocked to the ground have the bitterest feelings about this evil. They can bring no relief to themselves and scarcely dare to implore help from others. But he sits in heaven who does not forget the needy and his eyes question the sons of man. At length the Lord will arise because of the groans of the poor. We do not doubt but that he has arisen in you, most honorable Duke, to repress through you the private cupidity of these times, which is growing beyond bounds. Know what place you protect, look around at the eyes of the needy looking toward you, and look yourself to God, who judges by his own gaze both judge and populace.

This we petition from you, we by our letter, and the entire nation by common consent, though no part of the nation has been attacked more vigorously during the invasion of this evil than the realm of learning. Other men are free to seek a living for themselves; students have no choice, but receive the living selected for them. If it is increased, it is not through their own effort, but through the kindness of others.

Finally, either we ought to have more money (which we desire) or the price of things--and almost all men now understand how high it is--ought to be less (which we hope will be through you), or else the fruit of our studies will be minimal (which we fear most of all). We are leaving out others; we are now speaking of ourselves and our college. The great expense of things and the non-existent charity of men have in the course of a few years driven away from this one college more youths of fine talent than there are now completely learned men in the whole University. Not only does it drive away those present, but it also removes all hope for those absent. What kind of college we are, what studies we pursue, how much support to religion and nation we can bring, John Cheke and William Cecil, formerly two students of this college, now two of the brightest lights of the whole nation, can explain to you.[10] They neither dare to speak false to you nor ought to hold back the truth in this honorable cause.

We seek only as much as you are willing to give. We are 170 and more who seek this, who desire to be sharers of this special kind-

---

[10]Cheke remained the tutor of King Edward, Somerset's nephew; Cecil had recently been appointed Somerset's Master of Requests, and would become his secretary in 1548.

ness of yours. We desire that this very distinguished college, which was founded to teach the doctrine of Jesus Christ, which has educated the best minds with the best instruction, which supports the most individuals with the fewest resources--we desire this, in our common prayers throwing ourselves upon your kindness: that some part of the spoils of Babylon may serve to support such a number of talented young men in this college as will later redound to Christ's glory. We understand that many citizens have obtained great wealth from the liberality of kings. That was excellently done; in this way other men will be encouraged to serve their nation. But if you want to provide through your individual effort for the public welfare, which depends upon many talents that have been well educated, you will easily see how much we should ask for honorably and how much you should rightfully grant--not to us, but rather to the nation.

The noble princes of Greece and Rome who achieved glory in war or peace erected memorials, statues, pyramids and triumphal arches in their own honor; certainly you yourself cannot erect for your honor a monument more bright for your glory nor more lasting for all posterity than if you establish some extraordinary testimonial of your feeling toward virtue and the gospel of Jesus Christ in this college. Such a pyramid in its height will top all those Egyptian pyramids-- nay, it will pierce the heavens into the sight of Jesus Christ, who will be much delighted by this work of yours. Act therefore, most distinguished prince; cherish and support our hope, which is placed in you according to the measure of your goodness, and we look for as much from you as we should hope for from a very good prince. Our Lord Jesus have your Highness ever in his keeping. William Bill, most devoted to your Highness, and the whole body of fellows and scholars of the College of St. John the Evangelist.[11]

---

[11]Ascham writes on behalf of the whole college, Bill being its new Master.

27 / To William Cecil[1]   (Giles I.lxxxiii)
Cambridge, January 5, 1548

In a letter (I.lxxvii) written less than a month before this one, Protector
Somerset accepted the University's offer of the Chancellorship (see Letter 25)
and emphatically urged the scholars to know their place within the kingdom: "let your study look toward truth; leave the changing of things to the
magistrates" (I, 146). When it came to religion, however, even a plain
warning could scarcely control the ferment at Cambridge. In a daring nocturnal prank during September a young Frenchman had secretly cut down
the pyx in the college chapel (see I.lxiii for Ascham's explanation to Archbishop Cranmer). In special meetings "at the break of day" the younger
scholars were being taught the new beliefs--though Ascham insists it was
being done "piously, Christianly, tranquilly, quietly" (I, 154). Then in late
1547, as this letter to Cecil indicates, Ascham embroiled himself in disputation and theological controversy that exceeded the authorities' tolerance.
This is the first of many letters Ascham would write to Cecil, his friend
since their days together at St. John's and, in the future, his most reliable
patron. Properly speaking, it is a personal letter, not written in an official
capacity, though Cecil, now Somerset's personal master of requests, was
rising fast in the service of the Protector, and Ascham was president of St.
John's and was forced, as he says in this letter, to take responsibility for the
conduct of affairs in the college in the absence of the master (see also
I.lxxxii, Ascham's account to William Bill, the absent master, and thus a
complement to the account given here).

Most accomplished sir, a month ago, or even more, we held a disputation in this college according to our habit, about whether the Mass
was the Lord's Supper or not. This question was handled with great
learning by Thomas Lever and Roger Hutchinson, whom I believe you
know.[2] They are truly learned men. Some in the University were
angry about the matter. Finally the affair came to the point, or rather
I was forced by the common demand of many in the college to trans-

---

[1]Giles' heading "To Sir W. Cecil" is erroneous: Cecil was not knighted until
1551.

[2]During his days at St. John's Cecil would have made the acquaintance of
both of these younger fellows: Lever commenced BA in 1542, MA in 1545, having
been elected fellow in 1543; Hutchinson commenced BA in 1541, MA in 1544,
having been elected fellow in 1542. Lever would go on to preach before King Edward at Paul's Cross, and to become noted for his passionate sermons about justice and Reform. Hutchinson's career as a divine would be less distinguished.

fer the debate from our domestic walls into the public schools. Our intent was to find out from learned men freely and without reserve what could be drawn from the founts of the sacred Scriptures in defense of the Mass, which not only occupies the highest place in religion and in men's consciences, but also has carried Christians away from the nearly all of the faithful ministry of the word of God and the use and observance of the sacraments. We approached the subject very quietly; we conferred among ourselves about what we had studied together, and proposed the scriptural canon as our guide, desiring that the entire question might be decided by its authority. We brought to the topic the ancient canons of the early church, the councils of the Fathers, the decrees of the Popes, the judgments of the Doctors, with a multitude of questionists, and all the modernists we could find, both German and Roman.

Certain members of our University took notice of our proceedings in their public sermons and finally brought it about that Mr. Madew, our Vice-chancellor, prohibited this disputation by letter. We obeyed, as was proper, but we were angry that the right to dispute was taken from us even though others were allowed to say as much as they pleased in their sermons. We have heard that the Archbishop of Canterbury was hostile to us. That is not surprising since our adversaries (I hate to use so sharp a word), most prudent sir, have reported the matter to him in a fearful clamor. One hesitates to say whether they have shown their malice more than their ignorance. For Thomas Aquinas proves that the Mass has many prerogatives by which it surpasses the Lord's Supper, and that it diverges very widely from the Supper in many respects: with respect to gender (women ought not to participate in the Mass, though they are not excluded from the Supper), with respect to age, with respect to the sin of one's parents, or with respect to disabilities (children, bastards, and handicapped people are excluded from the dignity of the Mass, but are admitted to the humility of the Supper), and in many other ways, so that if anyone were to affirm that the Mass and the Supper were the same, our adversaries would cry out much more loudly.

But what shall I say about those men to whom I have alluded? Only that "Herod was moved and all Jerusalem with him."[3] They say

---

[3]Matthew 2:3.

that we are hasty. Surely no one is so hasty but what he can easily
be called back. Thus all Cambridge needs the spur rather than the
checkrein.

But I have decided to tell you that although our disputation was
prohibited, yet our inclinations with respect to this matter were somehow stronger than before. For we have written nearly a whole book
about the Mass, which we propose shortly to present to the Lord Protector unless you and Master Cheke think it best not to do so.[4] When
it comes to the handling of this matter, I would prefer that you choose
to keep your judgment focused on the issue itself, and not on what
others are saying. We do not say this because we dare not promise
anything on our own part, but because we fear that certain men are
too eager to hinder by any means in their power what they themselves do not approve of.

We have read the most holy confessions of our Queen, together
with your most eloquent letter.[5] I wish that you could find it in your
heart to devote some of your time to the cultivation of English so that
men might know how readily our language admits the whole range of
eloquence.

We all enjoyed Master Cheke's letter to our College very much.
In just a few words he summarized both his and your very ample
goodwill. The Lord Protector's letter[6] to the University, which you
wrote for him, gave us all an amazing pleasure. It is our common
prayer that Cambridge may some day, and very soon, see John Cheke
the provost of King's College. That bishop[7] does not further learning;
I wish that he did it no harm. I do not say this to capture anyone's
favor, but for the good of the entire University. There are many reasons which make us think so, and in your wisdom you will see still

---

[4]Ascham almost certainly refers to his own *Apologia . . . pro caena Dominica*,
which after all did not appear until the posthumous edition of 1577, ed. Edward
Grant. See Ryan 94ff.

[5]The reference is to *The Lamentation of a Sinner* by Catherine Parr, the Dowager Queen, printed late in 1547, with a commendatory introduction by Cecil.

[6]See my introduction to this letter.

[7]The reference is to the conservative Catholic George Day, Bishop of Chices-
ter. At the time of this writing, Day was in the process of giving up his position
as Provost of King's, and Cheke did indeed acquire it in April 1548.

more.   We are talking with each other as friends, perhaps not the most discreetly, but yet very cautiously, and at the very least, very lovingly.   Consider this thing as you please, but advance it as far as you can. I am too troublesome. Farewell in Christ.

PART THREE: 1548-1550

Court Splendor/Court Tempest

The handful of letters from this period points the chief irony of Ascham's whole correspondence: that for which he has been celebrated for centuries is in fact scarcely recorded in his letters. Thus although shortly after the middle of February 1548 Ascham secured such an appointment as an aspiring humanist might only dream on, an appointment to tutor Princess Elizabeth in the learned languages and literatures, nearly two years of service bring forth no account of his royal prodigy's temperament and talents.[1] In fact his letters from this period are lackluster and few. No letters at all survive from 1549; indeed, one and a half years are "lost," for between a chatty, uninformative letter of mid-1548 to William Ireland (Letter 30) and a desperately anxious and apologetic one to Cheke in early 1550 (Letter 31) we have nothing from Ascham the tutor. Moreover, this great triumph within Ascham's career also precipitates his greatest disgrace: within two years he either resigned in the embarrassment of some quarrel, or he was fired (see Letter 31).

Some of the reasons for this lacuna are not far to seek, and render the irony understandable, at least in part. For example, although Ascham had good friends in the Princess' household, and lived and worked in the comfortable surroundings first of Queen Catherine's home in Chelsea, then of Sir Anthony Denny's country home in Cheshunt, and lastly of the Princess' Hatfield House, his young charge was never removed from political intrigue. Ascham's safety and security lay in his silence. From the moment of his arrival until at least March 1549, when the Lord Admiral was executed, Ascham cannot have been

---

[1]In later letters to Sturm, beginning with the famous account in the April 1550 overture (Letter 39), as well in *The Schoolmaster*, Ascham does pay tribute to her learning.

unaffected by the turmoil of Thomas Seymour's unseemly designs on the Princess (see introduction to Letter 30), but he was much too discreet even to hint at it in any letter.   Moreover, if anything at all questionable had somehow been preserved within any of Ascham's letters, it was surely suppressed by editor Edward Grant, who, we recall, dedicated his editions of Ascham's letters to Queen Elizabeth.

There is also the matter of Ascham's own ambivalence, the product of both apprehension and exhilaration.   When his beloved former pupil William Grindal, Elizabeth's tutor since about 1544, died in January 1548, Ascham campaigned for the position coyly but directly with the Princess herself, notwithstanding the opposition of her guardians (see Letter 28).   Even then, however, he would not, he wrote to Cheke, "give myself to this new way of life" without his mentor's approval (Letter 29).   The pleasures of the job itself apparently did little to assuage his ambivalence, for after only a few months he confided to his friends back at St. John's that he might become like many courtiers, unable to "give up the splendor and the display of life at court," but he professed to "have some plans" and announced that by Michaelmas he hoped to back in Cambridge for good (Letter 30).

Perhaps we can understand what he had in mind from a comment in a letter to Cecil written some years later.   During his months at Cheshunt, he reports, he commonly had dinner and supper with "the worthy Mr. Denny," "whose excellent wisdom . . . I can never forget: 'The Court, Mr Ascham, is a place so slippery, that duty never so well done, is not a staff stiff enough to stand by always very surely, where ye shall many times reap most unkindness where ye have sown greatest pleasures, and those also ready to do you most hurt to whom you never intended to think any harm'" (I, 350-51).   In the event, Ascham's ambivalence, strengthened by such sentiments as Denny's, would prove to be an accurate, indeed prophetic assessment of the situation.   Less than two years after his appointment, he experienced a "disastrous shipwreck" and was overwhelmed by a calamitous "court tempest" (Letter 31).

To Cheke Ascham asserts his own innocence, blaming "court violence and injustice," as well as bad fortune (Letter 31), but the real reasons for the separation remain obscure.   Some have speculated that Ascham was somehow a victim of the Lord Admiral's jealousy for Elizabeth, but that is hardly plausible in view of the fact that Seymour had been executed some ten months earlier (March 20, 1549).   Neither is it likely that this "court tempest" was connected with the fall of the Lord Admiral's brother, Protector Somerset (October 1549). Ryan has judged that this tempest "seems to have been a personal rather than a state matter" (112-13), but we are likely never to know for certain. In any case, at the outset of the year 1550 Ascham found himself once more in an "abject and humble condition," petitioning Cheke to help him find some new manner of living.

28 / To Princess Elizabeth (Giles I.lxxxiv)
[Cambridge], January 22, 1548

In late 1544 John Cheke had secured the appointment of William Grindal, Ascham's favorite pupil, as tutor to Princess Elizabeth (see Letter 9). Grindal's death of the plague a little over three years later left a vacancy to which Ascham here obliquely lays claim. The letter's thought and language are allusive, if not "metaphysical," as Ascham playfully teases out implications of the classic idea that friends are "one soul in bodies twain," and that if he, Ascham, is not another Grindal, yet at least Elizabeth might either transfer to him her opinion of her Grindal or preserve unchanged the opinion of him which she learned from Grindal.

I can readily appreciate the magnitude of your sorrow at our friend Grindal's death, most illustrious Lady, from the magnitude of his love and regard for you. I would be more afraid of increasing your sorrow by referring to it now than of diminishing it by consoling you if I had not observed your wisdom, so fortified by the sound advice of a very prudent woman, Mistress Katherine Astley,[1] and once so well taught by the very good instruction of my very good friend Grindal. I readily understand that the healing which time is accustomed to bring to the sorrow of fools is so lodged in your thought, your mind, and your wisdom that you can easily bring it forth to mitigate all your keen sense of sorrow. But if you expect consolation from this mournful letter and from me, who am held back by my own considerable sorrow, I can offer only the smallest remedy for others or for myself. In my judgment there can be no more certain fruit of consolation, whether it be drawn mainly from your dignity or from the good will of your Grindal, who died on his appointed day, or from the expectation of all of us, than if you seek to bring to its expected maturity his very great hope for your excellent learning, aroused by his labors. After that Grindal of yours, you cannot hope for a more skilled teacher in effecting this maturity than this Grindal. In both name and relationship he comes closest to your Grindal, since he comes very near him in excellence of learning by both the gentleness of his manners and his gravity. So much for this subject.

---

[1]Elizabeth's beloved and affectionate governess, Kate, married to John Astley (Ashley); cf. Letter 16.

From the very close union of study, good will, kindness, love, intimate relationship, and piety, which linked me with my Grindal for many years, I could never see any greater fruit than that which your great good will, evoked by his efforts, imparted to me. Now nothing ought to be more in my daily prayers than that your old favor towards me may rest upon the old opinion of Grindal concerning me, and may not retreat into new language or a new opinion of some other man. For although to my very great sorrow I have lost my Grindal, yet I do not wish in any way to lose the opinion you have from Grindal of me.

And I shall labor to serve you with all my diligence in so far as I put my hope in your kindness, so that my devotion, faith, and complete observance will be directed forever to your wish, favor, honor, and dignity. And I shall consider it my greatest happiness if that time comes when my services can be of use to your Highness. May our Lord Jesus increase your Highness daily in virtue, learning, and honor. January 22, 1548.

29 / To John Cheke (Giles I.lxxxv)
[Cambridge], February 12, 1548

You can easily understand, most honored sir, how keenly grieved I was at the death of my friend Grindal. But at his last breath his frame of mind, so unhampered by worldly cares and most intent upon God, gave me great comfort, so that the testimony of such a spirit seems to relieve a little my longing for so great a friend. Grindal and I were united by the strongest bonds of friendship, and I always enjoyed his company immensely. Moreover, he was never more gracious or more ready to exert himself on my behalf than when, as he had opportunity, he focussed the great kindness of the illustrious Lady Elizabeth on me. This goodness of our most illustrious Elizabeth appeared very great during Grindal's lifetime, but now after his departure it so shines out and overflows on all sides that I seem to have fallen heir to all her good will for Grindal and not to have lost possession of her old favor for me. For the most excellent Lady is thinking of having me in place of Grindal.

Although I have not decided to reject such a great favor from so great a woman, yet I am unwilling to give myself to this new way of life if I do not approach that position with some testimony of your good will and opinion of me. I do not attempt to get this from you either for the sake of increasing her favor, already most considerable, or in the interest of fishing for your commendation, which is plainly evident. Rather, I somehow credit so much to you that I believe I should really pursue nothing major without thinking I have undertaken it under the guidance and leading of your counsel. As for what I have done at this time, my own volition moved me much, but your gentleness moved me most of all, as well as something of our old familiarity. I can quite understand how important you believe it is to sustain your judgment of another person's character, and I am certainly not ignorant that advancing the desired testimony of so great a man leaves me open to some reproach. May you do, therefore, whatever you consider best to be done.

I was with the illustrious Lady recently; she spoke her mind to me and I did not exercise myself to my own advantage by any crafty storekeeper's evasion, but openly showed myself willing and very ready for her service. She told me also how much the Queen and the Lord Admiral were laboring in favor of Goldsmith.[1] I advised her to comply with their recommendations. I commended Goldsmith to her and urged her as much as I could to follow your judgment and advice in the matter, and entreated her to set aside all her favor toward me and to consider before all else how she could bring to maturity that singular hope which was awakened in her by Grindal's teaching.

You would hardly believe, most accomplished sir, how much skill in Greek and Latin she will achieve if she continues in the course begun under Grindal's guidance. We finally agreed on this point: on account of her supreme kindness for me she wanted only me, and on account of my loyalty to her and the respect I owe to her I wanted anyone who would be the best teacher for her. I can say nothing of myself, but I am led into the hope that even though I am a nobody,

---

[1]The Dowager Queen Catherine Parr and her new husband, the grasping and reckless Thomas Seymour, Baron Sudeley, Lord Admiral, and younger brother to the Lord Protector, were Elizabeth's guardians; she was living with them in Chelsea. Nothing further is known of this Goldsmith, Ascham's rival for the position.

unskilled in almost everything, still I can surely amount to something in teaching her Latin and Greek and in serving as her secretary.

When the lady Elizabeth comes to London, she will discuss this matter with the Queen and my Lord Admiral; I do not believe anything will be settled without consulting you. As far as I am concerned, I surrender all my work, my studies, my way of life, and myself to your wisdom; and I shall ever try to follow the guidance of your counsel. Our Lord Jesus have you ever in his keeping. February 12, 1548.

30 / To William Ireland (Giles I.xc)
Cheshunt, July 8, [1548][1]

In May 1548 Princess Elizabeth was packed off to live with Sir Anthony Denny at Cheshunt in Hertfordshire. Apparently she and her guardian Queen Catherine, who was now pregnant, were not getting along in Chelsea. Moreover, Catherine's new husband, Thomas Seymour, the Lord Admiral, was behaving with unseemly familiarity toward Princess Elizabeth, whom the Council had earlier forbidden him to marry. He was 38, she was 14. Sometimes he would tickle her as she lay in bed; in one amazing sexual romp, his wife Catherine pinioned the young girl while he cut away her gown. Although these disturbing affairs would not come fully into light until after Seymour's arrest in January 1549 for new intrigues to marry Elizabeth (Catherine died in September 1548 of complications after childbirth) and to overthrow his brother, they were scandalizing the royal household of which Ascham was now a part.

Ascham is much too discreet, however, to mention any of this sordid business in this chatty letter to his friend and one-time pupil William Ireland, now a fellow of St. John's College, though he does indicate that even after so few months of service he is already willing to give up "the splendor and the display of life at court." Neither does he give any account at all of his royal pupil and their studies together; that would first appear in a more formal and self-conscious letter to Sturm (Letter 39). Here Ascham's thoughts are with acquaintances back in Cambridge. Years later, first in a letter to John Astley prefacing the *Report of Germany* (III, 3-4), then in a eulogy of John Whitney within *The Schoolmaster* (III, 171-74), Ascham does grow nostalgic about this sojourn at Cheshunt.

[1]Giles erroneously gives 1549 as the date of this letter: by then Elizabeth was living at Hatfield.

Your letter, which Peter Perusini[2] brought me, was most welcome. Along with my John Whitney[3] I would very gladly have visited you during your last meetings if my most illustrious mistress had not vetoed my plan, either because Huntley[4] died recently among you or because she never willingly sends me away. I plan to be with you again at Michaelmas, that is, to stay with you permanently, if I can get my Lady's permission, which, to be sure, I scarcely expect, for she favors me wonderfully. Many courtiers express particular approval of their former quiet life, but they are unwilling to give up the splendor and the display of life at court. I cannot promise anything about myself, but I have some plans.

I would that you, my dearest Ireland, would wish to spend a day or two with me here at Cheshunt so that I could pour all my innermost thoughts into your most trustworthy bosom. You send to me your great thanks, albeit undeserved, for I know not what kindness of mine toward you. I know your heart is very grateful, but my kindness is nothing. If you are thinking of those two letters for hunting wild game which I procured for you and my Raven[5] from the Marquis of Northampton and from Sir Francis Bryan,[6] I am glad if our Grinwood[7] gave them to you and should like to know it. I wish you could be here to learn how I spend my time or could learn it from

[2]Pietro Bizari, called Perusini from his Italian origins in Perugia. He had adopted the Reformed faith, and left Italy for England. He studied at Cambridge, and would be admitted fellow of St. John's in 1549.

[3]A gentleman-in-waiting in Elizabeth's household, Ascham's "bedfellow" and "dear friend" (III, 171-72). A few years earlier Ascham had addressed to him a very complimentary letter, praising him for "following the leisure of letters in the midst of the great business of court" (I.xxxvii); see also Ascham's eulogy of Whitney in *The Schoolmaster:* "A court full of such young gentlemen were rather a paradise than a court upon earth" (III, 172).

[4]Unidentified. Elizabeth is understandably afraid of the spread of the plague, from which Grindal had died in January.

[5]Edward Raven, also a fellow of St. John's and a close companion of Ireland.

[6]Both Bryan and the Marquis, William Parr, were prominent Privy Councillors.

[7]Probably John Greenwood, admitted fellow of St. John's in March 1547 at the same time as Raven and Ireland.

conversation with someone, although if I find out that you want to know, I shall tell you fully in another letter.

Greet that most grave man and my great friend, Mr. Madew.[8] I have not forgotten how much I owe him, but remember every day. God willing, I shall presently write to him. Greet the most noble Stafford,[9] for whom I wish what he wishes for himself, namely, the union of the highest learning with the highest virtue. Lately I was in court with His Majesty. I saw many noble men in Somerset's room, friends of Mr. Stafford at court. I heard talk about the most frivolous subjects. Oh those fools, I thought, and how happy our Stafford, who now speaks with Cicero at Cambridge about the most weighty matters and those altogether worthy of a worthy man.

Greet the Master of our College,[10] and Masters Crosley, Langdall, Fawden, Fawcett, Browne, Bullock, Eland, Hutton, Lever, both the Pilkingtons, my Thomson, whom I have appointed to have seniority in my place, Patrick, my Pindar, Tayler, Leet, Thexton, Salt, Squire, both Wilsons, if the older is among you, and my Lakin, for whom I wish as much virtue and erudition as I always hoped and expected from him. And I say this also to my Callibut,[11] whom I see somehow estranged from me, since he never writes to me. I hear things, and I hope much is false. I cannot approve an injury done to anyone, unless I should want to hedge on my Christian sentiments. I wish I had been present. I think I would have either gotten rid of these commotions or put them to rest.

---

[8]John Madew, a graduate of St. John's, a doctor of divinity, and vice-chancellor of the University.

[9]Sir Robert Stafford, a courtier who was spending time at Cambridge (but apparently without taking a degree). His mischievous servant cut down the pyx in the college chapel in a nocturnal raid (see I.lxiii). Sir Robert himself got into trouble several times during his later European travels: see Christina Garrett, *The Marian Exiles* (Cambridge: Cambridge UP, 1938) 293-94.

[10]William Bill. Those on the list which follows were all fellows and scholars of St. John's, appearing in one of more of the standard authorities (Baker's *History of St. John's College*, Cooper's *Athenae Cantabrigienses*, and Venn's *Alumni Cantabrigienses*). Along with Raven and Ireland, John Thomson, John Pindar, and Thomas Lakin were apparently Ascham's own pupils.

[11]Robert Callibut (Callybutt), matriculated from St. John's in 1546.

I certainly have the highest opinion of Stafford, but for all that I cannot think the worst of my friend Hutchinson,[12] for he has, if I am not blind, a great wit and singular erudition.   He yields to very few in having a good character and a sound judgment in religion.   He is faithful and hates papism from his heart.   You readily understand how someone can stir him up by an undeserved injury.   The wit, the erudition of the man drive me to say these things, not any benefit received or expected.   But is his temper rather hot?   What sensible person would not easily bear with this fault when there are so many compensating virtues?   How much joy this flare-up brings to our papists I see plainly, and I also see what firebrands they have added to the fire.   A greater injury is done to pure Christian doctrine than to any one man.   If Mr. Stafford would forgive everything, he would carry away a greater glory than he brought back from the siege of Boulogne.[13]   I do not doubt but that he will do it, since I know his mind is as balanced as it is exalted and great, thus conceding something to someone for the increase of Christ's glory.   And I hope that now everything is settled and resolved between them.   If I knew of anything remaining which might keep their two spirits apart, I myself would be ready to fly into danger to find out whether or not I could join together those whom I have bound to myself with bonds of piety, an offer which I think neither could decline.

Meanwhile you must take care, my Ireland, to do what you think I would do if I were among you.   I have easily borne Hutton's harsh words directed against me at Hilton without any basis.[14]   I did not, moreover, reject the love of the man, but won him over into a very close friendship.   I hope the same thing will happen to Stafford, whom I know to be much wiser than I am in accomplishing this.

---

[12]Roger Hutchinson, chosen a senior fellow of St. John's in 1547, had debated the Mass vs. the Lord's Supper late in that year (see Letter 27).   In this passage Ascham apparently alludes to a quarrel over religion between Hutchinson and Stafford; it suggests that Hutchinson was as outspoken on behalf of the Reformation as the noted preacher Thomas Lever, his partner in the debate.   Hutchinson's works have been edited by John Bruce for the Parker Society.

[13]Stafford was knighted for his part in the action at Boulogne.

[14]The episode is unexplained, the parties unidentified.

Greet the most venerable mistress Cheke[15] most dutifully and Mr. Blythe[16] and his wife.   Greet that good man John Barnes,[17] his wife, and his whole family, so that he won't think that I have forgotten him.   Greet Dickinson and William Cook.[18]   I deliberately did not greet my Raven, since I write this letter to him as well as to you. Katherine R., a most charming and honorable girl, has been with me. I was at court on the day when she came to Chelsea, but if I hadn't been, I would have taken her to my most illustrious Lady.   I told all our noble girls that I loved her dearly, and that she was to be my bride, which almost everyone readily believed.[19]

If you should go to Witham, greet all most dutifully.   Keep my room and its humble furniture clean and neat as you always have done.   Write at great length and very fully.   You can send your letters easily.   Reluctantly I am torn away from talking with you.   Farewell in Christ Jesus.   Cheshunt, July 8.

31 / To John Cheke   (Giles I.xciv)
                     [Cambridge], January 28, 1550

> Nothing in Ascham's life raises more questions than this anxious, but cautious letter, for here Ascham discusses his "shipwreck" at court without really explaining it, earnestly seeking to keep Cheke's favor and support, but reserving the whole story for another occasion.   Was the real story too sensitive to tell?   Did he after all have something to hide?   Was he the

[15]John Cheke's mother, Agnes Duffield, married to Peter Cheke, a bedell of the University.

[16]John Blythe, first Regius Professor of medicine, was married to John Cheke's sister Alice.

[17]Perhaps a tavern keeper: in February 1551 Ascham would send greetings from the Continent to "mine hostess Barnes" (I, 280).

[18]Dickinson: unidentified; Cook held a variety of posts within the University over the years: councillor-at-law, steward of various manors, vice-steward of the University, Recorder of Cambridge, and sergeant-at-law.

[19]This is one of Ascham's rare displays of playful wit.   He was not married until 1554, and then to Margaret Howe: see Ryan 114-15 and 200ff.   Katherine R. is unidentified.

victim of political intrigue or instability? The facts are not clear. In this letter Ascham's strategy is to blame Elizabeth's *oeconomus*, most likely her steward Thomas Parry, who had weathered the investigations surrounding the scandal of the Lord Admiral and who would continue to serve Elizabeth for years to come. Did Ascham perhaps run afoul of him?

I always give great thanks to God, and will do so as long as I live, that in his extraordinary kindness to me I have spent a large part of my life in study at Cambridge in a most distinguished college, and especially that I have had you as my dearest friend and most learned teacher. For whatever aids I obtained, whether they were modest ones from fortune for life's necessities, or very slender ones from learning for the improvement of my abilities, they certainly all flowed from your singular and abundant love for me and from those springs of learning which you have happily and constantly discovered for us these many years through your great intellect, precept, example, and advice.

The more pleasant my recollections of the very delightful style of life which I enjoyed with you at the University, of those talks we had sitting together in your room, when you very often declared your special interest in me and aroused my firm hope in you, and finally of the past kindnesses which you always in both the University and the court poured out abundantly on me--the more pleasant these recollections, frequently occupying me night and day, the more bitter now is the alienation I suffer because of my recent disastrous shipwreck, overwhelmed as I am by court violence and injustice, more through bad fortune than through any fault of mine. Certain men are even trying hard during these difficult and very trying times to block the course of your kindness toward me.

But in this parade of very serious injustices, this especially sustains me: by no means could it be as painful to me to be accused to you through open hatred and invented falsehoods as it would be delightful to be defended by the silent testimony of your judgment concerning me, a judgment which I easily discerned from your conversation with me the last time I was at court. I have never yet been persuaded, nor shall I ever be, that I should have more fear of new slanders from malevolent people than I have had confidence in the strength of your old benevolence.

This would appear to be a good time and place for me to explain the whole conduct of my life at court and my reasons for leaving it. I would certainly do it now, except that the matter can be more suitably explained in conversation face to face than in a short letter.

I do not want any credence to be placed in my own speaking about myself in my own defense unless the most weighty testimony of the most worthy men shall have attested to my innocence in all my words and deeds. In this most just cause of mine I can produce one man, R. S.,[1] a serious and upright man, to oppose the reproaches of these light-weights, if I may speak lightly of them. But I am not bringing him forward, this sharer of my thoughts and my fellow in fortune. Cumberford[2] and Wilkinson,[3] however, known to you for many years as men of good reputation, will not want to lie or conceal the truth in this affair. And so if even their testimonies do not explain where all the injustices with which the court tempest overwhelmed me came from and why I should be enjoying the fruit of office rather than the fear of offense, then certainly I will readily suffer your kindness to be cut off from me, a kindness from which all the more pleasant aspects of my past life have flowed and from which a bright hope still shines for the many opportunities to come. But if it is otherwise, and you learn that I have been attacked without any fault of my own by the injustices not of my most illustrious Lady, but of her steward,[4] let me obtain this favor of you (which you would give of your own accord): do not let the letters of men or the injustice of the times dislodge you from your old kindness in defending your old friend Ascham and acknowledging him as yours.

I strive for this the more earnestly because I have always valued your love more than your approbation and I shall labor always with all my care, diligence, and respect to keep it so forever. Truly, now

---

[1]Ironically Ascham does not give the full name of the one defender he cites; he remains unidentified.

[2]Probably Henry or Richard Cumberford (Comberforth), both contemporaries of Cheke and Ascham at St. John's.

[3]Christopher Wilkinson? Richard Wilkinson? Both are listed as Cambridge students, but neither at St. John's.

[4]Thomas Parry, Elizabeth's longtime servant.

in my abject and humble condition nothing can arouse me to more hope than if you, next to the King and my most illustrious Lady (whose favor I should be most unwilling to lose), would still give some weight and value to my goodwill, fidelity, and service, which already have sometimes received some of your approbation. Surely you will not blame me for wanting that, since it arises from nothing else but a certain inclination and the tendency of a mind devoted to you for many years.

The other matters about which I was going to write--concerning either establishing myself comfortably at the University or undertaking two years of study abroad, plans for which I promise myself some of your assistance and favor--I shall shortly explain to you in another letter or, more suitably, in a conversation face to face. Our friend Eland[5] has recommended to you Henry Wright,[6] a young man of our college who, if I judge rightly, has entered upon a most correct course of studies with great talent, industry, perseverance, and promise; that is to say, so happily has he joined Aristotle and Plato to Cicero that, if he goes on as he has begun, he will surely prove worthy of your favor and support and that of men like you, those who are appointed by God to promote learning. May Christ Jesus ever have you in his keeping. January 28, 1550.

[5]Henry Eland (Ailand), a fellow at St. John's.

[6]Henry Wright, from St. John's Sedbergh school in Yorkshire, transferred to St. John's College from Christ's in 1549. He would be admitted a fellow of St. John's later in 1550. He entered a career in the church.

PART FOUR: 1550-1553

"the wit and wisdom used in travelling"

The "court tempest" and "shipwreck" of early 1550, to use Ascham's own metaphors for the events severing him from his position as tutor to Princess Elizabeth (Letter 31), ironically made literally possible a stimulating voyage to the Continent later in the same year. His well-placed friends secured him a position as secretary to Sir Richard Morison, newly appointed ambassador to the court of Emperor Charles V. Ascham left London for Augsburg on September 21, 1550. Some months later he allowed with an uncharacteristic dry wit that "seeking company and experience of men's manners abroad is a fit remedy for the sore, wherewith learned men . . . be much infected withal, which is 'the best learned [are] not always . . . wisest'"(I, 352).

Travel did indeed ripen and season Ascham's knowledge. His letters from this period bring out all the most attractive qualities of his character. His interest is kindled in history, culture, learning, the affairs of state, and the practices of religion. He was never so alive. Ever the humanist scholar, he delights to cite the ancients as his guide, particularly the "wit" and the "wisdom" of Homer's Ulysses, "the wisest traveller that ever travelled," as he would say in *The Schoolmaster*, "set out by the wisest writer that ever spake with tongue, God's doctrine only excepted" (III, 149-50). Gracefully alluding to Homer and Horace, he promises friends in England that in every city he intends to visit "the churches, monasteries, ancient monuments, bookshops, libraries, goldsmiths, marketplaces, walls, castles, and ports" (Letter 32; cf. Letters 34, 37). His Latin letters to Cheke and Edward Raven, a friend at St. John's (Letters 32-34), as well as several letters in English, one of which is very long (I.cxvi), form a remarkably vivid travelogue. One can see Ascham sharpening the skills exhibited in the more analytical and political *Report of Germany*, which he would write (but not publish) at the close of his three-year sojourn in high and low Germany (see Letter 52).

During Morison's tenure religious conflict, intrigue, treachery, siege, and reversals of fortune were everyday realities within the Empire. The Turk threatened by land and sea, and Protestantism continually challenged the Emperor. He was increasingly demoralized by flight, displacement, and his failure to establish a permanent religious peace and to preserve the old faith within the Empire. Pressed by the Lutheran forces of Maurice of Saxony, he was forced in 1552 to retreat from his seat in Augsburg to Innsbruck, and then to flee precipitously across snow-filled Brenner Pass. In 1553, as Ascham was nearing the conclusion of his tenure of service, the Emperor was seeking safety in the Low Countries, and moving toward abdication.

Nevertheless, one reads surprisingly little about political and imperial affairs in these letters. Moreover, though numerous lively dispatches from Morison are preserved and calendared in the state papers of the period, virtually none of the letters Ascham himself composed in his official capacity survives. One might offer several reasons for these unexpected omissions. The most sensitive political information, for example, was apparently transmitted orally by courier (see Letter 36), but clearly the chief reason is that Ascham continued to prefer the world of learning to matters of state. In fact, we read more about the ambassador's classical studies that we do about his diplomatic activities at the Emperor's court. Ascham's letters to Cheke and to friends at St. John's show him nostalgic for Cambridge and yearning for news from home. Other letters, especially those to such noted humanists as Johann Sturm (which I have grouped together in Part Five of this volume) and Hubert Thomas Leodius (Letter 38), are clear indications that he remained the enthusiastic and scholarly Cantabrigian, eagerly debating Cheke's and Smith's reformed pronunciation of Greek and extolling Princess Elizabeth and other paragons of English learning.

32 / To Edward Raven (Giles I.cv)

Antwerp, October 1, [1550]

On the morning of September 21, 1550, Ascham sailed from Billingsgate with the ambassadorial party. The day before he paid one last visit to his dear friend Cheke; they talked for hours about religion, the court, the country, and the University (I.civ). This letter to his former pupil and friend at St. John's is the first of Ascham's travel letters from abroad. The holograph is preserved in British Museum MS Lansdowne 98.

My most gentle Edward Raven, the recollection of my country is very dear to me, but the remembrance of your companionship so full of all humanity, benevolence, and devotion is even dearer to me, I know not why. From this my most pleasant journey I easily suffer myself to be absent for two or three hours and to be enclosed within my chamber at home in Cambridge so that into your bosom, with my dearest friends also present--the Pilkingtons, the Levers, the Elands, the Bees, the Wilsons, Wryght, and Washington--I could pour all the delights of my journey.

On September 21 we arrived at Gravesend, Neptune favoring us, but Iris somewhat angry. On the 22nd, on a small and weary horse, via a long and muddy way, we reached Canterbury. On the same night John Hales,[1] that learned and wise man, entertained us sumptuously. By merely descending from my horse, I put myself inside the most holy church of Christ.[2] I examined all the ancient relics, the tombs of Henry the Fourth and of the noble prince Edward, son of Edward the Third, the place where Becket was killed, and almost all the nooks and crannies, etc. Next I went to the booksellers, then to the goldsmiths' shops. Later I looked at the layout and the walls of the city, all the while carefully noticing as I wandered the customs and the general habit of the people. For I have resolved, my dear Edward, wherever I shall go, to visit in every city, as far as I can, its

---

[1]Hales, Edward VI's clerk of the hanaper, was the older brother of Christopher Hales, a St. John's man. Later we read of his activities in connection with Morison's embassy, perhaps as one Cecil's intelligence agents. He and Ascham would also correspond: see Jean Rott and Robert Faerber, "Un Anglais à Strasbourg au Milieu du XVIe Siècle: John Hales, Roger Ascham, et Jean Sturm," *Études Anglaises* 21 (1968) 381-94. See also Garrett 172-74.

[2]I.e., Canterbury Cathedral.

churches, monasteries, the oldest monuments, bookshops, libraries, goldsmiths, marketplaces, walls, castles, and ports. These are not matters for a short letter, but ought to be reserved for a long talk.

On the 23rd we visited his reverence, the Archbishop of Canterbury, who went with us almost to Dover. The castle there is situated on a very high and steep promontory, which can easily be seen from France and Flanders. It seems to menace quite imperiously not only the whole sea, but France itself as well. When we were in midchannel, England itself was the higher, France much lower. Dover Castle is very full of monuments of the very distant past.

On the twenty-fourth we crossed the strait. Only I and a certain young noble from Lincolnshire, Thymlibey, did not get sick; Mrs. Morison got a little sick, and the rest of our company were very seasick. On the twenty-fourth and twenty-fifth we recuperated at Calais. I immediately walked around the whole town, noting its position and its fortifications and its port. I saw Risebank and Newnhambridge, two exceedingly strong forts; from a distance I saw Ardres, Guînes, Hammes Castle,[3] and the layout of the whole region, so that it can never escape my memory.

September 26: if you now wish, my dear Edward, accompany me into Flanders up to Antwerp (provided always that Washington be your lackey), glance at my map of France, and you shall be our fellow travellers from now on. First we came to Gravelines, which is on the border of Flanders, separated from English soil only by a river, about nine miles from Calais. That night we lodged at Dunkirk, a very fishy town indeed, but one which can be compared with any city in England by reason of its magnificent buildings, and there we eagerly inquired whether Mrs. Morison had arrived or whether, as they said, they awaited her. On the twenty-seventh we reached Nieuwpoort, not inferior to Dunkirk by reason of its excellent harbor. On the twenty-eighth we finally reached Bruges, a very large city, but over so muddy a ten-mile road, called Sili, that it surpasses the wooded roads of Kent.

If I were allowed to tarry longer in this city, my Raven, I would trouble you with a long account; the city far surpasses London. On the twenty-ninth we came to Calf, an obscure place about which I

---

[3]Ascham names castles, fortifications, and villages which the English held in and around Calais.

shall write nothing, because we were so wretchedly lodged there, for we spent the night in our clothes. On the thirtieth we reached Antwerp, the most splendid seat of trade not only of Brabant, but--good God--of the whole world! Its splendid and magnificent buildings stand out so much that it surpasses every other city I have seen, just as after its anniversary the hall at St. John's, set up as a theater, surpasses itself. We are there now, safe, sound, and merry, thanks be to God. Antwerp has not yet received the Emperor's edict concerning the changing of religion.[4] In almost all of Flanders, papism is so fat and gross, not to say puerile, that if anyone in England who especially seems to favor it should come here, he would spit it out quickly. My friend Gipkin showed me a list of new books, including Sturm's *De periodis* and Sturm on Aristotle's *Rhetoric*. I have not seen the books themselves, but you can guess how much I want to.[5]

I hear that Bucer's wife is in England.[6] I think she has a letter for me from Sturm: take it, save it, send it if possible, but keep a copy of it. I shall write to my most reverend father Mr. Bucer when I have something in hand which will interest him. Greet him most dutifully for me, and my dear friend Pember,[7] of whom I think daily, Barwick,[8] John Scarlet,[9] the Barnes family,[10] all our fellows. When I

[4]Ascham apparently refers to the *Interim*, promulgated on May 30, 1548, by the Diet of Augsburg for Emperor Charles V in an effort to bring Protestants nearer to the old faith. Because of popular Protestant opposition throughout Germany and the Empire, however, execution of the *Interim* was sporadic and uneven.

[5]Sturm's *De periodis* was published in 1550, but the translation and commentary on Aristotle's *Rhetoric*, eagerly awaited by Ascham and the subject of many comments in letters to Sturm (see Part Five), did not appear until 1570, two years after Ascham's death. See Jean Rott, "Bibliographie des oeuvres imprimées du recteur strasbourgeois Jean Sturm (1507-1589)," *Actes du 95e Congrès National des Sociétés Savantes (Reims, 1970)*, Section de philologie et d'histoire jusqu'à 1610 (Paris: Bibliothèque Nationale, 1975) I, 319-404.

[6]See Letter 35.

[7]Robert Pember was Ascham's tutor at St. John's; although he remained Catholic, he continued in Ascham's affection (see I, 261-62). They shared an interest in old coins (see I, 316-17).

[8]Thomas Barwick, fellow of Trinity College, Cambridge?

[9]Matriculated at St. John's in 1549.

[10]See Letter 30, note 17.

say all, I except not a one; although I do not mention each one by name, I always think and shall think of them every day. Write what letters you have had from me, on what day, from what place. Farewell in Christ. Antwerp in Brabant, October 1. Your R. Ascham.

33 / To Edward Raven   (Giles I.cvi)
Cologne, October 14, [1550]

> Here is a continuation of Letter 32. In this case the holograph is again preserved in British Museum MS Lansdowne 98. Giles erroneously gives the date as October 12.

My dearest Edward, if I knew that my Thomas Lever were near you, I should write this to him. I shall write to you as often as a courier is available. But expect no *thrifty management*; I shall stuff items into my letters in a disordered way. Antwerp ought not be described in a letter, but in a long talk. Great events are occurring in that town, which I should fetch very fully to a problem fire.[1] First, hear this: the edict of Caesar about religion in lower Germany, at the order of Caesar himself, has been made invalid.[2]

On October 3rd we set out from Antwerp to Mechelen, a city which can hardly be compared to London. It surpasses Norwich by far. Here I was wondering how such a great number of people living in the very densely populated cities of Bruges, Antwerp, Ghent, Mechelen, and Brussels can be supported. These five cities are situated only twelve miles from each other. If five Londons were placed in such a confined space within England, they would exhaust our country immediately. Both flocks and herds are rarely seen here, even if you were to look all around Flanders, Brabant, Liège, and Gelderland. But I cease to wonder: they have almost nothing to add to their bread except vegetables and herbs. Certainly Brabant, and especially Liège and Gelderland, are equal to and surpass not only any shire in

---

[1] A fire for talking through an academic problem in logic. Cf. this from a letter in English: "if I were with you at a problem fire, I would make you partakers of a great deal of my journey" (I, 247). The phrase is not in the OED.

[2] See Letter 32, note 4.

England, but even the area around Cambridge in the quality of their soil and in the bounty of their crops, which is evident far and wide. By their diligent cultivation they grow a great plenty of vegetables everywhere. Here men never experience hunger, so long as crops do not fail. We reached Mechelen. On the outskirts is a convent full not of idle, but of busy nuns. There are 1600 in that place making linen garments, earning their bread; they marry and leave as they will.

On October 4th at Caesar's residence in Mechelen I very much enjoyed seeing the noble Landgrave of Hesse, whom the Spaniards treat badly.[3] Every day at eight in the morning the Landgrave distributes forty stivers to the poor, i.e., 6s. 8d. It was an opportune time for me to observe him.

But I am distracted from writing, although I am unfolding scarcely one day's journey. When I write, I seem to be among you, oh my dearest friends, and therefore I am writing gladly and frequently and fully. I shall pass over no day of my trip. And so in the next letter, picking up at October 4th, I shall pursue the rest of my way up to Cologne, where I write this. Billick is here, and I have seen him.[4] And I have heard Josse Velsen[5] reading from Aristotle's *Ethics* in Greek.

But Mr. Morison calls me from my writing: the boat on the Rhine is ready to take us to Mainz. I gladly greet all of you in my letter. I think of you each day most joyfully, and commend myself to your prayers. Nothing on the whole journey has been troublesome, I am never tired out, and everything has been supplied for our great pleasure. Write. Farewell in Christ Jesus. Greet the most reverend father Bucer, Pember, the most honored Haddon. Cologne, October 14. R. Ascham.

---

[3]Philip, Landgrave of Hesse, a Protestant leader in Germany, was defeated by Charles V in June, 1547, at the close of the Schmalkaldic War, and thereafter kept in humiliating imprisonment.

[4]Edward Billick (Eberhard Steinberger), an opponent of the German Reformation, was warden of the Carmelite friary in Brussels (see I, 247). The meeting was not productive: see Ascham's fuller account of it in letters to Cheke (Letter 34) and to Raven (I, 254-55).

[5]Velsen (Velsius), learned in many fields, with a doctorate of medicine from Louvain, was professor of Greek and Latin at Cologne.

34 / To John Cheke[1]   (Giles I.cviii)
[Augsburg], November 11, 1550

> On October 28, five weeks after departing London, the ambassadorial en-
> tourage reached Augsburg, the seat of the court of Emperor Charles V (As-
> cham here calls him "Caesar"). The delights of travel so took Ascham that
> in this letter, written two weeks after his arrival, he is already asking for
> money to travel further.

Most excellent sir, I would write to you gladly, frequently, and in
much detail, and now after our departure from England I would set
each day's journey before your eyes except that I fear that when you
read over our news, you will think you are looking at a good deal of
trivia and judging my follies. If I knew that along with serious news
you expected to be delighted occasionally by recollections of how we
spent our days and hours together, I could often write at length.

But however I shall write, I think you will be content, as will I,
and you would rather do without good judgment in me and *thrifty
management* in my letter than reproach either my goodwill or my neg-
ligence. Look therefore in all my letters not for the pleasure of things
proceeding orderly, but for a heap of things jumbled together. Although I am bothering you less with this practice at this time because
there is not very much important news which I think you would be
interested in knowing, nevertheless there is nothing small, big, or in
between which comes into my hands, whether pertaining to religion or
to the private or public sphere, which I do not eagerly and attentively
examine. Monasteries, temples, libraries, old books and coins (when I
return home, I shall give you the most elegant and ancient ones), the
customs of cities, their government, their layouts, structures, walls,
resources, ports, all the good qualities of the surrounding land and
water--all these I shall describe in such a way that when I dare to
bring my thoughts forth freely, many days of conversation will scarcely be able to exhaust the recollection of these things. Pardon me
therefore that I now write briefly to you, until you indicate that you
want me to employ another style of writing.

---

[1]Giles erroneously heads the letter "To Sir John Cheke": he was not knighted
until 1551.

Lower Germany, as all call it, although many think it infernal, as I plainly perceive, the noble concourse of merchants excepted, is in every way the lowest and most desperate. Flooded by the vilest inundation of Roman dregs and filth, she now seems to stagnate. At Antwerp I saw *Commentaries on Plato's Timaeus*, but by a Latin author. We stopped at Louvain, but no longer than it took us to eat. Still, in the College of Three Languages I heard that supposedly famous man Theodore Lang[2] reading Sophocles' *Oedipus Tyrannus* for a whole hour. In everything he followed our pronunciation. If he should be compared with our Carr,[3] or Louvain with Cambridge, he clearly is out in the cold. At Cologne I heard Josse Velsen,[4] once from Strasbourg, now by fear made an Herodian, beginning *The Ethics* of Aristotle in Greek. I could approve but not admire. On the same day I heard Alexander Blanckaert,[5] a Carmelite, lecturing on the Acts of the Apostles; he is a famous papist. He translated the ninth letter in the first book of Cyprian as an offering on behalf of the dead. He is considered more learned, but worse than Edward Billick,[6] who lectures publicly on Genesis, but he was not reading that day. I went to Billick's monastery and saw the great man. I pretended that I had heard that he had certain books of Saint Bernard not yet published. I did this so that I might by some means engage the man in a personal conversation and see what kind of mind he had. But his servant said he was busy and had no free time. Put off to another time, I myself put him off too as an arrogant papist.

I have visited many libraries, but have not seen one famous book. At Spires they say there is a famous library crammed with old Latin, Greek, and Hebrew books. The man in charge was away; if he

---

[2]Theodoricus Langius (properly *Lang*, not *Laud*, as in Giles), or Thierry de Langhe, was a visiting professor from the University of Bordeaux. Educated at Louvain, he eventually settled there permanently. See Henry De Vocht, *History of the Foundation and the Rise of the Collegium Trilingue Lovaniense 1517-1550*, Humanistica Lovaniensia 13 (Louvain: Librairie Universitaire, 1955) 265-68.

[3]Nicholas Carr, Cheke's successor as Regius Professor of Greek at Cambridge.

[4]See Letter 33, note 5.

[5]Blanckaert (Candidus) was Professor of Theology at Cologne; he had recently published a Dutch translation of the Bible.

[6]See Letter 33, note 4.

had been there, I would have gone through them all. At Günzburg,[7] a town nine German miles from Augsburg, I went to the Jewish quarter, where many live. They have a great many ancient Hebrew books beautifully written. I could not buy a single one, though I tried. I also saw very fine old coins; I bought two, a Nero and an Augustus. I also saw a fine ancient Hebrew gold piece, with very fine Hebrew lettering. I would have bought it if the price had been reasonable. This city of Augsburg has a very well-stocked library, with many ancient Greek and Hebrew volumes. Those in charge have put away up to sixty of the best books so that Caesar or the Caesareans do not carry them off. They have the Greek Chrysostom complete, and many other famous authors. A good man has promised me that he will try to get me in to see it for myself.

The Christian religion flourishes at Augsburg with Caesar present in much the same way that your pronunciation of Greek flourished at Cambridge despite Gardiner's raging.[8] We all rejoice, and I too am very glad. But I myself fear that in religion Caesar will easily through deceit while he is present, or even more easily, without suspicion, while he is absent, manage to break up the political forces, and with political disintegration religion also will slide to ruin. But he is on high who will command his angels--you know the rest of the psalm.[9] Hamburg, Bremen, and especially Magdeburg defend religion with heart and pen and sword.[10] I have seen the Magdeburg confession. This is the argument of the book: if the higher magistrate exercises force against his subjects contrary to either natural or divine law, the lower magistrate is allowed to resist. I applaud the city of Magdeburg and its spirit, but I do not approve this *thesis*, for thence grave disturbances readily arise.

As a gift I am sending you this book, which can scarcely be procured here. I would send you many other mixed and indifferent

---

[7]Emending *Gavisburg*; see parallel account in English (I, 264), employing the name Gamsbroug.

[8]See Letter 2.

[9]Psalm 91:11 (Vulgate 90:11), adapted.

[10]Protestant opposition to the *Interim* was strong in these northwestern cities; Magdeburg was the center of the resistance. There Matthias Flacius began to draft his *Magdeburger Centurion*, a polemical Protestant history of the church.

tracts except that I thought that Gipkin had taken care of all this for you. Wittenberg with Melanchthon and Leipzig with Camerarius are criticized here by many good men because they admit mixed and indifferent doctrine.[11] In an oration at Leipzig last year Joachim Camerarius upset the hearts of many with respect to religion. When anything reliable, having to do with either the state or religion, reaches my hands, I shall write fully to you. Just now upon our arrival I do not have many things to write, and nothing big or surprising.

In our whole journey the thing that amazes me most, like nothing I have seen, is how my lord ambassador can support the magnitude of the expenses, for in recent days costs are increasing an immense amount, even for individual items, and he throws his English money everywhere. I know the level of the King's support, and I have seen the daily expense. Careful supervision and moderate caution are being applied, but expenses overflow, converging from unexpected sources along multiple lines of expense, so that they can readily absorb and exhaust even an immense supply of resources. Thus unless abundant provisions are made for this problem, I fear that of necessity his liberality will dry up in a short time, and that the door, not without some recrimination from this country, will finally be closed, a door which at home has always been kept open with great glory. And that *aporia* does not cling to him alone. It also touches those who on account of their prudence and erudition are the next ones going on similar business for the prince. You can readily understand this, and also help out with timely advice there.

George Wheetley,[12] whom you know, dwells nearby. He is wealthy by virtue of his own business, and experienced in German affairs, and so obliging to all Englishmen with respect to their privileges and business in this region that they are unable to do without him at all. He wishes to be a servant of his Majesty, seeking not a purse of money from England, but petitioning for a testimony of commendation

---

[11]In the raging conflict over religion Philip Melanchthon, Professor at the University of Wittenberg, and Joachim Camerarius, Rector of the University of Leipzig, took a more moderate approach by accepting some Catholic views as nonessentials, or *adiaphora*, in the *Leipzig Interim* of 1548-1549.

[12]Once a fellow of St. John's, admitted 1541.

from his fatherland.   Mr. Hoby,[13] I know, will take great pains on behalf of this petition, tendered more by good will than by necessity.
His motives are very sound, and thus I want him to owe this kindness to you, not to another.

On the day before the Lord Ambassador made his departure
from London, you planted in me by that talk in your study at London
the seed of true religion and of the correct method of study, which
can never escape me.   I was very glad that you were on such familiar
terms with Demosthenes.   If you were to translate his and Aeschines'
opposing orations *On the False Legation* into Latin, you would undertake a task very well-suited to your place, interest, talent, judgment,
and ability.   You would shine a great light on the imitation of Demosthenes and Cicero in Greek and Latin.   As for your pronunciation, lest
it should hide any longer in England, if you will send me copies, I
shall have them published in a short time.[14]   I do not doubt but that I
could use Johann Sturm's work to add luster to it.

If you wish to hear something of me also, my progress is immensely satisfying, and in all this progress nothing is more satisfying
than my very enjoyable practice with my lord.   His conversations are
sprinkled with the salt of humanity, and are so remarkable for the
marks of his prudence.   And if some debate crops up, his arguments
are so pointed, and have such force and strength, to which he adds an
extensive knowledge of affairs and a strong memory, that I seem not
to be torn away from my studies, but rather not to have lived in them
until now.

Let me tell briefly that which is more objectively true.   After the
departure of Mr. Hoby, when we acquired a little more leisure, we
talked over all the best Greek authors in our studies together.   I treat
my lord with the same humanity and liberality which you often used
to preach.   Until now I have not lacked anything.   His style is that he
is much quicker and prompter in giving me his benevolence than I in
my bashfulness am in asking for anything.   And although he does this
with good sense, spontaneity, and geniality, still he is much moved by
your commendation of me.   I hope, therefore, that by means of some

[13]Sir Philip Hoby, the ambassador preceding Morison.

[14]Cheke's writings on the pronunciation of Greek were eventually published
as *De pronunciatione Graecae* . . .(Basel, 1555), but not with Ascham's assistance.

token of gratitude he will understand that what was done for your sake has made you grateful as well.

When my lord sees me greatly delighted by the second line of Homer's second work,[15] he readily promises that I am to go not only to Italy, but also to those parts which you have enkindled my ardor of seeing when you lectured on the *Euterpe* and *Polymnia* of Herodotus,[16] an ardor that can never be quenched by any dread of labor or peril. For I possess a body prompt and willing for study, not indeed robust, but enduring labor, cold, or heat well enough, and staying healthy on any sort of food and drink. If I can have your help in getting together some resources to take advantage of these opportunities, you yourself can perceive some of the fruit of this journey. For beyond my diligent acquisition of memorials of ancient times, I can surely report to you in my conversation the current ways of life, customs, and appearances of places which you have always held in admiration.

In England many nobles are favorable to me, and you know that saying of Hesiod, *If you add a little to a little*, etc.[17] For this trip I am not asking for any annuity, but for a little ready cash. My most illustrious Mistress,[18] I do not doubt, will advance much to my petition. Just last year the Duchess of Suffolk, after I had spent some months teaching her son Charles Greek and fine penmanship, gave me large and generous promises.[19] I have saved her liberality for this time and this use. My most excellent Duke of Suffolk, since he favors me and owes to me the elegance of his handwriting, in which he excels, will

---

[15]Ascham alludes to the proem of *The Odyssey* concerning the cities Odysseus saw and the minds of men he learned of in his travels. In *The Schoolmaster* Ascham cites Ulysses as "the wisest traveller that ever travelled" into Italy, and offers Horace's Latin and Thomas Watson's English renderings of Homer's line (III, 149-50).

[16]Books II and VII of Herodotus' *Histories.*

[17]"If you add a little to a little and do it often enough, soon the little will be much" (*Works and Days* 361-62).

[18]Princess Elizabeth.

[19]Katherine Willoughby Brandon, widow of Charles, Duke of Suffolk, was a noted patron of Protestant learning. Before he left Cambridge for the Continent Ascham assisted in the education of both her noted sons, Charles (the younger) and Henry (the elder and thus the titular Duke of Suffolk).

support this request with his mother. I look for much from both mar-
quises,[20] who are rather generous to me.

But let me hush my noisy letter, which shame would long ago
have thrown into silence if my unwillingness to take my leave had not
banished all sense of modesty from it and from me too. But your old
kindness toward me and the not dishonorable reason for my petition
increase my hopes. I am more wordy than I had planned at the outset to be. If I could know that you have received this letter along
with the confession of Magdeburg, I would be more ready to write
you at other times as well. Farewell, most honored sir, and love me
as you do. November 11, 1550.

35 / To Martin Bucer   (Giles I.cxi)
                   Augsburg, January 7, [1551]

> On the invitation of Archbishop Cranmer, Martin Bucer had come over to
> England in 1549. One of the most illustrious leaders of the Reformation on
> the Continent, he was highly valued as a theological consultant and guide
> to the proper course of English Protestantism. Late in 1549 King Edward
> named him Regius Professor of Divinity at Cambridge, with a very gener-
> ous salary. Soon after Bucer's arrival in England Ascham first made his ac-
> quaintance. The relationship was warm and deep; Ryan terms Bucer As-
> cham's "spiritual father and teacher" (116).

Venerable Master Bucer, it is not because I have forgotten you that
you have not yet had a letter from me, nor have I forgotten what you
said to me on my departure: those present expansively promise to
write, but absent they immediately toss their faithfulness and their
concern for their friends to the wind. That's not the way it is, my
Bucer, for since I first arrived in Augsburg my leisure has not merely
been scarce, but non-existent. No messenger is available except the
common one to whom I cannot and dare not entrust anything, and it
would be utterly ridiculous to write this silly letter to you unless it
bore some token of my gratitude and my memory of you. If I were

---

[20]William Parr, Marquis of Northampton, and Henry Grey, Marquis of Dorset.

to write you about weightier matters, I fear lest they be lightened by being read on the way. The messengers here are searched, and whatever one writes runs the risk of being destroyed, discovered, or intercepted. But I am wasting my scanty pre-dawn leisure.

The glory of Christ flourishes here at Augsburg more than can be imagined, bringing into view a most abundant harvest. The Protestant churches could not be more crowded, could not be more glowing. The ministers are very diligent. On the other hand, Popestant churches could not be more uncrowded, nor more cold. The General Council will resume at Trent on the first of May. The Emperor has received the Papal Bull. The rumor is prevalent that Cardinal Reginald Pole will preside over the council.

African affairs are in a great uproar.[1] The town called Africa was captured this year by Andrea Doria, but after he had pacified everything there and then departed, behold, suddenly the prefect of the town, cast out by Doria, turned around and to everyone's surprise occupied the island of Djerba and killed its king, a friend of the Emperor. This prefect, a bloodthirsty Turk, is a dangerous plunderer and a pirate, and no doubt the Emperor will gladly crush him for his insolence.

But a greater danger threatens Hungary, which the Turks will shortly attack, according to very frequent rumor. The Emperor will resist them in Hungary with huge forces enlisted from Spain, Italy, and Germany. Preparations are in full swing, and there is growing expectation of our departure. Shortly we shall move from here to Ratisbon. From there we plan to go to Hungary by way of the Danube, unless perhaps, as some say, we will journey through Saxony and Poland. The forces at Magdeburg recently captured George, Duke of Mecklenburg. My friend Edward Raven--and I commend him especially to you--will show you a letter from which you can piece together the state of affairs.

Clement of Alexandria was recently printed at Florence in a most elegant edition: *Exhortation to the Greeks*, one book; *The Pedagogue*,

---

[1]See Ascham's *Report of Germany* (III, 10ff.) for another account of the victory of Andrea Doria, Doge of Genoa and the admiral of the Emperor's Mediterranean fleet, at Mahdia (here "Africa") in present-day Tunisia.

three books; *Miscellanies,* eight books.   The Italian Paolo Giovio has
written a huge two-volume history of the times to this year.[2]

Christopher Mont,[3] a great admirer of yours, is with us here.   I
urge him every day to write at length and with care about the whole
state of affairs here.   He is better situated than I am since there is almost nothing which does not come to his attention.   I hope to send
you a longer letter shortly, if I have the chance, if I feel like it, etc.

I must ask you, noble teacher, to undertake some trouble for me,
your absent son, and in an important matter.   You remember how I
once approached you when you had first come to England and were
living at Lambeth.   A stranger to you, I declared to you how badly
treated I was, not by my Lady Elizabeth, but by one in her household.[4]   I asked you then if you would restore me to my lady's favor
by writing a letter on my behalf, since she had been somewhat estranged from me, not, as God is my witness, through any fault of my
own, but by the evil work of others.   Before my departure from England I went to my most illustrious lady; she received me very kindly,
and even more kindly reproved me because I was minded to leave her
without endeavoring through anyone to get back into her favor.

I entreat you, noble sir, by all our friendship, to indicate by a
letter to our most illustrious lady how much I have endeavored to
have you do this, something I think you would indeed have done if
your health had not prevented you.   My good conscience is safeguarded, my Bucer, by my upright words and deeds in the court, and
if modesty did not restrain me, I would explain to you what excellent
things my lady has gotten from me.   Your kindness to me and mine
while I am absent will make me very, very grateful.   You know that I
sought this favor from you once at Lambeth.   I pray that I may know
even here at Augsburg how *blessed* I am as I again seek the same
kindness from you.   Christ's own pursuit *of mediation* is most appropriate to those fashioned after his image.

---

[2]Paulus Jovius, *Historiarum sui temporis* (Florence, 1550).

[3]Mont (Mount) was an English agent at Strasbourg; he often served as a
courier between Augsburg and Strasbourg, and thus figures frequently in Ascham's correspondence with Sturm.   Years later Mont speaks with nostalgia of
good times with Ascham at Morison's residence in Augsburg (II.lxxiv).

[4]See Letter 31 concerning his "shipwreck" at court.

If the auspicious gentle breeze of my most illustrious lady's favor blows again toward me, I shall attribute it in large part to you. I shall learn from your letter how much you will do for me in the matter. I shall await nothing more eagerly than the talk of your letter. Greet our most honorable friend Haddon. I commend all Johnians to you. Love me, which you do. Farewell in Jesus Christ. Augsburg, at the monastery of St. George, on the day after *Epiphany*.

36 / To John Cheke   (Giles I.cxiii)

Augsburg, January 14, 1551

I doubt whether my last letter sent to you by Francis the letter-carrier[1] ever came into your hands. I do not expect an answer, most honored sir, for I see that you are so occupied with weightier affairs that you cannot even spare three words in reply to the letters my lord ambassador sent you each week with the greatest show of goodwill. Nevertheless, there is no delight of friendship so immediate as when the absent one feels his welfare safeguarded by the obligations of friendship or his memory kept alive by frequent letters. On the other hand, nothing hurts more than the sort of men about whom Cicero as proconsul bitterly complained: they destroy the absent one with silent ingratitude or the rebuke of injustice. We obscure and humble folk are happier in this respect, since we do not sorrow if we are passed over in silence, nor dread to be wounded by ill-will. We are not accustomed to being upset very much by a sense of *ingratitude* nor mortified very quickly by the sting of *injustice*.

I certainly want to write you frequently and at great length, but there are sound reasons and definite considerations why I do not. The most important things which are happening here are being written in the ambassador's private letters to you or in his public ones to the King's council. If I were to write the same things in my letters, I should betray a trust committed to me, and take on a task as useless to me as it would be troublesome to you. But if I were to bring up lesser matters which are daily tossed about in the street, fathered by

---

[1]Probably Francis Yaxeley, a courier for William Cecil (see I, 344, 350).

falsehood and disseminated without authority, I should seem to have
little consideration for your dignity, prudence, or judgment. Besides, I
have very little leisure, so that even if I very much wished to write, I
have very little opportunity.

My lord ambassador, whenever he is free from public duties,
takes long, daily excursions into the Greek language. He does not rest
quietly in any lodging place or turn aside on any bypath. Already he
is beginning to run fast, and I hope he will soon be flying along, so
that he may think he has everything he needs to surpass the rest of
the Englishmen in this race--unless he catches up to you Olympians,
which he will, even if you are on guard.

This is how I spend my time: I either study or read with my
lord, or copy the letters which he himself writes to England. Very
rarely do I roam into the city, but I find all my pleasure in my duties
at home. In all kinds of service in which I can make myself valuable
to my lord (for I hope that he will not exact from me what I cannot
do), I shall show my best effort, diligence, and respect, with the greatest goodwill, loyalty, and constancy. And although this conduct demands integrity on my part and generosity on his, still you, most honored sir, are the one I daily set before my eyes, as if I considered you
to be present here, looking at what I am doing, so that I engage in
nothing while you are absent which you would not approve of if you
were present. And since your efforts alone got me here, I shall always remember Cicero's maxim: "it is a greater matter to guarantee
someone's integrity than his debt."   When I am so far away from
you, nothing occurs to me more frequently than that I must labor diligently so that every day there will be a new accumulation of your old
kindnesses toward me.

In the Greek language I am diligent, in Italian somewhat, in
Latin not at all. I have infrequent practice in reading it, less in speaking it, and least in writing. I should enjoy a visit to Italy for a few
months. As I wrote you in an earlier letter, I would bring especially
to you any profits of my journey. For if I were free, undivided, and
undistracted, I should so set myself to the recording of times and
places, manners and men, that there would be no movement in the
commonwealth, no status of religion, no progress of literature, no level
of morals and behavior, no changes, hopes, open counsels and secret
plots which I could not fish out in some manner and report fully to
you. If your influence were to assist me in this project, I would be

doubly grateful for your kindness at this time and in this my absence. With just a word of support from you I could readily secure what I seek. I am not so hard on myself that I do not know what I myself can do, and I also know what others are not capable of, those who nevertheless have received handsome prebends, as they are always called.

The position of keeper of the King's library is being withdrawn from me, as you know.[2] If some other advantage does not compensate me for this loss, I must deplore my *bad luck*; other persons cannot excuse their *injustice*, unless it is considered no crime for one man to circumvent another. I love Bartholomew Traheron for many reasons, and would readily give up the library for the sake of so worthy a man, provided that there was a way open to me for a similar post. If you, kind sir, would require any light labors of mine, I believe you know with what attitude, what interest my whole self should bend to it. I know that I happily give myself over to you and entrust my business to you. I have no one else who is better disposed toward me or who is better situated to accomplish this for me.

Clement of Alexandria has been printed at Florence: *Exhortation to the Greeks*, one book; *The Pedagogue*, [three] books; and *Miscellanies*. Theodoret's *On Heresies* has been published at Rome, and recently at Venice eighty Greek orations by Dion Chrysostom: the book treats the famous common places *On Kingship, On Greed, On Law, On Character, On Belief and Unbelief.* Camerarius once translated this last one and other similar ones designed for civil use. I should gladly send you this book and others if they could be carried handily into England. John Jacob Fugger, a prominent merchant of this city, has had a great number of the best Greek books from Italy, France, and Germany elegantly transcribed for himself. His library I have not yet seen, but if I

---

[2]As a result of a mistranslation of Ascham's phrase *mihi conceditur* (properly "is being withdrawn from me," not "is granted to me") error and confusion have surrounded the question of Ascham's position as the royal librarian. Giles first created the confusion with his mistranslation (I, p. lxxiv); even Ryan, who says little about the whole question, perpetuates the mistake (107). All the details of Ascham's appointment, including the date, remain unknown. However, records do indicate that on December 14, 1549, Bartholomew Taheron, a much-travelled graduate of both Cambridge and Oxford and one-time servant of Chancellor Cromwell, with strong ties to Continental Protestantism, succeeded Ascham in the position.

do I shall note whether any old classics are to be found there. Musculus last year dedicated an ecclesiastical history to his royal majesty.[3] At this point he does not know whether the book has been presented to him. If you, Cecil, and Cooke[4] preserve the cause of virtue and learning there, you will be answering everyone's wish. If in your next letter to the ambassador, you indicate that you have received this letter, I shall be obliged to you. But I would be far more grateful if I could learn of your old benevolence in a letter from you, which I long for very much. Farewell, most excellent sir. Augsburg, January 14, 1551.

37 / To Lady Jane Grey   (Giles I.cxiv)
Augsburg, January 18, 1551

The drama of Jane Grey's life and death is poignant and memorable in its own right, but Ascham must be chiefly credited with memorializing her devotion to classical studies, and securing her a place with Catherine Parr, Queen Elizabeth, the talented daughters of Anthony Cooke, and others as one of the learned women of Renaissance England. Indeed, Ascham's tributes to Lady Jane are legendary, the inspiration for a still growing series of romanticized accounts of this unfortunate girl's achievements before she was executed in 1554 for her unwilling and unwanted role in Northumberland's succession schemes upon the death of King Edward in 1553. Her wealthy and prominent father, Henry Grey, Marquis of Dorset, was married to Frances Brandon, daughter of Charles and Mary Tudor Brandon, Duke and Duchess of Suffolk. Mary Brandon being the younger sister of Henry VIII, Jane was thus cousin to Edward VI and especially vulnerable to coming into harm's way in the struggles over who should succeed to Henry VIII's throne.
　　As Princess Elizabeth's tutor, Ascham first came to know Lady Jane when she was a resident in Queen Catherine Parr's household in Chelsea,

---

[3]*Ecclesiasticae historiae autores* (Basel, 1549), a collection of writings on church history by Eusebius and others. Wolfgang Müslin (Musculus) was displaced from his post in Augsburg by the *Interim*, and became professor of theology at Berne in 1549. He edited numerous Biblical commentaries and collections of writings by Church Fathers.

[4]Sir Anthony Cooke, William Cecil's father-in-law, a strong advocate of Protestant learning, and a good friend of most of the members of Ascham's Cambridge circle.

and apparently he worked at keeping up the relationship. In 1550 as he journeyed from his native Yorkshire to London, where he would join the embassy to Germany, Ascham stopped by Bradgate Hall, the Grey home, to make the visit recounted here. An account parallel to this one is found in *The Schoolmaster* (III, 117-19). See also Ascham's tribute in a letter to Sturm (Letter 41).

In this long journey of mine, most illustrious lady, I have traversed large territories, seen the largest cities, and with all the diligence I could muster I have witnessed the customs of many men and the institutions, laws, religion, and government of diverse peoples.   But nothing in all this variety of things has prompted me to so much admiration as when last summer I blundered in on you, so noble a maiden, while your tutor was absent and you were in your most noble father's hall.   While all the others, both men and women, were giving themselves over to hunting and to pleasures, I blundered in, I repeat--O *Zeus and the gods*--upon you, a divine maiden sedulously reading in Greek the divine *Phaedo* of the divine Plato.   It is on that account that you are happy, rather than because you trace your family back to kings and queens *on your mother's and your father's side*.   Continue to press onward, most accomplished maiden, bringing pride to your country, happiness to your parents, glory to yourself, praise to your tutor, congratulation to your friends, and the greatest admiration to all strangers.

Oh happy Aylmar[1] to have such a pupil, and much happier you to have him for a tutor!   I certainly rejoice and congratulate both of you, the one who learns as well as the one who teaches.   These are the words of Johann Sturm to me[2] concerning my position as teacher of my most illustrious mistress Elizabeth.   But they can be more truly applied to you two.   I give you this happiness unimpaired, although without any cause I myself have drawn a bitter injury out of a relationship from which I should fairly have expected the sweet fruit from my labors.   But this is not the time to reopen the wound of my sorrow, which should by now have healed and become calloused, if not through my good sense, certainly through time itself.   I will say this

---

[1]John Aylmar (Elmar), a Cambridge graduate (MA in 1545), though not from St. John's; future Bishop of London during Elizabeth's reign.

[2]Letter 40.

much: I cannot accuse Lady Elizabeth, who has been very good to me, nor Mistress Astley either. But if I ever happen upon my Aylmar, into his bosom I shall abundantly pour all my sorrows.

I seek two favors from you, my Aylmar (for I suppose you will read this letter of mine): first that you will persuade and encourage Lady Jane Grey to write to me in Greek as soon as she can. She promised she would do it for me. I recently wrote to Johann Sturm also that she promised me this. The way is long, but John Hales[3] will very readily take care of getting a letter to me. If she would also write in Greek to Johann Sturm himself, neither you nor she will regret undertaking that task. The second favor that I seek, my Aylmar is that you look into how the two of us may spend our whole life together. How pleasantly, how freely, how like philosophers we should then live! What would prevent at least us, my dear Elmar, from enjoying all those good things which Cicero at the very end of the third book of *De finibus* attributes to this life-style? There would be nothing in either language, nothing in the whole history of the past or of the present from which we would not pluck something to sweeten our lives.

Concerning the news here, most illustrious lady, I know not what to write: letters would be worthless which contained worthlessness, and yet, as Cicero complained concerning his own times, no letter of any weight or importance could find its way to you without being lightened by its reading.[4] Besides, unrest, strife, and rumors of war fill these places and the conversations here. Many of them are devised by treachery or disseminated without authority, and you would derive little or no pleasure from my writing about them, nor would you have much interest in them.

The general council will commence at Trent on the first of May. They say Reginald Pole, the English cardinal, will be president of the council. Meanwhile, there has been tumult in Africa this year, there are preparations for war against the Turk, and expectations are high of an expedition by Caesar into Hungary. If I am not a soldier in this war, I shall at least, God willing, be an ally. What would it profit to write about the siege of Magdeburg, and how they have captured the

[3]See Letter 32, note 1.
[4]*Ad Atticum* 1.13.

Duke of Mecklenburg, and about the widespread disturbances which afflict Saxony, miserable in every way during these hard times? There is no time to explain fully the things which I have compressed into the narrow limits of my letter, nor is it safe. On my return, which I hope is not far off, my whole pleasure will be to weave this entire story for you, and to draw out each individual thread at length in conversation face to face.

Your liberality, most noble Jane Grey, was always welcome when I was present, but it is far more welcome when I am absent. With all my heart I wish your noble parents long happiness, I wish you daily victory in your studies and in virtue, and your sister Katherine the same as I wish you. For my Aylmar I wish what he would desire for his Ascham. And if I did not fear burdening my ladyship with the weight of my light greeting, I would pray you to greet Elizabeth Astley in my name. I love her much since in pleasantness and integrity I think she resembles her brother John, my very good friend.[5] Greet, I pray you, Mary Latin, my relative, and my wife Alice, whose word I more often remember than easily follow.[6] Greet also the noble youth Garret and James Haddon.[7] Farewell in Christ, most illustrious lady. Augsburg, January 18, 1551.

38 / To Hubert Thomas Leodius (Giles I.cxliv)
Brussels, March 6, 1553

Ever the confident warrior in the Cambridge humanists' campaign for a reformed pronunciation of Greek (see Letter 2), Ascham eagerly challenged conservative Heidelberg humanists to debate the subject with him in an exchange of letters. Only one of Ascham's letters survives, this playfully

[5]See Letter 16.

[6]Ascham was not yet married; by the Latin term *uxor* ("wife") he may mean someone who had promised to marry him, or perhaps he is merely being playful about a certain woman in Lady Jane's household. See Ryan 114-15.

[7]Jane's tutor, formerly fellow of Trinity College, Cambridge, and younger brother of the better known Walter Haddon, Regius Professor of Civil Law at Cambridge. Later, as a Marian exile in Strasbourg, James was responsible for the publication there of Jane's papers (1554).

combative one to Hubert Thomas Leodius (the last appellation is a contraction of *Leodensis*, "of Liège"), secretary and counsel to the Count Palatine,
Frederick II, and something of a diplomat, historian, and antiquary. Giles
also prints two of the Heidelbergers' rejoinders: I.cli (from Nicholas Cisner
[see note 1 below]) and I.cliv (from Hubert Thomas).

Ascham writes from Brussels, the Emperor's new seat, following
months of straining to attend a displaced and brooding court. In March
1552 a storm of battle had broken within the empire, and by the end of
May the forces of Maurice of Saxony had forced Charles V to flee first to
Innsbruck, and then, in a particularly tumultuous flight, to Carinthia across
Brenner Pass. During the remaining months of 1552 the Emperor did not
regain effective control, and early in January 1553 he gave up efforts to
wrest control of Metz from the French, and retreated to the Low Countries.

The sudden raising of the siege of Metz afflicted many men with great
sadness and gave me not a little sorrow, most learned Hubert, since
that was what prevented me from visiting Heidelberg. I would have
derived a special pleasure from your agreeable manner and learned
conversation, and of course from Micyllus' and Cisner's as well.[1] We
would profitably and fully have debated what each of us has determined about the correct way of pronouncing Greek. I know that I
would have reaped a great profit from your learning, and I believe I
would have reported at home that I won the victory by having a better case.

I think often and long about my friend Hubert, that is to say,
about your great kindness and extensive learning and about that disputation we planned. I am thinking that I should try now in a letter
to lay some part of the foundation for that which I would have completed in a conversation face to face. Following this plan, and using a
system of writing by turns, we shall have a double profit, for we shall
by the frequency of our letters stabilize our incipient friendship, and
we shall pursue the disputation we planned with great pleasure.
Moreover, let us pursue it in such a way that we never go beyond
exchanging letters. And let us handle only one letter of the Greek
alphabet in each letter. Thus our letters will never be too long, and
we shall have really abundant subject matter to write about.

---

[1]Jacobus Micyllus (Moltzer or Molshem), 1503-1558, Professor of Greek at
Heidelberg and distinguished editor of Homer; Nicholas Cisner (Kistner), 1529-
1583, appointed Professor of Ethics at Heidelberg in 1552, and later a leader in the
study of law and jurisprudence.

So, may the muses favor our undertaking, and approve our cause! Willingly I allow you three, whom I consider my opponents, to be the judges in this case. Now let both pronunciations, yours and ours, be brought forth, and let them battle it out with each other. With what weapons? With reasons? I accept readily. With learning? I expect it from you, most learned gentlemen. With witnesses? I agree to them also.

I know that you have no reasons except those which your extensive learning has provided. But who are your witnesses? Let them stand for examination. You have the chief witness, Usage, for everyone except the English pronounces Greek as you do. Then you will produce Greece itself, which today retains your pronunciation, whose authority is much to be preferred to those British Islands, so cut off from the whole world. Now if you understood Usage to be the custom of ancient times when Aristotle lived and wrote, he who has been preserved and is flourishing still today in the books of learned men, even I admit Usage. But if your Usage is this vulgar, unlettered, and mundane Usage, altogether foreign to the ancient and most learned Usage, corrupted by so many mutations, bound up with so many errors, and rotten with age, I certainly do not accept it. Usage, unless it depends upon learning and reason, always plunges headlong into errors. Hence it happens that no republic was ever so well governed, nor any law so righteously enacted but that it after all totters and is overturned by the fault of one custom.

I am silent about the fact that Usage alone produces and fosters errors even in the true religion of Christ himself, just as a stinking sow suckles its little pig, and bites to protect it. Do you want to correct something, or restore something that has been vitiated? Usage by itself fights back and defeats itself, crying out, "it's a habit, it's a habit." It is a habit from which the mob of unlearned men can be parted only very reluctantly. You leaders of knowledge will see, therefore, whether in this case Usage must not be designated in many respects the author and defender of all error, especially since there is nothing which is more liable to daily mutations than the pronunciation and the sound of words.

Since now the Greek language has for some time withdrawn itself from common use and exiled itself to the books of the learned, let your Usage remain silent and withdraw from this judgment, and bring forth those books which "neither the wrath nor the fire of Jove

nor all the ages can corrupt," those books, that is, of the more ancient
faith, though I do not reject the word and testimony of any book
which you three deem a worthy and suitable witness. But books, you
say, do not speak, and cannot express the sound of letters. I know
that all books and letters are speechless and will blush at speaking
about your corrupt and vitiated pronunciation.   But they will offer
abundant, clarifying testimony about ours.   And if any books have
something to say about your method, produce them; I shall not challenge one.   I in turn will bring forward on my behalf the most learned books of the greatest authority, and that shortly, as soon as my
discussion is under way.

Another witness in your defense is Greece itself.   Rightly so.
But it is a Greece, of course, which does not know how to speak.
Does she know correct pronunciation?   Does this Greece, which has
now long has lost her power, glory, talent, learning, and even her
name and her language, still retain, please God, her true pronunciation?   Has this Greece, with so many of her cities destroyed, her temples thrown down, the victim of so many invasions by the barbarians,
still preserve her pronunciation pure and inviolate, uninjured by any
mutation?   Surely you are obliged to seek other witnesses of a happier
fate and fortune than these unfortunate Greeks.   I gladly oppose not
only you three, but all living Greeks, for Greek no more belongs to
the Greeks than Latin belongs to the Italians.   Perhaps they will say
that they are accustomed to use a pronunciation better than, but different from, that employed by those old learned Greeks, and then I
shall fight them for having added their own impudence to the inveter-
ate and singular error of others.   Therefore whoever wishes to contend
in this case must fortify himself with the strength of knowledge, not
the error of custom.   He must continue this disputation using the
monuments of the learned, where now the Greek language wholly
dwells, not the Greece of some other time, now the territory of barbarians, from which all learning, even the language itself, has been
banished.

So much for the general question of pronunciation.   Now very
briefly let me write about one character, lest it seem I set out to make
a letter into a little book.   We do not disagree about the Greek *alpha*,
unless when it unites to form the diphthong *ai*, but we shall postpone
that matter until our disquisition on vowels.

Let *beta* come forth, for here we differ a good deal. But let us hear how you and how we say it, and you three be the judges whether both pronounce it correctly. The Greek word *kuberno* you pronounce *chiverno*, in which one utterance alone you commit three errors, in *kappa*, in *upsilon*, and in *beta*. The Latins have made this word their own, and they not only retain its meaning ["I steer"], but also its correct pronunciation, changing only the unvoiced first letter *kappa* into their own "g," as the ancient Greeks very often did themselves. And so we pronounce *kuberno* with the Latin *guberno*. (I shall deal with *kappa* and *upsilon* in their proper place.)

Now let us offer fitting witnesses concerning whether one should say *verno*, as you do, or *berno*, as we do. Produce your witnesses: they are all beginning to lose their tongues except for that liar Usage, whom his accessories Error and Ignorance have hustled in, dragged by the neck, with impudent looks. Now hear our witnesses, whom I know you will not reject.

First is the very learned Eustathius,[2] who thus explains the passage in Homer, *bê de kat' Oulympoio,* etc. *Be,* he says, is the very sound of the sheep pen. Now whether any sheep says *vee,* as you do, or *baa,* as we do, you judge. I know that all English, German, and Italian sheep testify for us, though perhaps Greek sheep formerly did not *baa,* but *vee'd!* But you will complain, what sort of learning is this, which is gotten from sheep? Surely we are not steeped in shame to learn from sheep, since in a similar case he for whom no one can find an equal did not blush to learn the Greek letter *rho* from a dog.[3] To learn from sheep is to learn from nature herself, which is ever constant and most like herself, not liable to variations and changes as your Usage and fluctuating custom is.

But I have another witness. Here is Marcus Cicero, who by speaking Greek stole glory, as he put it, from the Greeks themselves, and who said in a well-known letter about obscene words[4] that when he heard *binei,* a foul Greek word, it sounded just like Latin *bini.* But

---

[2]Twelfth-century metropolitan of Thessalonica and teacher of rhetoric, with an extensive knowledge of Greek literature. Ascham refers here to his commentary on Homer's recurring phrase, "He/she came down from Olympus' peak. . . ."

[3]See the account of Demosthenes in Jerome, *Adversus Rufinum* 1.17.

[4]*Ad fam.* 9.22.

if *bi* had sounded like *vi* to Cicero, as now it sounds to you, he would without a doubt have said *vini*, not *bini*.   Therefore either Cicero's *bi* was not correct, or your pronunciation is now at fault.

Would you care for a third witness?   He is not a trifling one either, but a most weighty one in all cases.   We produce Aurelius Augustine, who has decided this matter more plainly, if anything could be put more plainly, than Eustathius or Cicero.   In his book *On Christian Doctrine*--the chapter escapes me,[5] and I do not have the book handy--he says that when he heard the vegetable *beta* [beet] named, it seemed to him that the second letter of the Greek alphabet was pronounced, as we now utter it.   But if Augustine had pronounced it as you do, it would have sounded like *vita*, that is, "the soul," not *beta*, "the beet."

Do you want a fourth witness?   If I had not proposed limits for my letter, I could have produced a fifth and a tenth witness also.   But let us follow him who in more weighty matters says, "In the mouths of two or three," etc.[6]   I shall not exert myself to satisfy anyone for whom Eustathius, Cicero, and Augustine are not sufficient.   Therefore let us say frankly that either I have misrepresented my sources, or that those three witnesses have not written correctly, or that we have liberated the true and genuine pronunciation, the one most fitting for Germanic peoples.   Let us pursue in our future letters, God willing, our discussion of the pronunciation of the remaining letters in their proper order.

Greet the learned Micyllus and Cisner, whose letters and yours too about pronunciation I eagerly await.   Greet also in your letters that most accomplished woman Olympia.[7]   If with her singular learning and very good judgment she alone should undertake the patron-

---

[5]The reference is to 2.24.

[6]"In the mouth of two or three witnesses every word may be established," Matthew 18:16, AV.

[7]Olympia Fulvia Morata, 1526-1555, was accounted one of the learned and brilliant women of her time.   Born and educated in Ferrara, she married Andreas Grünthler, a young German studying medicine at the university there, and accompanied him over the Alps in 1551.   She endured months of siege and such terrible hardships that she never recovered her health after arriving in Heidelberg, where her husband became Professor of Medicine; she died at age 29.

age of our pronunciation, I shall struggle less with the rest of you. Farewell, best and most learned Hubert.   Brussels, March 6, 1553.

PART FIVE

Letters to Johann Sturm

Johann Sturm, Strasbourg's leading humanist and the rector of its Protestant Gymnasium, was the correspondent Ascham valued most. In this edition, therefore, I have omitted none of Ascham's surviving letters to his esteemed friend. After 1550 Sturm's influence over Ascham seems even to exceed Cheke's. All that is good in *The Schoolmaster* "is to be credited to you," he would write to Sturm in 1568, "for I have taken pains that what I write should be wholly Sturmian" (Letter 60). Although Ascham never managed to meet Sturm in person (see Letter 47), this German scholar-teacher was, Ascham once wrote, "the dearest friend I have out of England" (III, 216).

Encouraged by Martin Bucer, Strasbourg's leading reformer who had come to England in 1549 after repeated invitations from Archbishop Cranmer, Ascham inaugurated the correspondence nearly six months before his departure for Germany and well before he was awarded his position with Ambassador Morison. Once he was established at the Emperor's court, moreover, he readily found couriers to prosper their exchange, for there was frequent traffic between Ambassador Morison and Strasbourg, chiefly through Christopher Mont, an English agent who appears repeatedly in these letters. In May 1551 Ascham wrote friends back home in England, "I hear from Sturmius every week" (I, 284).

In every Renaissance edition of Ascham's correspondence, the letters to Sturm had pride of place; they constitute the opening book. Ascham's inaugural letter was particularly polished and substantial, glowing with his pride in English learning and the English church. Indeed, it stands as a kind of classic of mid-Tudor humanist ideals, a recitation of the articles of Ascham's midcentury creed: a pronounced preference for Greek learning, an admiration for the Protestant policies of the boy King Edward, a partisan commitment to Scriptural religion and a Reformed church polity, a marked preference for the kind of practical scholarship conducive to better pedagogy, an enthusiasm for Cambridge learning, and a glowing estimation of the literacy of both the royalty and the nobility of England. Sturm himself had a memorable phrase that effectively summarized their shared humanistic ideals: *pietas literata.* It was, Ascham wrote Sturm, his firm resolve to join Plato, Aristotle, Demosthenes, and Cicero to the faithful and constant study of the Scriptures (Letter 39).

Sturm's reply to Ascham's overture, though slow in coming, was no less impressive, and since Grant's second edition of the Ascham correspondence in 1578, it has always been printed with Ascham's letters. I have thus included it as well. We should also note here that Sturm soon arranged to have their inaugural exchange printed under the title "Epistolae Duae de Nobilitate Anglicana," included in Conrad Heresbach's *De laudibus Graecarum literarum oratio* (Strasbourg, 1551). It marks the only publication of any of Ascham's letters during his lifetime.

In general Sturm was not, however, a particularly good correspondent, confessing, "I write but seldom to my friends" (I, 292). After the first, his letters are largely reaffirmations of his love for Ascham and brief accounts of the progress of his projects. Later on, two or three years pass without any letters between them (see Letters 48, 49). Moreover, not all the correspondence survives. Their friendship did nevertheless continue to the last syllable, as it were, of Ascham's life. His final letter to Sturm, an inspired account of educational methods and ideals and the longest of all his letters, was completed only days before his death. I have reserved it for a separate section, Part Seven.

39 / To Johann Sturm (Giles I.xcix)
Cambridge, April 4, 1550

Inspired by conversations with Martin Bucer, the celebrated Strasbourg theologian and reformer who had come to England in April 1549, Ascham here inaugurates a long and fruitful correspondence with Strasbourg's most famous humanist. Sturm would presently have this elegant letter, along with his own answer to it (Letter 40), printed under the title "Epistolae Duae de Nobilitate Anglicana," included in Conrad Heresbach's *De laudibus Graecarum literarum oratio* (Strasbourg, 1551).

Ascham's famous words of praise for Princess Elizabeth in the second part of this letter are not mere disinterested compliments. Earlier he had asked Bucer to intercede on his behalf with the Princess, allowing that she was "somewhat estranged from me" (Letter 35), but he got no immediate result. Since he could reasonably expect that news about a letter as long and formal as this one would get back to Bucer and others in England, this communication to Sturm affords Ascham another opportunity to work strategically to restore himself to the full favor he had enjoyed for almost two years as Elizabeth's tutor.

No art for the guidance of life nor any science for the cultivation of the intellect, in my judgment at least, most accomplished Johann Sturm, has ever been discovered which can compare with the excellence of that faculty by whose aid reason is trained for thinking carefully and language for speaking clearly, and by whose aid the rest of man's life seems to be far removed from monstrous and savage custom and to come very near to the divine nature.

Hence that unbelievable sense of devotion with which almost all learned men at the present time follow after that Attic Athens, from which one city in one age, as you know, more leaders and teachers of the arts of eloquence and of logic have arisen than have ever appeared in the whole of human history. To be sure, Rome, once the dwelling of empire, far superior to Athens herself in her crown of virtue, equal or not much inferior in her excellence in eloquence (although now by her present customs, papist luxury, and domineering anti-Christianity she has subjected herself to good men's hatred) has been so commended to all posterity by her reputation for ancient eloquence and the genius of Cicero that the memory of the city of Rome, held in the greatest love and affection, shall endure as long as any men are sustained by the fruit of Latin letters or made illustrious by their glory.

We admire very much not only the erudite centuries of ancient times, but also the splendid learning of the present age, particularly in those men who have flourished by their supremacy in eloquence. I myself strongly love and cherish many excellent men from Italy, Germany, and France whom I have never seen, because of the notable brilliance of the learning which I perceive shining within them. And since you, most illustrious Johann Sturm, have imbibed the wholesome liquor of eloquence from Plato, Aristotle, and Cicero in ways that I have not seen for years in anyone else nor in anyone living in our time, and since you have focussed all that eloquence on making the doctrine of Christ more sound, if I were not writing to you about yourself, I should gladly explain in detail how much I think of you. Even if I should do it, I do not see why I should fear the stigma of flattery. To me it seems affected to try to write one way to one person, and another way to someone else.

That divine judgment of yours by which you evaluate individual authors, read with such discrimination, and remark, select, weigh, construct, refine, and finish, transports me into such admiration that whatever you have thus far written I have searched for sedulously and read over avidly. I have even happened upon transcripts someone made of some lectures of yours, namely, your very learned lectures on the whole text of Plato's *Gorgias*.[1] I acquired this volume three years ago in London. In this way, although I could not directly enjoy the pleasantness of your presence, I was at any rate always pleased to profit as much as I could from the wealth of your genius.

For many years now I have been marvelously inspired by my love for you. Mind you, my almost daily conversations about you with my reverend father and teacher Martin Bucer make me so enthusiastic that I do nothing more willingly than write to you, especially when I understand from what you have written about yourself that you are one who is content with gentility and benevolence. Besides, from conversation with Doctor Bucer I understand that you are not more skilled in the eloquence of Cicero than adorned with his humanity, and judge that nothing is greater in a man than responding in love to those who provoke love.

---

[1]Despite Ascham's pleas at several points in this letter, Sturm never published these notes.

But look how audacious I am: at the very outset of our friendship I have not only wanted to show a sign of my goodwill, but have
resolved as well to seek some fruit and reward.   For I have determined to ask you to do something for literature for the sake of your
own name and for my own use, unless there seems to be too much
self-love in this. With the favor of Christ I have resolved to build the
tabernacle of my life and studies above all on the reading of the Scriptures, and I have in mind to join Plato, Aristotle, Demosthenes, and
Marcus Cicero to the rest of my labors. The pleasure I take in this
kind of study is not so narrow, nor I am so lazy that I condemn altogether the doctors' and jurisconsults' books and never touch them at
all. For these books contain the arts and sound learning, and they
profit and enrich human life. But in view of the great variety of very
good scholarship, let everyone, as far as I am concerned, follow this
maxim: "To each his own bride, mine is for me," a crude saying by
Atilius, a very wooden poet, as <u>Cicero</u> says.[2]

In learning and judgment Aristotle not only surpasses all the
others, but in my opinion he surpasses even himself in those books
where he explains the art of eloquence with exquisite learning.
Thanks to his divine intellect the divine sciences of reason, nature, and
morals lie hidden in the rest of his books. In his *Rhetoric* he presents
and explains almost nothing which is not useful in practical, daily life.

The more I admire these books of rhetoric above all others, the
more I respect Daniel Barbaro and Pietro Vettori, who have certainly
commented on them with great diligence.[3] Although I earnestly desire
it, I cannot find out what Gregory of Nazianzus has to say in those
Greek commentaries in the books Erasmus says in his adage *Festina
lente* that he read in Aldus' printing house.[4] For I do not believe that
these are those *anonymous commentaries* printed in France. I freely acknowledge the diligence of all these scholars and strongly approve
their good intentions. But when I look at your works, which I know

---

[2]*Ad Atticum* 14.20.

[3]Daniel Barbaro (1513-1570) was a learned Venetian, and incidentally an ambassador to England in 1548; his commentary on Ermolao Barbaro's Latin translation of Aristotle's *Rhetoric* appeared in Venice, 1544. Vettori, or Victorius (1499-
1585), was a renowned scholar in Florence, where his commentaries appeared in
1548.

[4]*Opera omnia*, ed. Le Clerc (Leiden, 1703) II, 405.

through frequent reading and through the word of many men whom I meet often, I see clearly that you are translating these books on rhetoric with great talent and good judgment, and I have resolved not to review in a letter either what they teach on this topic or what I think about it myself, but to leave it to you.   This, then, most learned Sturm, is what I seek so eagerly from you: that you publish your skillfully developed commentaries on the supreme art of this supremely great thinker.[5]

Now truly, if I had any aptitude for persuasion or power of compulsion, I would use it all to urge you to do this.   Not I alone, but many others demand this from you.   Since their wishes involve the great usefulness of literature and the tremendous glory of your name, consider again and again how much your liberal knowledge owes them.   We do not seek to have you burden yourself with new labors; we long for the old ones, so that the mature fruit of your studies can be distributed very widely.   For we have seen and read a great deal of your work in explaining those books of rhetoric, and you have excited so much enthusiasm in us for seeing the rest of them that it can in no way be satisfied unless your talented work is published.   Therefore, best Sturm, hurry and make the prayer of one man work for the good of all.

And even if you wish to be too inflexible to be moved by the prayers of many good men, which I do not readily believe, still I assume that you are far too wise to allow someone to plagiarize your work on Aristotle's rhetoric or the *Gorgias* or your *Politics*, something that happens now and then, as you fear, something you might have to redress in the future.   Someone in the huge crowd of note-takers may easily pull off this very thing through the stupidity of a friend or the avarice of a greedy printer.   Erasmus and many learned men have often suffered this injustice, which you ought not dismiss lightly even if it should happen to you alone.   But since this injustice commonly happens to all men of letters, involving students of yours as well, certainly you should be more cautious.   Whether you take this as the honest advice of someone warning you, or the truthful eagerness of a

---

[5]Although Ascham read parts of the manuscript at various times, Sturm's translation and commentary on Aristotle's *Rhetoric* would not be published until 1570, two years after Ascham's death.

loving friend, or the zealous decree of a beggar, I pray you take it in that spirit in which I write and fulfill it because I especially desire it.

In recent years Aristotle has come out of France speaking with a Latin tongue, as all men reckon, but thinking very strange thoughts, as certain scholars judge. Many approve of Joachim Périon's efforts in joining Cicero with Aristotle,[6] and more think better of his diligence and energy in gathering and organizing passages from both than they do of that big mouth of Cephas Chlononius,[7] who by impudently attacking both the prince of Greek learning and the schoolmaster of Rome has insolently wronged their good work and misused his own intellect. I myself also believe that Aristotle's excellent ideas seem to be too little embellished and obscured too much to allow many readers to be enticed by pleasure into studying him or to be compensated for their efforts by the benefits they derive, since nearly everywhere Aristotle is taught without being carefully illustrated with examples, a matter in which Latin and even Greek commentators fall short. Yet the whole discipline of dialectic ought not be found wanting because of this defect, since in that whole subtle system of logic taught by Aristotle there is no rule for which there are not explicit examples within the Socratic dialogues written by Plato and Xenophon. This, most erudite Sturm, you wisely observe and teach frequently, especially in the explanation within your preface to Plato's *Gorgias* of the method of dialectical argument and composition. Every time I come to this passage, as I do very often, I leave with some new profit for my work and new admiration for your talent and judgment.

As for rhetoric, which is designed for a more illustrious use, I require nothing more than that examples chosen from Demosthenes, Cicero, Thucydides, Livy, and the books of similar orators and historians be organized so that whatever there is of splendor and equity in virtue, of foulness or fraud in vice, of seasonable opportunity in wis-

---

[6]Périon, or Perionius (c. 1499-1559), was a learned student of both languages, with a doctorate from the Sorbonne. As a member of the Benedictines he also wrote on behalf of Catholic faith and practice. Since about 1540 he had been translating the works of Aristotle into elegant Latin. He came under attack from Ramus for idolizing Cicero.

[7]Here Ascham plays scornfully with Greek forms for the name of Peter Ramus (Pierre de la Ramée, i.e., "rock" + "twig"), whose slashing attack on Aristotle first appeared in the famous *Aristotelicae animadversiones* (1543).

dom, and of unexpected good luck in fortune can be observed and collected from the heritage of all ages. I always look for rhetorical principles to be carefully linked to examples or to references to particular passages.

And although this ought to be a labor appropriate to an eager man of letters, yet when the attention, the delight, and the judgment of a superior mind are brought to bear on it, certainly this conjunction of art and imitation produces a new sweetness and pleasure in studies and makes the fruit useful. No matter whether you want to call it some error of mine due to ignorance or some sluggishness in me due to laziness, I indulge it the more freely because I see that very often those who cling to the bare principles of the arts are bloodless, cold, inept, without sense, feeling, or profit.[8] On the other hand, those who have not been instructed in the principles, but who have been content with only the reading of orators and historians, have been stuck in one place. I do not say these things because I in any way approve of the idle boasting of a tongue or the insolence flowing from a pen. But just as in handing down true religion one ought to join examples from life to points of doctrine, so indeed one ought to bring this practice to bear on the cultivation of the whole art of imitation, so that the course of study may seem neither unprofitably impeded by obscurity nor boldly led astray by deception. Besides, since rhetoric is *soul-winning*, as Socrates teaches, and since the whole noble science of the soul has a very close relationship to this art, many would heartily applaud this discipline and this age of ours if you would some day shine the light of your genius on the *Phaedo* of Plato and the *De anima* of Aristotle.

Since I see that I have already taken advantage of your kindness, and exceeded the limits of modesty, certainly I can now use the strategy of Cicero himself and "be out-and-out impudent."[9] Demosthenes himself, who up to this point has been rejecting the unsuccessful attempts of many a man, also entreats you heartily. Twice now Italy

---

[8] In this discussion of the value of examples as illustrations of principles, Ascham anticipates one of his major themes in *The Schoolmaster*: "For precepts in all authors, and namely in Aristotle, without applying unto them the imitation of examples, be hard, dry, and cold, and therefore barren, unfruitful, and unpleasant" (III, 231).

[9] *Ad fam.* 5.12.3.

has sent us Aeschines and Demosthenes speaking in Latin, but in my opinion these translations have not been worthy of those orators or of that land. Those two Germans whom I always admire and love also disappoint many in their translation of Demosthenes.[10] But truly when in your book *The Lost Art of Eloquence*[11] I read your translation of the first rhetorical period which begins Demosthenes' oration against Aeschines, and when I marked carefully your good judgment in weighing what force individual words have in each language and what structure the thought has, do not think, most learned Sturm, that I didn't cry out, "Oh Gods and Goddesses! What is this new head of Venus!"[12] Don't you think that especially in this present letter of mine, as well as in the public prayers long uttered by educated men, we are earnestly soliciting you to complete what remains to be done with the opposing orations of those two noble orators? By such a labor you will marvelously awaken the splendor of both tongues and ease our longing for the lost Ciceronian translations. And to this request of mine-- audaciously undertaken, I know--I hope you will give much thought, not only to a consideration of the work itself, but also to the burning desires and the sound reasons for my request. Finally, you must see that you would fulfill the expectation you aroused in all lovers of let-

[10]Throughout his correspondence, as well as in *The Schoolmaster* (III, 206-07), Ascham expresses his particular interest in two celebrated pairs of opposing orations by Demosthenes and Aeschines, one pair *On the False Embassy*, the other pair entitled *On the Crown* and *Against Ctesiphon*. Work on these orations constituted a kind of humanist set piece; Cicero himself had first undertaken the task in order to polish his style. The chief Italian to whom Ascham refers is Leonardo Bruni, whose translation was published in Venice, 1485. The German whom Ascham has chiefly in mind is Hieronymus Wolf, whose landmark translation of Demosthenes appeared in 1550; Ascham would become "well acquainted with him" (I, 284) in Augsburg. Soon he would also urge Cheke to undertake a translation of the opposing orations (Letter 34); in years to come Sturm, Melanchthon, Dionysius Lambini, and Thomas Wilson, among others, would also undertake this classic humanistic challenge.

[11]*De amissa dicendi ratione* (Strasbourg, 1538; enlarged edition, 1543).

[12]Allusions to the *Iliad* 8.5, and to the most famous of Apelles' paintings, that of Aphrodite (Venus) wringing from her hair the water of the sea from which she has just risen.

ters when you wrote those books *On the Art of Eloquence and Composition.*[13]

These words I have written about you and yours; now a little about us and ours. About the course of religion, the condition of the state, and the culture and fruit of learning among us here in England, I could deliver a quite loquacious sermon, if such matters could be included in so short a letter. But what cannot now be concluded in the space of this one letter, I shall reserve for many letters which, God willing, I shall write to you frequently.

The care of true religion stands guard first of all in our Josiah,[14] and at Canterbury, and in the whole royal council, so that we work to no other end than that Christian doctrine and church polity are drawn very purely from the well of the sacred Scriptures, and that the flow of the bilgewater of Rome, which has flooded the church of Christ with so much human filth, is completely stopped up. The unanimity and the obedience of the people in this matter are unsurpassed.

In our studies we willingly follow the counsels of the Fathers, where they themselves do not wander from the Holy Scriptures. We set the most store by Augustine. I would not yield to you in your preference for the Greeks Basil and Chrysostom, except that I love you very much. Dr. Martin Bucer, that man of God, arouses the glory of Christ among us with his deep spirit; his grounding in doctrine is so thorough and his life so temperate that his adversaries themselves have no complaint. We still do have some adversaries among us who are out of tune with us, their energies and their capabilities carrying them beyond the accepted boundaries and limits. Nevertheless, because many of them do so without bitterness and vituperation and commend themselves highly not only by the excellence of their learning but especially by the probity of their lives, we cannot but follow them in love, entrusting all things to the providence of him who even on the final day will lead some into his vineyard.

The state is in great expectation. What will follow this peace made between us and the French, the sons of the princes being hos-

[13]See note 11.

[14]Edward VI: see Letter 25.

tages,[15] we do not know. Certainly that utterance of Cicero always seemed pleasing to me: "The name of peace is sweet, peace itself is salutary."[16] What else is war than Sophocles' *Furies, many-handed, many-footed, with hooves of brass,*[17] radically overthrowing the course of religion, the control of morality, leisure time for literature, and all prospects for happiness in life? I am very grateful to the French, whom I have always particularly loved and whom in my judgment not even the Italians surpass in every excellence of literature and humanity. We hope that for both nations this peace will be good, auspicious, favorable, and fortunate, for the Earl of Bedford, Lord Paget, and John Mason,[18] the principal negotiators in our party, bring to the establishment of this treaty not only long experience in politics and extensive erudition, but also a true fear of God.

The languages and arts at Cambridge everywhere draw on those authors who are always considered the best teachers not only of rhetoric, but of logic also, so that thought does not swell up too much because of lack of speech, and speaking does not become insolently loquacious because of lack of knowledge. In mastering the knowledge of both languages we do not follow exactly the same age in both cities, but virtually the one unique age. Many have entered into this course of study, stimulated by the example, the precepts, the talents, and the counsel of John Cheke and Thomas Smith. These two, once of this University, now of the whole nation, shine brilliantly in princely splendor. If they had devoted themselves to writing books, neither Italy in Sadoleto nor France in Longueil[19] would have boasted more properly than England in these two. We see that clearly from the little book we use at Cambridge called *The Correct Pronunciation of*

---

[15]The Treaty of Boulogne, returning that town to France, was concluded March 24, 1550. Young members of the nobility were sureties for the agreement.

[16]*Phil.* 2.44.113.

[17]*Electra* 488, 491.

[18]Sir John Russell (1486-1555), a well-respected courtier and diplomat in the reigns of Henry VIII, Edward VI, and Mary, was created Earl of Bedford early in 1550; Sir William Paget had served as Secretary of State; Sir John Mason (1503-1566) was also an experienced courtier with a long record of loyal service.

[19]Two erudite and elegant Ciceronians, Jacopo Sadoleto (1477-1547) of Italy and Christophe de Longueil (Longolius) (1488-1522) of France.

Greek, a book which Cheke wrote in opposition to the Bishop of Winchester.

There are here at Cambridge a number of eminent men, among whom my good friend Walter Haddon, now Vice-chancellor of the University, stands out so much that he seems comparable to those two men I spoke of rather than to anyone in our circle. What all the Oxford men follow I certainly do not know, but some months ago I happened to meet at court someone from that university who preferred Lucian, Plutarch, and Herodian, Seneca, Aulus Gellius, and Apuleius, and thus seemed to me to confine both tongues to a decadent and declining period.

The nobility in England was never more literate. Our most illustrious King Edward, by his talent, industry, constancy, and learning far surpasses his own years and the devotion of other men. I am not influenced by the reports of others, but many times I myself have witnessed (occasions which I consider my greatest blessings) the whole choir of virtues that have taken residence within his soul. I'm sure France will find superior learning in the famous Duke of Suffolk and in the remainder of that delegation of young nobles educated in Latin and Greek along with our King, who have just today set out for France.[20]

We now have many honorable women who surpass the daughters of Thomas More in all kinds of learning. Amongst them the shining star, not so much for her brightness as for the splendor of her virtue and her learning, is my lady Elizabeth, sister of our King. Her light is so radiant that to commend her great versatility properly I have difficulty not in finding something to praise, but in setting limits for it. But I shall write nothing which I have not seen for myself. She employed me as her tutor in Latin and Greek for two years. Now freed from the turbulence of the court and restored to the pleasantness of my former literary leisure, I have by his majesty's beneficence an honorable place and position in this University.

It is difficult to decide whether the ornaments of nature or of fortune are more to be admired in my illustrious lady. All the qualities Aristotle praises have flowed into her: *beauty, stature, prudence,*

---

[20]Ascham refers to the group of notables, including Henry Brandon, the young Duke of Suffolk, who served as sureties for the agreements signed concerning the surrender of Boulogne to France.

and industry, all of the highest order.   She has just passed her sixteenth birthday, and her seriousness and gentleness are unheard of in
those of her age and rank.   Her study of the true faith and of good
learning is most energetic.   She has talent without a woman's weakness, industry with a man's perseverance, and a memory unparalleled
in its perceptiveness and retentiveness.   She speaks French and Italian
as well as she speaks English; her Latin is smooth, correct and
thoughtful; frequently and voluntarily she has even spoken with me in
Greek tolerably well.   When she writes in Greek or Latin, nothing is
more beautiful than her handwriting.   She is as skilled in music as she
is delighted by it.   In adornment she is *elegant rather than showy,* and
spurns *gold and headdresses* so that her whole style of life reminds one
of Hippolyta, not Phaedra.

      She has read almost all of Cicero with me and most of Titus
Livy.   From these two authors alone she has drawn her knowledge of
Latin.   She has always begun the day with the New Testament in
Greek, and then read selected orations of Isocrates and the tragedies of
Sophocles.   For I thought that from these she would derive linguistic
purity and intellectual acuity so that for the rest of her noble life she
would be well-prepared for every blow of fortune.   For religious instruction she added Cyprian and the *Commonplaces* of Melanchthon to
the fountains of the Scriptures, as well as others of a similar nature,
from whom she can drink in purity of doctrine along with elegance of
speech.

      In every kind of writing she readily notices any dubious or far-
fetched word.   She cannot endure those foolish imitators of Erasmus
who have tied Latin in knots with proverbs.   She freely approves of a
natural style appropriate to its subject, chaste in its propriety, and
clear in its perspicuity.   She especially admires modest metaphors and
apt antitheses contrasting felicitously with one another.   By careful
attention to these matters her ears have grown so sharp and discrimi-
nating, and her judgment so intelligent, that nothing in Greek, Latin,
or English composition is so loose and slack on the one hand, or
abrupt and choppy on the other, either so well-tempered or diffuse in
rhythm, but what she scrupulously attends to it as she reads, rejecting
it at once with great disgust or receiving it with the greatest pleasure.

      I am not making this up, Sturm, nor is there need to, but I
wished to sketch out for you this much of an outline of her excellent
talents and course of study.   While my mind has been so totally fixed

on the shape, as it were, of her accomplishments, I have freely and gladly been occupied with cherished memories of my most illustrious lady. If you should write anything to this noble princess, most learned Sturm, it would be gratefully received and perused with great judgment. But I fear that either in my delight in recording these things about her or in my enjoyment of writing to you, I have gone beyond my limit in the prolixity of this epistle. I will say more some other time about our approach to literary studies.

There is a rumor here that you are coming to England. Whether this is true or whether it arises wholly from the desire many people have of seeing you here, I do not know. As for me, nothing is more frequent in my prayers. In the meantime, while I await your arrival with high hopes, I beg you to alleviate my longing for you in your absence by means of your very pleasant letters, so that I may know at least that you have received mine. Meanwhile in your absence I am bestowing upon father Bucer, present here, all the love which I especially owe to you.

Enclosed in this letter is a gift of a silver coin of Caligula. Later Caesars added ever more wordy titles, as I have often remarked on the gold and silver coins of almost all the Caesars down to the Gothic invasions. On this one only a part of the name of Caesar is stamped. Because I am myself so fascinated by these relics of antiquity, I wanted to send this coin to you, and shall send you more later if I learn that you are delighted by this memento of ancient times and of my old friendship. Farewell in Jesus Christ. Cambridge, from the College of St. John the Evangelist, on the fourth of April, 1550.

40 / Johann Sturm to Roger Ascham　　　　　　(Giles I.cii)
Strasbourg, September 9, 1550

Fully five months after Ascham's grand inaugural letter, Sturm responded with this equally impressive epistle. He sent it along with Bucer's wife, who was coming to join her husband at Cambridge, but by the time she arrived, Ascham had departed for Germany with Ambassador Morison. He would not receive this letter until late in the year. Meanwhile, Sturm had arranged for this exchange to be published (see introduction to Letter 39).

Since the second edition of Ascham's letters in 1578 this letter has always been included in collections of Ascham's correspondence; in view of its merit and substance, I too have included it.

Look, my Ascham, what your letter has brought about: in my little book about oratorical periods, *I addressed your Elizabeth.*[1] Since she can unravel the most artful speech and the most complex webs, she can also judge this little work, which has been woven out of thick and thin threads at night. For I believe that the web of Homer's Penelope can justly be compared with the verses of the poets and the periods of the orators. Both kinds of art involve things not only being composed, but also taken apart and altered and even destroyed as often as they need to be mended. For young people and women, especially little girls, what occupation can be more honorable, what exercise more liberal? What pastime is more pleasant than that of the pen, of composition, of pure, elaborate, perfect, and consummate speech, toward which we all struggle and strive?

You are a literate man, a good person worthy indeed of the glorious name of evangelist, and everything is not merely apparent, but actually shines out in your letter. I believe there was nothing in your letter untrue to the virtues and glories of a royal princess. What in our times can be more desirable than that the families of the rulers and the nobility bring forth talented people in both sexes who delight in learning, cultivate and pursue it, and achieve a full knowledge of literature, the arts, and the sciences? England is more blessed with this kind of good people than Germany, where there are very few amongst the nobility who think that distinction in literature befits their class. In your country nearly all of the nobility strive to become educated, or if they catch on too late, they still think it pertains to them and theirs. Thus there is hope that the glory which once Italy always claimed as her own, and which later France and Germany, rivals of Italy, tried to assume, England can now appropriate completely for herself. And may the kind of dwelling the masters of speaking and knowing once had at Athens and at Rome, the two cities which you mentioned, be established for them now in England, so that your people, who strive to imitate their virtues, may equal their glory and achievement.

[1]See the preface to *De periodis unus libellus* (Strasbourg, 1550).

But when I come to you, my Ascham, I do not know whom to congratulate more, you to whom God has given such a pupil, or Princess Elizabeth, to whom God has given such a highly trained master. Certainly I rejoice and congratulate you both. Happy were the two years during which you taught and she learned. I am also glad to hear of the leisure that King Edward kindly gave you and bountifully bestowed upon you. Indeed the nature of our studies demands a busy leisure and a leisurely business, for to the common folk we seem to be leisurely in our work and to work in our leisure. When other men are hunting or fishing or building, they are considered to be working. When educated men read, write, or prepare commentaries, they are considered idlers, when as a matter of fact their minds while at work stir up anxieties and cares, not because of fear of danger or the hardships of their toil, but because they undertake to think about matters of great, eternal significance. Since you have the best kind of leisure, it will yield the ripest and most delightful fruit for me. For in your letter you promised me many, frequent letters, which I very eagerly await, not only because of the love for me which I observe in your letter, but especially because of your learning in the two arts in which I also have been engaged for many years now, dialectic and rhetoric. We both wish to be dialecticians and rhetoricians, and you already are, while I am striving to be. Certainly without the resources of eloquence the profession of dialectic is dark and vile, while eloquence without the knowledge of dialectic is puffed up and swollen, wandering in error, bringing us nothing by rhyme or reason, nothing artfully done. And so your judgment and mine are the same; we desire the same, follow and strive for the same. Everyone who aspires to live in literature and to reach fame through literature must also undertake the same course of study.

Now to return to your letter, I enjoyed it immensely, first because it demonstrated your good will toward me and then because it told me much about your country, which for centuries has been considered very noble and well-fortified. You also told me about your king, in whom is placed a certain and excellent hope with respect to his wisdom, clemency, and religion. You wrote about William Paget, whose probity and moderation and gentleness I discovered five years ago in Calais; about Cheke and Smith, whom many have praised to us; about John Mason, whom our Mont[2] embraced with great kindness and praised to me more often than I can count whenever I recalled Paget; about Haddon, your Vice-chancellor, whom you rank among the best; about the nobility of England, and those who have set out for France with the three negotiators. Finally you wrote about the lady Elizabeth. The more this passage grew longer than the rest, the more I wished while reading it that it were longer still.

Everything, I repeat, was thoroughly enjoyable. But when you credit me with so much, very little of which I can recognize in myself, then you strike me with shame, to use Horace's words,[3] because I cannot demonstrate the knowledge and good judgment which you ascribe to me. But when you ask me to translate and edit the *Phaedo* of Plato and Aristotle's *De anima* and his works on rhetoric, and to translate the opposing orations of Demosthenes and Aeschines and to publish the books I promised *On The Art of Latin Eloquence*, well, I do not so much shun the work, which might be undertaken, as I do the audacity of undertaking it and the suspicion of temerity and presumption in publishing it, which called me back, as it were, last year when I started down this road. For I decided to expound Aristotle's books on rhetoric with his own words on logic. I had already given a part of this to the copyist when I changed my mind, first because of the reason I have given, then because certain other matters intervened which deterred me from the undertaking. But I propose to resume my work on them this winter and complete what I have begun, if God grants me life and strength.

I am lecturing on the orations of Demosthenes and Aeschines to my students. Thus I am engaged more in explaining them than in translating them. For it is enough for me if I explain the thought and the force and power of the words. The rest of my effort is spent in pointing out the art of rhetoric, so that students understand invention, division, partition, arrangement, kinds of argument, syllogisms, figures of thought, elaborations of indefinite questions and handling of definite ones, amplifications of both, the kinds of rhetorical periods, rhythm, and clausulas for beginnings and middles.

[2]Christopher Mont (Mount), English agent in Strasbourg. See also Letter 35.
[3]*Epist.* 1.18.77.

Two of you must be content with this my wintry labor: you, my dear Ascham, who ask, and Bucer, who seems to have urged you on. As for the *Phaedo* and Aristotle's *De anima*, they will have to wait until I have the free time, if life continues and I am able. Even though I have observed in the *Gorgias* certain points which pertain to the function of dialectic, it does not follow that I can explain what makes the *Phaedo* a classic, and escape offending the ears and the minds of literate men; and even though I understand its rhetorical aspects and can perhaps publish something about them, it does not follow that I am capable of undertaking an analysis of the *Phaedo's* serious discussion about life, death, the immortality of the soul, the passing of good men from life, the heavenly rewards for the most distinguished, and the eternity of matter.

You touched a nerve when you ask me for the books about the Latin language, for I promised them some years ago. I can only confess that even if I had the talent, I do not have the resources, as I have often told Bucer. What a tall order it is to create just a short book which will, after a look at the rules, develop your ability to express in Latin prose whatever you have in your mind: the language must be not only pure, but also elegant, ornate, and graceful; you must have ready examples of how the material can be polished with figures of thought and expression; and you must have everything not only collected, but also classified and organized under headings. Although I have carefully considered this kind of work and it exists in rough form in my mind, I am constrained by my resources to leave it lie incomplete. Our school does push me to do it, but although it pushes me, it does not force me. I think I will do enough for mankind if I am not indolent in the rest of my duties.

Now concerning what you wrote of Augustine, I praise your judgment, and I am delighted by your gentleness and love in that section of your letter. Without hesitation I too consider this theologian superior to others in a great many things on account of his knowledge, for his teaching covers every thing, he makes shrewd conclusions with pointed refutations, erring not at all in proposition, division, argumentation, or development. But when I urge my students to cultivate eloquence, I consider not only knowledge of the subject matter, but also its arrangement and adornment. I think Augustine is superior in learning, while those with the skills just mentioned are superior in speaking, but those who are both learned and rhetorically skilled must be preferred from the start.

In teaching Latin and Greek one must constantly beware lest authors whose rhetoric is inferior are preferred to Cicero, Demosthenes, and other writers who are better because of the way they handle the material. The terms "wisdom" and "knowledge" are pleasing to everyone; knowledge of the material is not only desirable, but also valuable, for no one can either write or speak excellently who has mastered the arts and methods, but has no knowledge of the subject matter. Therefore I do not consider the man who is endowed with good judgment, but who limps along with a poor command of rhetoric to be among the eloquent, accomplished, and properly Latin speakers, writers, or craftsmen.

And I consider someone whose speech is inflated with verbiage not only an inept author, but also a stupid man. I do not think anyone should be praised who seized on words and their embellishment and neglected matter, whether it be Longueil, Sadoleto, Bembo, Navagero,[4] or anyone else in Italy, France, or Germany--though these men have in fact done very little of that. What should I say about Budé,[5] a man of excellence in learning? Even if we love and defend him, there are some who think him more a disciple of words than of matter in some books. Thus I would not rank the person who thinks that the excellence of speech consists in words and not in the matter among the best, but among the worst of writers and orators.

This must be the first consideration: is it permissible to read indiscriminately from any time period, or should there be some discrimination of times, periods, and abilities? The Greeks assigned Homer to be learned by heart by their young people. They could do that without difficulty because the children had imbibed the words of their fathers along with the milk of their mothers, so to speak. The

---

[4]All four of these eminent humanists were considered leaders in Ciceronianism: Christophe de Longueil (Longolius), born in Belgium, educated in France, based in Italy; Cardinal Jacopo Sadoleto, Italian humanist; Cardinal Pietro Bembo, from Venice; and Andrea Navagero (Naugerius), also from Venice, and an important editor of Cicero.

[5]Guillaume Budé (Budaeus), 1467-1540, the greatest humanist of France, active in the controversies over Ciceronianism, and professor of Hebrew, Greek, and Latin in the College of France.

Roman grammarians taught Virgil in their schools; there was no danger in that. From the beginning those same Romans read Homer; the alien tongue was no hindrance, though the language of public life in Rome was Latin. The Greeks could do the same if they liked the language. But what benefits with respect to the acquisition of a pure Latin can a boy derive from Cato's distichs, from Aquinas, Gerson, or Cocca?[6] I have named a few: many others from the same herd could be cited. I do not mean to be nasty, but they are simply not suitable for our purpose.

To these let us also add the barbarous welter of grammarians, logicians, physicians, theologians, and philosophers who would rather have the sordid than the pure, the utilitarian rather than the challenging. A great number of them are defending themselves today in our colleges of sophistry, and fight viciously for their own barbarousness as though it were another Palladium. What a charming bunch! Oh holy conspiracy! For them it is glorious to be conquered and shameful to conquer! What can be the condition of literature, the condition of religion, when speech, language, and eloquence is so foul? Who would not spurn them if he but heard the noise from their mouths, the deformity of their words, the stupidity of their thoughts, the emptiness of their judgments, the stubbornness of their spirits, the vulgarity of their habits, and their outlandish morals? They have displaced liberality with license, corrupted the arts and sciences, defiled history, religion, and ceremony, not only by a rotten kind of style, but also by ignorant opinions outside the mainstream of learning, and obscured things by their bickering and polluted them by their defenses. Are these people to be the instructors of our children, and their writings to fill the minds of young people, so that in our countries we have corruption in place of purity, barbarisms in place of good Latin, obscurity in place of clarity, and chaos in place of good order? Shall we not retain our standard of good and evil when it comes to matters of lesser weight and importance?

---

[6]Sturm lists mainstays of a conservative or scholastic curriculum: *Disticha Catonis*, a little metrical compendium of rules of conduct; Jean Gerson (Charlier), 1363-1429, French scholastic theologian, known for his crude Latin; Merlin Cocca[i], born Girolamo (Teofilo) Folengo, 1491-1544, an eccentric Italian who published macaronic poetry.

But the study of matter has always been considered more important than the study of words. It is plainly the duty of the eloquent to care first for matter, then for words. For it is a vice to speak what is inane or stupid. Although the orator needs not only wisdom, but also the embellishment of words, let us separate the two, which otherwise cling together by nature. Wisdom demands that you question what you speak: is it true, probable, certain, intelligent, disciplined, and complete? What does embellishment demand? That it be meaningful, sonorous, full, harmonious, ornate, and elegant. But if wisdom should demand of me to drop my system of adornment, I would be content with purity, I would not affect the rest of adornment, I would allow myself to be freed from great labors, extreme cares, and daily vigils.

But if wisdom should also demand that I abandon purity, surely I shall not conform to that kind of wisdom, even if it is offered. But if wisdom should reply it is good to be gifted with learning, but that it is really outstanding to join eloquence to that same basis of speaking and to learn both from the best rather than from the worst rank of authors, and that labors are best expended upon the most perfect writer, then I shall follow the advice of wisdom as though it was given by a divinely appointed oracle.

Therefore in the beginning those are the authors I want children to be taught. The first ones to be read for practice should be those who have joined eloquence to learning, not the ones who were content with knowledge and either despised eloquence or did not even aspire to it. The more nearly one approaches perfection, the more he should stand at the head of his age and rank and be considered as exemplary. This is the reason I put Chrysostom before Augustine, not because Augustine is not wiser or is not accomplished, but because he is less fluent than Chrysostom, who is after all erudite and scholarly. I give Chrysostom the first place with respect to his language and his time, but not with respect to learning and intellect, since in these points I put many others before Chrysostom himself. For by the study of eloquence one learns the importance of avoiding not only barbarisms, but also of always preferring the better to the good. But perhaps I shall seem to have too little confidence in your brilliance when I state my case so carefully. Nevertheless, since I think the order in which authors are read makes a very great difference, it has seemed good to explain my thinking to you. I do not think that you will find it strange.

I have spoken freely because you say in your letter that the
name of peace is sweet and peace itself is salutary. I know where
Cicero says that and gives his opinion in those very words.[7] I have
tried to imitate the form of that passage here so that I may play *rhet-
orician* with you. And having set the example, unless you keep watch,
I shall sport again in a little while when I again petition for what I
want and how much I want from your mistress Elizabeth. For I cannot forget that she joins the art of eloquence to her great knowledge
of things, as you wrote, and stays in practice, which greatly becomes
her sex, yet lies spurned by almost all. But she thinks rightly with
herself: for if the shape of the body in young ladies is pleasing, why
not also the shape of modest, chaste, pure, and beautiful speech?
Young women of both noble birth and obscure birth engage in spin-
ning, weaving, and embroidery, and often we see low-born women
working more skillfully than the nobility. However, elegance of
speech apparently prefers to dwell in the houses of the nobility and in
the distinguished families, so that the nobility differ as much from the
masses in their refined speech as in dress and accomplishment.

Moreover, the expensive clothes, gems, bracelets, and other
adornments of noble women belong to fortune and often abound in
rather bad natures. But elegance of speech and beauty of voice cannot
be separated from beauty of mind, and they are the mark of an excellent intellect and a noble nature. And while the titles and ornaments
of riches are celebrated only at home, an artful utterance, once it is
noticed, often wings its way to foreign nations and peoples, who consider it admirable.

Thus I am the more positive about the lady Elizabeth's industry.
It will have such effect that young girls, maidens, and mature women
will be deemed noble not only by virtue of the antiquity of their families, but also by virtue of the elegance of their learning and speech.
Therefore it is most fitting that I have sent her this little book. For
when it comes to the publication of books, it is foolish to address
them to those who know nothing about what is dealt with, or who do
not really love the same things. Thus since my book cannot speak for
itself, for it is not fluent, you may deprecate it as far as it errs, and
commend it where it does not err, and in both cases act as its patron,

---

[7]See Letter 39, note 16.

especially to King Edward, to whom I also sent a copy, so that it may be defended by a tripartite patronage: first by you to Princess Elizabeth, then by her to her brother, King Edward. And if with his authority he wishes to be its supreme patron, what greater blessing could my little book ask for?

As far as power is given me, I shall do my best to please the English people, for I love that people on account of their faith and on account of the fame of their great king in these times. I hope that the King can guard, defend, and strengthen the faith which he learned during his boyhood years and which his Council unanimously established, so that it may not be opposed. Although it pertains to God and his providence and will, there is this to think about: reform and improvement in the use of ecclesiastical funds, in the control of morals, in the doctrines of religion, in the sanctity of the law, and in the dignity of office can not be established without some trouble, and can not be maintained without fear of some danger. But there is less fear now in view of the steadfastness of the Council, for it has set policy concerning religion, has established it, and has strengthened it by its decisions. And in order that this state of affairs may continue, while the kingdom and religion require it in order that the King may not be ruined by any intemperance of the times, we must earnestly pray to God the Father of all mankind and to Christ the Savior of all men. We must praise those men who are engaged in the negotiations and those in the King's Council. We must urge the King to constancy and highmindedness, so that the Council may not repent of its policy and the King may not be wearied by the dangers which seem to loom.

Therefore the authors of this reformation are to be given praise, not only for their piety, faith, and learning, but also for their courage, for they were not terrified by those dangers which they in their prudence foresaw, but which in their devotion they disdained. What a holy Curia, which preferred honor and faith to profit and an easy life! They seem to be men born to renovate the name of England, so that during this reign England may again occupy her place as a cornerstone of the church and be a refuge, not only at present by taking in and protecting angels and messengers of freedom, learning, faith, and merit in the Christian state, but in a short while by also sending them forth and equipping them. For ungodliness makes nations instable; faithfulness normally makes them stand firm. No change in kingdoms needs to be feared unless it follows upon a contempt for or a corruption of godliness. Thus a country is insecure which has men who in their wicked lives are fearful of the sanctity and purity of godliness and sound doctrine. But those who patronize, cultivate, and defend godliness and sound doctrine can only change the state into something heavenly and divine, where there will be perpetual and eternal felicity. For not only are the kings and princes and magistrates of this world frail and fleeing, but cities and nations and kingdoms also flourish in their brief bright moments and then collapse and crumble away. Everlasting happiness is the end of good men in all walks of life; in this felicity they have their rewards.

Unless there are these rewards, what sensible man would expend great effort or endure great danger in sacrificing himself for his country or dying for his religion? For this reason the most farsighted men have wisely taken thought: they have regained for their homeland that without which no state can be stable. At their own peril they have established what they wanted most for their posterity. They preferred to take the risk of maintaining godliness and the piety of their country rather than hand it over without risk to their posterity.

This glory is more splendid than any triumph whatsoever, a glory not to be compared to the slaughter of enemies, but one which is radiant in piety and godliness. It demanded not the blood of enemies, but the moral purity of its own citizens. It has not chased after new things, but restored the lost. For after religion was settled, peace was established with the king of France, laws for life and morals were promulgated, the schools of learned men were reformed, the light of truth again appeared, as well as the lamp of the gospel. So long as there are men who love goodness and delight in the memories of brave souls, good men will never cease talking about these things.

The credit for this action, or rather this wisdom, belongs in very large part to his most serene Majesty, King Edward. If the Council had not noticed that as he grew older, he simultaneously grew in prudence and in seriousness and strengthened his interest in and devotion to godliness, it would have pushed and demanded and undertaken for itself, at greater risk, the very thing that he has established and decreed. Therefore every class in the nation is to be congratulated: the King because he obtained what he wanted with the unanimous consent of the Council, the Council because it wanted the same thing as the King and because it knew that no more godly policy could be established, and the people because they saw what passed between the

King and the Council as something that came about not through popular agitation but through the voice of the commonwealth, just as the
better part of the people hoped. Finally, all levels of society are to be
congratulated, because with this conjunction of minds there need be no
fear of dissidents. Peace and concord blossom again, the true faith is
renewed, the gospel's word of salvation resounds, and the dominion of
Christ holds supreme sway in England.

This benefit, nay this glory, of the nation ought to banish fear
from everyone's mind, to stir up the King into amplifying that glory,
to exhort the Council to fortitude, and to arouse the people to charity
and respect. Thus the authority of the King, the policy of the Council,
and the will of the people will stand like a bulwark against the trick-
ery and the treachery and the might of the enemy of our God, an
enemy by whom we cannot be vanquished as long as we stand firm.
For if we must die, mortality will be exchanged for immortality; if we
live, what is more glorious than through our devotion to experience
heaven in this life?

Excited by your letter, my Ascham, I have been carried away,
more than I had intended. Although I had heard before from many
people about your King and his sister, I took more pleasure in learning their glories than in receiving Caligula, whom I had not previously
seen in this way upon coins. Still, I'm grateful for the gift because it
came from you and because of its age and because it bears the image
of one who with respect to glory in war can be compared with the
most courageous, the most skillful, and the most fortunate of emper-
ors. Farewell. Strasbourg, September 9, 1550.

41 / To Johann Sturm (Giles I.cx)
[Augsburg], December 14, 1550

In November Sturm learned that Ascham was no longer in England, and
therefore missed his letter of September 9 (above). He quickly sent another
copy directly to Augsburg, along with a brief note (printed by Giles as
I.cix), dated November 18, 1550. This response from Ascham refers to both.

That fine man Christopher Mont, now our common friend, delivered
both your letters, my dear Johann Sturm, the first of September 9 and

the other of November 18. I have read both letters with the greatest joy, and I read them over frequently, and never finish reading them without an increase in the amount of pleasure I take from them.

The praise which you give me I do not acknowledge as alien, but it is like a cloak generously placed upon me, but not fitting very well, and with a blush I take it off. Nevertheless, I consider it the highest praise to be praised by so praiseworthy a man. You were kind about what you call my blind love for you, suffering it to remain blind lest it open its eyes and swerve from you and be transferred to another. Blind love, my Sturm, is vagrant and errant. Since it adores, it does not discriminate; it tends to be rash, not steady. But my love for you is so sharp-eyed, so much a Lynceus,[1] that no desolate wastes of Earth or Ocean can stop its vision from penetrating the farthest reaches, and from shining with enthusiasm wherever the lamps of virtue and learning burn brightly. In your wish for both of our letters to be published and to stand as a witness to our eternal friendship, you certainly wish no more than what I myself long for--though you also want more than I can solicit from anyone without displaying the mark of impudence, or more than I can beg from you without creating the suspicion of imprudence. But since you make me shameless, unless you yourself wish otherwise and unless the letters themselves have already gone to the printer, I desire above all that our letters fill some blank page in your *Aristotelian Dialogues*. But I am foolish to ask, since you know best what ought to be done. Still, I write this because I fear that my letter may be too much trouble and somehow take it hard if it is separated from that book about which it has been so demanding, persistent, *always-pressing*. Yet I promise this: it will be not only content but positively exhilarated if by some strategy it gains admission into the society of your literary works. If your book is printed in quarto, as the term is, and not in octavo, as is usual in the case of your writings, I shall approve the more, and in the business of publication I always praise not only the expertise of the French, but also their good taste.

I was wholly steeped in joy, my Sturm, when I came to that place in your letter where you say, "I have picked out a place for His Majesty in my *Aristotelian Dialogues*, on which I whet my pen daily, so

---

[1]An Argonaut whose eyesight was so keen he could see through the earth.

that it can show what it can do against barbarousness. I have also been cultivating friends, etc. . . ." What you are doing for the King, my dear Sturm, you will not be doing for that most famous prince alone, but for his whole kingdom and for learning in general and for eternity. For when the King hears from you that it is glorious when *kings are philosophers* and when the state is guided by policy, not by fortune, and that the best policies are derived from the best books, and that after you have left the sacred sources, no one is better for shaping policy than Aristotle himself, do not doubt but that in instructing our prince you will be pouring out the richest pleasure, which will flow to your singular honor into the whole of England and into all Englishmen. And although the prince--such is his noble nature--does not need to march onward into the unencumbered study of wisdom and learning, a course into which he has already entered, yet from your delightful, flowing discourse, attuned to this fact, he will receive a new impetus to his labors and a greater hope of glory, just as if from the applause of a distinguished man who supports him as he runs. You know that very delightful verse of that most delightful poet, which I often repeat to myself:

> He who exhorts you to do what you are already doing
> Praises you by his exhortation and by his advice
>   shows his approval of your actions.[2]

Fortune vies with nature in our prince, and his virtue surpasses both. Rather, as it befits a Christian man to speak, the manifold grace of God wonderfully outdoes his own youthfulness, with his eagerness for good learning, his zeal for the true religion, his disposition, good judgment, and constancy, which you praise especially in his studies. Scarcely any part of his happiness involves more blessings, I think, than the fact that as a youth he had John Cheke to teach him sound learning and true religion. He understands, speaks, and writes Latin exactly, skillfully, and fluently, all with good judgment. He has studied logic and is now studying Aristotle's *Ethics* in Greek. He has progressed far enough in Greek to have no difficulty in translating Cicero's philosophical books from Latin into Greek. On the day before I left England, when I visited Cheke in London and asked him in our

[2]Ovid, *Tristia* 5.14.45-46.

conversation why the King should study the *Ethics* of Aristotle rather than Xenophon's *Education of Cyrus*, he answered most wisely and learnedly, as he always tends to do: "in order that the mind, grounded first in those universal and timeless precepts and categories of virtues and vices, may bring sound judgment to the particular, everyday examples of conduct which are amply displayed in histories. Also," he said, "it scarcely happens that the mind, softened and dulled in the beginning by the charms of history, is sharp enough to penetrate into the abstruse and recondite thoughts that are thoroughly necessary for corroborating any judgment about specific issues. Nevertheless," he concluded, "I do not want to advance any precept without illustrating it with a notable example." No one can understand better than you, my Sturm, how happy England is when a young prince of his age--for he has but recently passed his thirteenth year--is molded by this superior instruction. Soon he will complete the *Ethics* and go on to Aristotle's *Rhetoric*, so that he has not only a timely, but an almost divinely ordained opportunity to take up your book. For I believe that it has not happened without divine assistance that his royal majesty should be ennobled by the great power of your intellect, judgment, and learning.

If I had just a little more free time, I would initiate a longer conversation with you about our royal majesty, about my noble Princess Elizabeth, and about the noble daughters of the Duke of Somerset: they certainly have been brought up under the finest instruction in learning.[3] However, I cannot skip over two English women, nor should I want you, my Sturm, to skip over them if you are considering cultivating English friends, than which I can think of nothing more desirable. One is Jane Grey, daughter of the noble Marquis of Dorset. Since her grandmother was the Queen of France,[4] she is a close rela-

---

[3]The second wife of Protector Edward Seymour, Duke of Somerset, was Anne, daughter of Sir Edward Stanhope. Both the Duke and Duchess were active patrons of Protestant learning, and promoted the education of their ten children. At least three of their six daughters--Anne, Jane, and Margaret--achieved some distinction in learning.

[4]Mary Tudor, daughter of Henry VII, was married briefly (October 9, 1514-January 1, 1515) to King Louis XII of France; after his death she married Sir Charles Brandon, Duke of Suffolk; their daughter Frances married Henry Grey, Marquis of Dorset.

tive of our King Edward. She is fifteen years old.[5] I was very friendly with her at court, and she has written learned letters to me. Last
summer when I was visiting friends at York and was summoned to
court by a letter from John Cheke, I took a detour through Leicester-
shire where Jane Grey was living with her father.[6] I was admitted at
once into her room, and found the noble girl--good God--reading Plato's *Phaedo* in Greek, which she understood so well as to inspire me
with the highest admiration. She speaks and writes in Greek so well
that one can hardly give her the credit she deserves. John Aylmer
was her teacher, a man well-versed in both languages and my very
close friend on account of his gentleness, prudence, experience, true
religion, and many other bonds of warmest friendship. When I was
leaving, she pledged that she would write me in Greek if I would
challenge her with a letter written from the court of the Emperor. I
expect her Greek letter any day; when it comes, I shall send it to you
immediately.

The other woman is Mildred Cecil,[7] who speaks and understands
Greek about as well as English. It is difficult to decide whether she is
happier in this superior knowledge because she was born to that noble
man Anthony Cooke, her father and teacher (because of his extraordinary erudition Cooke was John Cheke's partner in the education of the
King), or because she married William Cecil, a young man, to be sure,
but a young man with the prudence of an old man and a great understanding of life and letters. He is gifted with such restraint in
managing daily affairs that by the common consent of Englishmen he
merits the complete, four-part tribute that Thucydides gave to his rival
Pericles: *he knows all that is fitting, is able to apply what he knows, is a*

[5]Born in October 1537, Jane Grey was actually 13 years old, not 15, at the
time of this letter.

[6]See other accounts in Letter 37 and in *The Schoolmaster* (III, 117-19).

[7]Mildred was the second wife of William Cecil (his first wife, John Cheke's
sister, died in 1543), and the eldest daughter of Anthony Cooke. The learning of
both Cooke himself and his family of daughters was widely celebrated.

lover of his country, and is superior to the temptation of money.[8] After my departure from England he was made a Principal Secretary.[9]

I am afraid, my Sturm, that I have troubled you with my prolixity, but because I want nothing more than your longest letters, I write at length now, and shall write at more length if I have the time. Never in my life have I been busier than I am now. No one can write you more reliable or more timely news about events here than our Christopher Mont, and I ask him daily, and shall continue to ask him, that he write you in detail. I myself shall not fail to write as often as a suitable courier is available. And lest in these momentous times my letter come to you light or empty, here's news about Magdeburg,[10] which by itself so occupies the suspicions, rumors, conversations, discussions, and planning of all men at Augsburg that everything else, large, small, or in between, has almost fallen silent. All reports concerning that city's hope of safety or fear of destruction are so involved with rumors either devised with treachery or disseminated without authority that I have nothing definite or confirmed to write.

About one matter, however, I am most certain: this city is now pressed hard by the enemy, but it is defended courageously by its own citizens, because neither by prayer nor price, neither by fears nor forebodings, can it be driven to betray and abandon its beliefs or to accept badly corrupted ones, since all good men, wherever they are, cherish their beliefs as doctrines drunk from divine fountains. It should not surprise you if Cerberus of Rome and Geryon of Spain, the two three-headed ones, try to take this city by assault.[11] If its gate was either stormed or opened voluntarily, the way into all of Germany would immediately lie open to Cerberus, and almost all of Europe would be open to Geryon, so that no purity in religion and no political privileges in the state would remain which would not be, in a word, either defiled by the habits of the one or ravished by the occu-

---

[8]*History of the Peloponnesian War* 2.60. Ascham confuses Thucydides the historian with Thucydides, son of Melesias and rival of Pericles in Athenian politics.

[9]On September 5, 1550, Cecil was appointed to serve with William Petre as Principal Secretary.

[10]A major center of Protestant resistance to the Imperial *Interim*.

[11]Ascham is alluding the threat posed to highly Protestant Augsburg by the Imperial Catholic presences of Emperor Charles V and his son Philip II of Spain.

pation of the other. The remaining matters--Turkish, Papist, Imperial, Satanic, and Christian--lie in great silence. I shall write shortly about them if anything certain comes into my hands. Farewell, most learned Sturm, and, as you do, love me. Augsburg, December 14, 1550.

42 / To Johann Sturm (Giles I.cxvii)
Augsburg, January 24, 1551

> Although Sturm wrote Ascham on November 18, 1550, that their first ex-change of letters would be published "in the next few days" (I, 223), As-cham here offers a last-minute insertion into his text (i.e., into Letter 39). The courier is again Christopher Mont, the English agent now returning to his home in Strasbourg.

Since so suitable a courier is at hand, I must send you a letter. There is no need for a long one, my dear Sturm, when Mont alone can be equivalent to our longest letter. I consider the departure from us of a man of such honor and integrity as most unfortunate in these times and in this place, but I am not so hard on others, nor so full of self-love, nor so oblivious of my friends that I am not moved by the sense of his desire to see those who are dearest to him.

You write by our Mont that both our letters have been pub-lished. You will see, most learned Sturm, how to your peril you have brought to light a man who until now has been concealing himself in the shadows. Although I am telling you frankly what I feel, I value the testimony of your judgment, or rather of your love, more than I fear the word or the opinion of any man. This statement can appear either too arrogant or too conceited, I admit. If I sin because there is error in me, not evil in others, I expect you who love me to pardon me. From others whom I do not hurt, I do not fear attack.

If my letter is not yet printed, I earnestly desire these two or three words to be inserted into that passage where I was explaining Princess Elizabeth's progress in the study of literature:

> The fundamentals of both languages were instilled in this princess most readily by the assiduous and diligent tutelage of my William Grindal. I say "my Grindal," and if there were another appellation in the whole course of friendship, intimacy, fondness, or piety which

would designate a closer relationship than "my," I should most gladly apply it to the memory of my Grindal. For he was my pupil at Cambridge for a period of almost seven years, and since the time he was little boy he learned Latin and Greek within the walls of my room.

He had such high morals, great talent, keen memory, and good judgment that I have scarcely seen his equal in England. The numerous excellent men who were very closely associated with him at court know I am not making any thing up in these tributes to him. I do not fear the stigma of flattery, for he is dead. I disdain the criticism of the envious, for they cannot bear the praise of virtue in others when they cannot find it in themselves.

He was summoned to court from the University by Mr. Cheke, and in a short time was appointed tutor to the Princess. Some years later, when the most noble Elizabeth both by her own genius and by his work as her tutor had attained an extraordinary level of understanding, and my Grindal both by his own merit and by God's favor had come near distinction, lo, he suddenly died of the plague.

At court he left such an empty space that I hardly know whether over the years anyone else besides him has afflicted me with a greater sorrow than I felt at the death of both my parents, who on the same day at nearly the same hour, after being happily married for 47 years, ascended together to Christ, being joined even in death.

I have been appointed to fill the place of my dearest pupil and most intimate friend. In him the foundations of both languages were so well laid that I do not know which to admire more: the genius of her who learned, or the diligence of him who taught. With diligence and assiduity I have tried to build upon that which was so well begun by my Grindal, without my help perhaps, but not without my advice.

If, my Sturm, you can set these words aptly in their place and refine them according to your judgment, polishing them with a file, as it were, so they fit neatly into the rest of the letter, you will be doing me a kindness which I have much desired. If I did not love you much and give everything to our friendship, I should fear to bother you so inconsiderately. But one needs a close acquaintance for whom friendship is not an idle tale. You know what your Cicero says about sharing with a friend: "I want to speak without affectation, deceit, or concealment."[1] The "wise ones" who put on a show of friendship give no delight, and always bear more foliage than fruit.

[1]*Ad Att.* 1.13.

In my last letter I mentioned that most noble girl Jane Grey. If my judgment has any value, human eyes have not seen nor has there ever come into view a more worthy model, by whom the rest of the nobility can be challenged to true glory and magnificent splendor. Pardon me, my Sturm, if I want these luminaries of my native land to be illumined by the light of your talent, so that although they are illustrious in themselves, they may yet be elevated into an eminent and conspicuous place by your testimony.

I avidly await a long letter from you, although I do not wish to disturb you when you are working on your *Aristotelian Dialogues*, about which I do nevertheless want to hear.

When I told the ambassador that I am sending a letter to you, he asked me to greet you cordially in his name, and said that he wanted very much to become closer friends with you, whom for years he has loved very much. This, however, will be somewhat difficult because he is daily distracted by all the work, so much so that he frequently cannot pursue the study of literature, by which he entwines himself with you.

I do nothing more cheerfully than write to you, but until I find a reliable courier, I shall beware what I commit to paper, for I fear that which your Cicero wittily complained about with respect to his own times: "There is scarcely anyone who can carry a weighty letter without lightening it on the way by reading it."[2] If a good, sure messenger from you or from our Mont comes to me with your commendation, I shall gladly let you know about what I have heard concerning developments within the government, the status of religion, public policies, and secret deals.

I much prefer your very pleasant letters, full of Sturmian qualities--that is, learning, eloquence, and humanity--to all that Turkish, Papist, Imperial, and French business. However, I would write something at this time about these things, except that our Mont, full of all the important news, is returning home to you. You have a better opportunity to learn about different things from talking with him than

[2]*Ad Att.* 1.18.

from my writings. Farewell. Greet John Sleidan and Valentine Erythraeus for me.[3] Augsburg, January 24, 1551.

43 / To Johann Sturm   (Giles I.cxxvi)
                    [Augsburg], June 1551

> This is written in response to Sturm's brief letter of June 15, 1551 (I.cxxv), a
> date which helps to resolve the confusion which surrounds the dating of
> this one. Ascham received Sturm's letter on June 22, exactly one week after
> it was written (see first sentence below), yet this answer to it is dated, with
> manifest error, June 18 of the same year. The error originates in the early
> editions on which Giles' text is ultimately based: the closing of this letter
> in the 1576 and 1578 editions of Ascham's letters reads only "June, 1551,"
> but the 1581 edition, for unknown and obviously erroneous reasons, speci-
> fies the day: "June 18, 1551," a mistake which subsequent editors, including
> Giles, have perpetuated.

Your letter, prudent and delightful, along with the two books sent to
me as a gift from Master Toxites,[1] was delivered to me on June 22.
You write in kindly fashion about my complaint concerning your silence, although you please me so much simply because you write, my

---

[3]Sleidan (Philippson) and Erythraeus were two of Sturm's learned humanist
associates in Strasbourg. Sleidan was highly regarded in his own day as an historian. His friendship with Sturm dates back to their student days in Paris. In
1544 he settled in Strasbourg, and came under the influence of the city's great
reformer Martin Bucer. During the Schmalkaldic War, he spent some time in
England under the patronage of King Edward VI, but he returned to Strasbourg,
where he was appointed Professor in 1554. He was especially noted for his important history of the Reformation, entitled *Commentaries on the Religion and Political
History of Charles V* (1555). Erythraeus studied under Sturm at Strasbourg, and
then under Luther and Melanchthon in Wittenberg. He returned to Strasbourg to
become Professor of Rhetoric, a position he held for 29 years. Besides writing
books on various aspects of rhetoric, he also edited some of the work of Sturm:
see Letter 59.

[1]Michael Toxites (Schütz), 1515-1581, taught in Sturm's gymnasium after he
settled in Strasbourg in 1544, and was supported by Sturm with editorial and
diplomatic assignments even after he was dismissed for drunkenness. Toxites and
Ascham would soon correspond directly, and Ascham would visit with him during a stopover in Strasbourg in 1552. Later in life Toxites became a strong pro-
moter of Paracelsian medicine.

dear Sturm, that even if you did not write, you could not be otherwise than most pleasing to me. For I do not want my friendship to prove empty and troublesome to you, but welcome and timely. I know what you are busy with, and I am such a strong supporter of your free time that I shall be very sorry if even the least part of that time has been taken from your work on the *Aristotelian Dialogues* or on the speeches of Demosthenes and Aeschines, and directed toward other things.

As for how much I love our Toxites, I shall soon write to him, always offering him all my service, and acknowledging the love and concern he has for us both, the goodwill, or rather the piety, with which he has extolled my country and my sovereign, his enthusiasm for the true religion of Christ, his favorable opinion of the refined learning of Sturm, and finally the numerous other bonds of genuine friendship by which he has bound himself to me forever.

You ask me to assist you with my ideas and resources in the composition of a life of Bucer.[2] Although in this matter you do not need my resources, I still would have done something in support of your good intentions, even if it were not enough, except that I knew that the English collection of writings commemorating Bucer's death would reach you before this letter would.[3] In that book one can readily observe the friendship and the good will of England toward Germany and of Cambridge toward Strasbourg, as well as the devotion of both peoples and cities to true religion, to learning, and to the saintly and learned Bucer.

What our Carr says of Redman is admirable; let me add a few words to give you an idea of what kind of man he is. He is a close relative of Cuthbert Tunstall, Bishop of Durham; from boyhood he enjoyed the Bishop's advice about the study of literature. For some

---

[2]In view of Cheke's efforts, mentioned below, Sturm chose not to bring this *Vita* to completion, though he did eventually write a preface to the volume of memorials to Bucer entitled *Scripta Anglicana* (Basel, 1577).

[3]The death of Bucer in Cambridge on February 28, 1551, brought forth a flood of letters, poems, and memorials from grieving English Protestants, including two epitaphs by Ascham (III, 287-88). Sir John Cheke edited and published these materials in a volume entitled *De obitu doctissimi et sanctissimi theologi doctoris Martini Buceri, epistolae duae* (London, 1551). One of the long letters indicated in the title was by the Regius Professor of Greek at Cambridge, Nicholas Carr, whose comments on Redman are referred to below.

years he dwelt at both Cambridge and Oxford. Later he went to Paris. After staying there for a while, he returned to England before his twentieth year or a little after. He was so well versed in Greek and Latin, and so polished by his careful study of Cicero that either by emulation of his excellence or by imitation of his precepts John Cheke and Thomas Smith, both quite young and equal in all respects, were aroused to reject the sordidness of the barbarians and to drink deeply of the rich liquor of wise eloquence from the fountains of Plato, Aristotle, and Cicero, a liquor you will notice is abundant in their pupils and my most intimate friends, Haddon and Carr.[4]

Redman, about whom I started to write, has dedicated himself wholly to the study of sacred letters, so well fortified by the garrisons of intellect, learning, and eloquence that he surpasses almost everyone. He has a very delightful character; he lives very modestly; he is open with every one, and good even to his adversaries, and he is not difficult or harsh with anyone. I confess I have scarcely ever heard a preacher so gifted in framing sermons to nurture the Christian life. In the public schools of Cambridge he has thoroughly explained his views and his judgment concerning such points of doctrine as the marriage of the clergy and other controversies.

About justification by faith alone, however, he has differed somewhat from us. He always does it commendably and without harsh words, not so much, in my view, because he has doubted the truth of that doctrine as because he feared licentiousness, into which the ghosts of virtue and forward, verbose men were being swept. Therefore, whether you consider Redman's extensive learning or his very well-attested goodness, shared with our Bucer, you can boldly set his famous good judgment against all the Babylonians--the Ecks, the Billicks, and the rest.[5]

[4]Walter Haddon was the Regius Professor of Civil Law, Nicholas Carr the Regius Professor of Greek.

[5]Ascham names two stalwart Catholics: Johann Eck, 1486-1543, was Professor of Theology at the University of Ingolstadt; he opposed Luther in a memorable debate in 1519, and continued to lead Catholic attacks on Lutheranism. Concerning Billick, another German Catholic, see Letter 33, note 4.

I would write at length about how our noble Duchess of Suffolk[6] enfolded Bucer with tenderness, and how she nursed him with care and medical attention night and day, but Bucer's wife will have a better opportunity to tell you everything. I know that you will not skip over this topic and this most noble peer, my Sturm, for she is a model for the rest of the nobility, and she holds you in her favor, and has often thought of sponsoring your coming into England. Also, Mr. Cheke recently promised another writing, a separate one, about Bucer's death. When I have received it, I shall send it to you immediately.

The mention of these things, my Sturm, arouses a feeling of very deep sorrow within me, and a tremendous longing for that most saintly man, who loved me much and assisted me much in my education, by whose efforts alone this friendship of ours, than which nothing is sweeter to me, was founded most firmly. In my most recent memories flourish those frequent conversations he had with me about religion, about the conditions and the changes within the state, about the correct course of learning, about you and your extraordinary gentleness and knowledge, about his plan for us to write a joint letter to get you moving on your explication of Aristotle.

But I shall be silent lest I augment my own sorrows and not diminish yours, although in bad times reopening the painful wounds in private and in conversation with a dear friend affords some consolation. Farewell in Jesus Christ. It is enough if I know that you have received these words, and when you get enough free time and a break from more weighty matters, I prefer your briefest letter speaking about your Aristotle, Aeschines, and Demosthenes to one about all those Turks, Papists, Italians, etc. If there is anything in our Mont's letters,[7] he will tell you. June, 1551.[8]

---

[6]The widow Katherine Willoughby Brandon, Duchess of Suffolk and patron of Protestant learning, had settled near Cambridge while her celebrated young sons were attending the University.

[7]I.e., in the diplomatic correspondence he is carrying as courier.

[8]Giles' text erroneously reads "June 18": on the dating of this letter, see my introduction to it above.

44 / To Johann Sturm   (Giles I.cxxviii)

Augsburg, August 21, 1551

> The curious tone of the abrupt opening of this letter reflects Ascham's dis-
> covery that although he had urged his friend to shine the light of his favor
> on the matchless lady Jane Grey (Letter 42; see also Letter 41, and the last
> paragraph of Letter 45), Sturm had chosen to dedicate his eagerly awaited
> edition of the orations of Aeschines and Demosthenes to Bishop Julius
> Pflug, and not to the English prodigy Ascham was so fond of. (Sturm's
> dedication is dated November 27, 1549; the edition itself bears the imprint
> "Strasbourg, 1550.")

I was giving more thought to our friendship and to your kindness
than to my own modesty, my dear Sturm, when I revealed in my last
letter written to our Mont how eager I was to see your Demosthenes
and Aeschines appear in the name of that most noble maiden Jane
Grey. For I was not then totally unaware of the kind of involvements
you have within your elaborate affairs. If, then, there is some fault (I
hope that there has been none), assign it to our Mont, who had written to me a short time previously about the publication of those orations. I very strongly approve of whatever you want, and yet I have
written what I myself especially desire. For I want you to dedicate
something to that most excellent maiden, always most devoted to you
and yours, as I well know. Her mind is more adorned with the
teachings of Plato and the eloquence of Demosthenes than she herself
is illustrious by virtue of fortune or royal birth, or by virtue of her
accession to the very ample, but also very mournful inheritance of her
famous maternal uncle, the Duke of Suffolk.[1] It is this Jane Grey, who
has now become heiress of one half.

And always I see before my eyes that moment when I stumbled
upon that exquisite maiden reading the *Phaedo* of Plato, about which I
think I wrote to you once.[2] And why do I say all this? Least of all
my Sturm, because in this or in any other thing I wish to be trouble-

---

[1]Within the space of a couple of hours on July 14, 1551, both Henry and
Charles Brandon, the young, precocious Dukes of Suffolk, died of the sweating
sickness, leaving no issue. Upon their much lamented death, Henry Grey, Marquis of Dorset, married at the time to their sister Frances, came into the dukedom,
and his daughters Jane and Catherine stood in line as its joint heirs.

[2]Letter 41.

some, but in order that I may show, since I have long been most loving of you both, how I am now most devoted also to the cementing of a mutual friendship between you. That friendship cannot more worthily be added to you nor more desirably be offered to her.

I have written to Mr. Cheke on behalf our Toxites, and have done so very eagerly. I shall write also, if you wish, to Mr. Paget. If I were in England, I would act with much diligence and get something done. I would write at length about the rumors of the Turk, Parma, and Saxony, except that the one who bears this letter, our mutual friend, will have a better opportunity to explain everything. Whatever we have for certain about which ambassador will stay, or whether both will go, our Mont can tell.[3]

Hieronymus Wolf[4] has been put in charge of the Fugger Library.[5] From Fugger I have obtained a manuscript of Aeschines, with a commentary; Wolf has not yet been able to find the printed book. I happened upon the commentaries of Simon Grynaeus on the second book of Aristotle's *Rhetoric*;[6] I am working on having them copied for me, for in my opinion they are learned. If I find out that you want them, I shall send them to you, although I think that the heirs of Grynaeus, who are in Strasbourg, have this and many other of his writings.

---

[3]In Letter 45 Ascham speaks more specifically about the possibility of the French and Spanish ambassadors being sent home as the Emperor's dream of consolidating power was dying in the face of the opposition of European princes: during the first half of 1551 the Emperor's brother Ferdinand and his son Philip of Spain were not able to agree to Charles' plan for succession, for example, and France was on the verge of agreeing to the Treaty of Chambord with Protestant German princes.

[4]Cf. Ascham's comment to Edward Raven: "Heronimus Wolfius, that translated Demosthenes, and Isocrates, is in this town [Augsburg]. I am well acquainted with him" (I, 284).

[5]The Fuggers were celebrated Augsburg merchants. In January Ascham had marvelled about their wealth in a letter to Raven, noting also that Johann Jacob Fugger "is learned and hath gathered such a library of Greek and Latin books as is thought no man else to have. I will see it if I can" (I, 266-67).

[6]Simon Grynaeus (Greiner, Griner), c. 1494-1541, was a lifelong friend of Melanchthon, and in the course of his life he taught Greek and Latin in Buda, Heidelberg, and finally Basel. Aristotle was the subject of much of his scholarship, including some translations and a 1531 edition of Aristotle's works with a preface by Erasmus.

I am anxious to know about the recovery of your health. Please greet John Sleidan, Valentine Erythraeus, and our Michael Toxites.[7]
Augsburg, August 21, 1551.

45 / To Johann Sturm   (Giles I.cxxxi)
                    Augsburg, September 27, 1551

> In this letter Ascham introduces his correspondent to a new courier, the Englishman John Hales, who a year earlier had graciously hosted the ambassador and his entourage in Canterbury as they made their way to Germany (see Letter 32, note 1).

I do nothing more gladly than write to you, most learned Johann Sturm, but I am especially glad now because I understand that John Hales, a very distinguished man, is about to depart for Strasbourg. I'm sure that you know what sort of man he is from the frequent comments of our Mont, and I think that you will be pleased to hear a few words from me also.

He is very well grounded in the doctrine of the true religion of Christ. In the control of his conduct he is a diligent watchman and a serious, taciturn censor. Many think it is his nature to be rather serious; I think it is by design, although on that score there is no one who is more candid and affable when it comes to gentility. He is highly experienced in all kinds of English affairs, engaging in them for years with prudence, diligence, and praiseworthy temperance. Thus, my Sturm, if you desire to know the feelings and talents of our men, especially of our leaders, or why there has been so much change and so many revolutions within our history in recent years, there is certainly no one who better understands people's conduct, who has so wisely predicted certain occurrences, or who has more strongly resisted making a profit for himself out of difficult circumstances.

He is endowed with a great love for literature, as well as an excellent knowledge of it. His distinction is the greater because it was not from quiet fountains of the university, but from the middle of the turbulent English torrent that he drew his perfect knowledge of Latin,

---

[7]See Letter 42, note 3, and Letter 43, note 1.

his moderate knowledge of Greek, his total command of Italian, his smattering of French, and even a bit of your own German. Besides all this, my Sturm, he is also a great admirer of your excellent learning, and he is very eager to enjoy a closer relationship with you. He has read your books avidly and has very often conversed with me about you. He thought about traveling to Italy, but wholly captured by an admiration for your learning and a love for you, he sets out for Strasbourg.

I take his departure from us very hard, but my frequent thoughts about your friendship, a friendship whose closeness I shall rejoice in, will comfort me in his sad absence. Thus I do not so much sorrow for myself because his sweet companionship has been snatched from me as I applaud both of you and your delightful and pleasant union. After you have become accustomed to each other and known each other for a long time, all these things, my Sturm, will appear clearer than I have intimated.

Concerning the mutual beastliness which the Turk and the Hungarian practice against each other, concerning the storming of Tripoli, concerning the Mediterranean entirely overrun by Turkish terrors, concerning the devastation of the Piedmont, concerning the great eruption of war between Spain and France, now no longer expected, but actually happening, concerning the ambassadors of both being sent home, what shall I say but,

> What follies so ever great princes make,
> The people therefore go to wrake.[1]

About the courage and the perseverance of the Neapolitans, about the calamitous upheaval of religion in this city, about the grief of its people, their perseverance, and their increased hatred of false doctrine--about many other things I would write you at length except that Mr. Hales will have a better opportunity to tell them all to you orally than I have in writing.

---

[1]This couplet is the free translation Ascham himself gives elsewhere (in *Report of Germany* [III, 15]) of the line from Horace's *Epistles* (1.2.14) which he quotes here. Horace in turn is alluding to Homer's *Iliad*. In an English letter written two weeks later to the fellows of St. John's, Ascham also cites Horace's line (I, 312).

If the Emperor should settle in Spires, as the growing rumor has it, I shall gladly visit Strasbourg. In the meanwhile, although I always look forward very eagerly to your letters, you will not displease me if you write nothing, for I support your free time to work more than I wish to bother you in any way.

And as you wrote me in a certain letter,[2] insofar as you are happy that I love you so much without being offended by your silence (although indeed you are not silent), so too I am delighted, since you write in the same place that you are soon going to prove to me that you have not been indolent. I applaud the immortal glory of the Werters[3] since by virtue of your design and their own merit they dialogue with you in your *Aristotelian Rhetoric*. For you will accomplish this in such a way that the name of the family will seem to posterity to be famous not only for its nobility, but also for its virtue and erudition. I too, especially in many of my letters, have used the Werters as models for stirring up the English nobility to the same zeal and a similar excellence.

As I came to this place, behold, this letter of mine, rather impudent as it is wont to be and perhaps somewhat too imprudent, seemed to me to ask whether I should politely demand anything of you about Aristotle, about Aeschines and Demosthenes, and about the *Ciceronian Analysis*, etc. I have remained silent, and although smiling pleasantly to myself, nevertheless have somewhat rebuked the actions of my letters lately, not only because they have importunately asked all this, but because they have demanded it too rudely. I have mentioned your various and manifold involvements, and how you are squeezed by the weight of things you have already undertaken. I have explained that you reprimand their rather immodest cheekiness, in accordance with your own prudence, although in your kindness you pay little attention to it. They fell silent immediately, suffused with shame, and if after this, my Sturm, they continue in ignorance or foolishness to bother you, let them understand that you are angry and that they have caused you the displeasure about which you write so charmingly

[2]Sturm's letter (I.cxxv) was dated June 15, 1551.

[3]The Werter brothers, Philip and Anthony, were wealthy, aristocratic students of Sturm.   Elsewhere Ascham reports that they were giving Sturm 400 crowns a year for four years "to find him writers" (I, 316).   To these brothers Sturm addressed his book *A Literate Nobility* (Strasbourg, 1549).

to Julius, the Naumburg pope.[4] But even I myself am silent, lest you become angry with me more justly than with my letters. You see how much credit I give to our friendship, within which I boldly dare[5] to present any and every absurdity of mine.

But to speak what I'm thinking, my dearest Sturm, I must confess that I am controlled by a great longing; indeed, I am subject to a very great longing for the project in which you are now engaged, and I was also laboring for it in my recent letters: I long for you to make that noblest of maidens, Jane Grey, famous by your writings.[6] Nevertheless, understand that the whole thing comes to this: I wish to desire nothing else than what accords with your own judgment, plan, and free time. Farewell in Jesus Christ. Augsburg, September 27, 1551.

46 / To Johann Sturm   (Giles I.cxxxv)
Hall in Tyrol, January 29, 1552

The storm of the Protestant princes' opposition to the Emperor is about to break as Ascham writes this letter; within a few months the Emperor would be scrambling to safety across the Alps in order to escape Maurice of Saxony. Nearly all of Ascham's attention, however, is focused on another kind of imminent battle: rumor has it that he and Sturm have been attacked by the great French iconoclast Peter Ramus. In his inaugural letter to Sturm (Letter 39) Ascham had taken a nasty crack at "the big mouth of Cephas Chlononius," that is, Ramus. Now he is thinking somewhat disingenuously about rewriting his differences with Ramus and about defensive strategies, particularly about how Sturm might help to ease tensions by comments within his own *Aristotelian Dialogues*. Ironically the rumor was apparently without foundation; there was no attack. Years later, in fact, Ramus would write Ascham a letter without a hint of antagonism or bitterness (II, 96-97),

[4]Julius Pflug was the Catholic Bishop of Naumburg to whom Sturm dedicated his 1550 edition of the orations of Aeschines and Demosthenes.

[5]Here I follow the early editions in reading *audeam* (dare); Giles' *audiam* (hear) perpetuates Elstob's typographical error.

[6]See my introduction to Letter 44 concerning Ascham's persistent efforts on behalf of Jane Grey.

and Sturm, notwithstanding his disagreements with Ramus over Aristotle, would invite the celebrated Frenchman to join the faculty of his school.[1]

At this writing the Emperor was settled in Innsbruck; Morison and Ascham were living nearby in the town of Hall.

For a long while I have been eagerly expecting a letter from you, most accomplished Sturm, and now I require it almost as a necessity, for certain friends of mine write from England that Peter Ramus has written something against our letters which you had printed at Strasbourg. But you know, best Sturm, what I have written to you about Ramus in my other letters,[2] and how much credit I give to his intellect and learning, and even to his intentions, since I think he was flailing inept and dull Aristotelians rather than refuting Aristotle himself.

You know in addition, unless it has escaped your memory or my letters have been destroyed, how much I preferred Peter Ramus to his brother Joachim Périon, whose ineptly stitched and poorly fitted Ciceronianisms against Martin Bucer and Philip Melanchthon I ridiculed.[3] I believe that Ramus thinks rightly about Christian doctrine, and that in his way, at this moment and in that place, he is concealing his own thinking, though he is nevertheless publicly displaying his interests by writing against those whom he sees as being intent upon being open adversaries of the true religion. Our Hieronymus Wolf,[4] who was first in Paris and then in Augsburg, has confirmed the truth of my opinion of Ramus.

Although I criticized his loose tongue in that letter of mine, and still do not approve of it, I did openly give him credit for his excellent intellect and learning, and I also tacitly sanctioned his intentions in the following words, saying that I think Aristotle's ideas are excellent, "but they seem to be embellished too little and obscured too much to allow many readers to be enticed by pleasure into studying them or to be compensated for their efforts by the benefits they derive, since nearly

---

[1]See Charles Schmidt, *La vie et les travaux de Jean Sturm* (1855; Nieuwkoop: de Graaf, 1970) 151-52.

[2]No "other letters" to Sturm before this date survive in which Ramus is mentioned.

[3]See Letter 39. The term "brother" is ironic: Ramus attacked Périon for his slavish devotion to Cicero.

[4]See Letter 44, note 4.

everywhere Aristotle is taught without being carefully illustrated with examples." For you know how I have been requiring students who are cultivating the arts to make use of imitation, lest their course of study seem to be either unprofitable, impeded by its obscurity, or unattractive, leading far afield.

In my heart I am certainly well disposed toward Ramus, and if the matter stands thus, I am sorry that he rejects my friendship. I suspect that certain Englishmen at Cambridge who differ somewhat from us in religion have turned Ramus against us on those very grounds, which is also the reason why they themselves have left England for Paris.

But however this matter turns out, I shall worry little about myself and wonder little about you. For to tell you the truth, the fellow has an amazing mind who doesn't set himself to attack anyone except the Aristotles, the Ciceros, and the Sturms. "One doesn't envy the dead, nor engage them in hostilities."[6] But perhaps because he even teaches the Aristotle whom I quoted, Ramus prefers to follow a strange and churlish way of thinking rather than not to fight with Aristotle about everything.

Moreover, Ramus acted contrary to practice and custom when he singled me out, an obscure man. He would never have heard of my existence except from you. But this should be pardoned because of his diseased mind. For just as the sick always reject the best remedies, so also when they never lie quiet, they have the severest relapses.

I am not surprised, nor am I very upset, that I displease Ramus, whom even the Aristotles, the Ciceros, and the Sturms cannot please. He will press on, I believe, and rush at you with greater vehemence when he understands that you assign *invention*, which he removes from his school of rhetoric, to the foremost ranks of the art of speaking, and that with Aristotle you properly and learnedly assign *delivery*, which those little Ramists prize, to a place within practice rather than within theory. But I understand Ramus' strategy: he does not want to be an *imitator*, lest he appear to follow Aristotle.

If Ramus has done this, you can find out in due time and will determine prudently what our course must be. Perhaps you have

---

[6]Aristotle, *Rhetoric* 2.10.

heard from Mr. Hales that I am somebody with the bow and arrow, and yet not a man of great stature. Hidden under my Sturmian shield, therefore, why shouldn't I, like Teucer, be able to ward off those blows of Ramus, or at least disdain them? At some convenient place in your Nidrusian dialogue[7] you could easily refute his insolence and vindicate me with just three words, although I have not intentionally written anything to criticize Ramus publicly. But if silence will please you more (and it also pleases me the most), I shall silently skip over this discussion at this time, and carry myself back to the delightful thoughts which occupy me every day, reading your Nidrusian discourse.

But look, those same thoughts, blushing modestly, are hiding themselves again and bashfully fear your eye. But they are behaving foolishly, since we have the kind of friendship that does not fear with suspicion the ambush of adulation, nor repel because of modesty the frank and open truth. Still, my thoughts, although they certainly long to be led forth, nevertheless cannot be; however, at another time and place they pledge themselves to be expressed. Meanwhile they often marvel with me at the book's introduction, designed to raise expectations, and then at your mature approach to the subject. They think about those eminently suitable for playing roles in it: Sapidus[8] could undertake the defense of nature because he is a poet, and could propose the more difficult questions about learning because he is serious and very learned. Both the Werter[9] brothers are eager to listen be-

[7]I.e., Sturm's *Aristotelian Dialogues* on rhetoric. The dialogues are set in the rector's country residence, Sturm's "Nidrusian," which might be compared to Cicero's Tusculan villa: see Jean Rott and Robert Faerber, "Un Anglais à Strasbourg au Milieu du XVIe Siècle: John Hales, Roger Ascham, et Jean Sturm," *Études Anglaises* 21 (1968) 385. In November 1551 Ascham had received a copy of Book One of the *Dialogues*, which he reports to friends at St. John's with great enthusiasm: "Sturmius goeth forward in *Rhetor. Aristot.* The first book is sent to Mr Cheke, which was purposed to me, but I had rather it should be sent to him. Mr John Hales, my singular friend, sent me a piece of this rhetoric this week. I never saw any thing more to be compared with antiquity" (I, 315-16).

[8]Johann Sapidus (Witz), 1490-1561, once the rector of the noted Schlettstadt school, settled in Strasbourg in 1526, and soon became one of the Latin teachers in Sturm's Protestant gymnasium. Some of his Latin poetry appeared in Sturm's publications in 1540 and again in 1542. Sturm married his daughter.

[9]Sturm's aristocratic patrons (and students): see Letter 45, note 3.

cause of their curiosity, and modest in their questioning because of their age. You used good judgment in assigning the explication of terms to them. If I were to take part in the discussion at that point within your Nidrusian dialogue, I would help them with their shyness, for on account of my ignorance I would put many questions about the connections between the two languages to you as the supreme craftsman in both languages, and in my ignorance I would more frequently have created some confusion on account of my impudence.

And for that very reason, if I did not love the noble Werters very much, I would want them, at least for those nine days, to act either less erudite or more impudent. And in that passage, my dear Sturm, you do seem gently to laugh at these foolish and inane thoughts of mine, but you ought either to put up with my stupidity or not acknowledge me to be your friend. Your cherry trees are to be preferred, in my judgment, to Crassus's plane tree, because that imitation in Cicero, as I see it, is not concealed enough.[10] And here I think even Ramus would praise me because I dare to criticize something in Cicero.

Fairly and correctly, my Sturm, you criticize the error of theologians who do not develop the parts into which they divide their sermons. And although I want to urge you strongly to finish those nine books as quickly as possible, nevertheless I assign less value to my own longing than to your glory, which will become immortal upon the completion of these books. For that reason I want you to let this work ripen rather than to rush it in any way. Nevertheless, do it such a way that you always keep fixed before your eyes that which you are wont to criticize in the preachers.

I have been pleased beyond measure by that work you have begun about what the authority of the law and the duties of a judge ought to consist of. But if I would set down at length all those things about which I am pleased in your discourse of the first day, I would have to write you a book in instead of a letter. I was glad to see the Strasbourg Gremp here at Augsburg, but I would much rather hear

---

[10]Sturm's Nidrusian dialogues on Aristotle's *Rhetoric* imitate Cicero's dialogue *De oratore*, whose interlocutors sit under a plane tree, explicitly remarking as they do that they are following Socrates' ways in Plato's *Phaedrus*.

the other Sturmian Gremp.[11]   I do not doubt but what that man is going to be thoroughly immersed in the most important affairs of these times, not unlike Laelius, or even Scipio.[12]

You will never have a more suitable place, my Sturm, for expounding your most serious advice and your opinion of the affairs of our day: concerning the Turks, the Italians, the French, the Germans, and the English.   Perhaps you would find this plan much more convenient than if you undertook some other work about the same matters.

I love Philip Werter much because he loves you and cultivates the study of literature and makes his noble family illustrious by the splendor of literature.   But I love him more because he himself is so ready to hear you speak at length about the religion of Christ and urges you, as I do also, to incorporate your most substantial and lengthy discussion of God and his doctrine into the remainder of your dialogue.   I normally put you ahead of all other men of our time when you begin a discourse on any subject, but I prefer you even to yourself whenever you speak of Christ.   And it is only just that he who has lavished on you the greatest learning, setting you above all others, should in turn, through his own gift to you, be glorified by the light of your talent.   Nor do I believe you disagree with what I am writing.

Perhaps I have troubled you with my long talk.   Since I am very eager for your longest letters, I wanted to be more wordy myself. [Farewell in Christ.]   Hall, January 29, 1552.

[11]Ludwig Gremp von Freudenstein, 1509-1583, had been a noted teacher of law at Tubingen before he came to Strasbourg in 1541, where he served as an attorney, ambassador, and parliamentarian for the city.   The Sturmian Gremp, of course, is a character in the *Aristotelian Dialogues*.

[12]Both Laelius ("the Wise") and Scipio Aemilianus were consuls, leaders in war, and great orators; they were also close friends.   Cicero honored both with prominent places in various of his dialogues, and considered Scipio the greatest of the Romans.

47 / To Johann Sturm (Giles I.cxlii)
Spires, October 20, 1552

During the spring of 1552 Emperor Charles V was on the run. The French advanced into Lorraine; Maurice of Saxony took Augsburg in April, and in May he cut off the Emperor at one pass, forcing him into a desperate, ig-nominious escape across another into Carinthia. Ascham apparently used the occasion to visit Italy briefly, for it was then within striking distance; afterwards he joined the Emperor's court in its summer retreat westward. By September they were close to Strasbourg, and Ascham eagerly seized the opportunity to look up his beloved Sturm, only to discover that his friend was out of town.

I am not able to express it in writing, but you can very easily imag-ine, most accomplished Johann Sturm, how I arrived at Strasbourg in a happy frame of mind, and how sad I was when I found you were not there. I have cheerfully wandered over a great part of Germany and some of Italy, but in all my travels nothing was more delightful and more frequent in my thoughts than that sometime I wanted to see Strasbourg, and most of all to see my Sturm in his Nidrusian.

In a long, confidential, and private conversation I was thinking to open my heart about the various things that have transpired recent-ly in the court of the Emperor, and about the excited, actual discus-sions which have taken place, and the false rumors which have been circulating. For ever since our flight from Innsbruck up to this day I have kept a continuous record of each day.

You would have laughed to hear me tell how we were gripped by an even greater fear at Villach on July 2 than at Innsbruck on May 19, when we were scattered every which way and put to flight. Some Pan or Nymphs from the Alps must have sent this terror upon us, and rumors about the Turks, however groundless, and suspicions of the Venetians attacked us. These and many other things I would have recounted to you, and I would in turn have heard from you about many things which occurred elsewhere during the same turbulent times.

We can perhaps at another time repair that kind of damage in some way, but I cannot redeem the damage which I incurred to my

hope of interrupting the most learned Nidrusian[1] during his disputation.   I believe I would have been silly and troublesome as I took
part, but I know that I would also have been eager and friendly as I
did it, especially when I think that I might have stumbled in on that
day which was designated for conducting the dialogue with Gremp.[2]

With very great kindness Anthony and Philip, brothers as truly
noble as they are German, alleviated somewhat my disappointment at
missing you.   They showed me the second book.[3]   I was certainly
pleased at the delay and Gremp's difficulties, and I think I see your
strategy in that passage.   Certainly I approve your judgment.   Unless I
am mistaken, you are reserving Gremp for an extended exposition of
those five points which have to do with how the most important deliberations in every state are framed.   If I had been present to hear
these things from the mouths of both of you, and with attentive ears
had listened to the good counsel and the illustrious examples not only
of the ancients, but in particular of our own princes and their times, I
should have thought myself no less happy than those famous men
who enter this kind of dialogue in Plato and Cicero.

I believe, my Sturm--and as much as I dare, this is also what I
urge--that you are preparing and designing this whole work not so
much with the intent of giving erudite instruction as of being useful to
civic life in our times and situations.   You have everything you need
in abundance; the materials are of top quality: the purest religion,
very unusual times, a zeal for the better things, the experience of life,
renowned princes, opportunity, judgment, eloquence.   You see what I
am looking for, and I understand what you can do.   In my opinion,
you must not underestimate how much weight you ought to give to
the true religion, to the better causes, to the freedom of a country, to
the injustice of others, even to your own disposition and the desires of
all good men.   You see what I am driving at, my Sturm, and perhaps

---

[1]See Letter 46, note 7.

[2]See Letter 46, note 11.   Gremp plays a role in Sturm's *Aristotelian Dialogues*.

[3]Ascham alludes to Sturm's *Aristotelian Dialogues*; the noble Werter brothers,
students of Sturm (see Letter 45, note 3), were able to show him Sturm's manuscript.   Previously Ascham had seen the first book (see Letter 46, note 7).   In May,
1553, Sturm would promise to send Ascham soon a copy of the second and third
books (see I, 358), but in September 1555 Ascham still had not seen the third (see
Letter 48).

you wonder what kind of judgment I have that I require these things in the exposition of rhetorical precepts: it is that very judgment which he used who prayed his friend to ignore all the laws of history in extolling himself. And I think that in this argument I am more nearly correct than even the very master of learning and eloquence, because he seems to connect it somewhat to self-love, whereas I refer everything to the supreme glory of a friend, to the greatest present good, to posterity, and never to fleeting admiration.

I am afraid, my Sturm, that I seem stupid, silly, and haughty in this entire passage. If when I write to you I were not always accustomed to giving as much credit to your good sense in judging me as to our friendship, I would think you would dismiss me.

But I proceed to other matters. With us here at Spires is the distinguished signore Marc Antonio Damula, Venetian ambassador to the Emperor, very interested in you, very friendly to me, versatile in learning, skilled in languages, and experienced in important affairs.[4] With great renown, he stands preeminent in prudence and self-restraint among the islands and the remaining territory of the Venetians. From him I hear many stories of Contarini, Bembo, and Sadoleto,[5] and he in turn often inquires of me about Sturm. He told me that he had sent you a gift the last time he was in Strasbourg, and was very sorry that he missed getting to know you, which he had been looking forward to. He asked me to take some care to let you know of his fondness for you and to greet you most dutifully in his name. If he were not lying in bed ill at this time, he would have lightened this my very pleasant labor by his own letter, more pleasant by far. Let him understand, I pray you, in your next letter to me or, if you wish, in a letter to him, that I was mindful and that you were delighted. I hold no wealth to be more magnificent than the addition of a magnificent friendship. He has asked me to visit him tomorrow and to bring with me your commentaries on Aristotle's *Rhetoric*, so

---

[4]See also a May 1553 letter from Ascham to William Cecil: "This last day as I talked with a Signior Marco Antonio Danula [sic], the ambassador of Venice, to whom I am exceeding much beholden, he said unto me if I had desire to live for a year or two in Constantinople, Damasco, or Cairo, he would provide I should be in place where I should be partaker of weighty affairs. . ." (I, 354).

[5]Gasparo Contarini, Pietro Bembo, Jacopo Sadoleto were cardinals in the church of Rome, and leading figures in Italian civic humanism.

that with that sweet discourse we may obliterate, as it were, the sharp pains with which he is racked. And when I cheerfully read and he eagerly listens, both of us will delight in your acquaintance.

See how talkative I am, my Sturm. Whenever I write to you, I write at such length because I love you very much or because I seem to be talking face to face with you or because I want to draw you into writing at great length yourself.

When I was at Strasbourg, I thought I saw old Sparta as I looked at your strongly fortified walls. I gave high praise to that Laconian frugality in life style, that sober appearance, those simple, rustic customs, rough rather than smooth and superficial. I certainly praise your spiritedness, though in truth you are also reserved, in the Laconian mode.

My Lord Ambassador, you know, has a tremendous fondness for you, and writes to England about you in ways that I could not improve upon or wish to change. When you write to him, write carefully, for I have discovered no one among all the Englishmen who evaluates what is prudently or learnedly written with more seriousness or who receives it with more gratitude. Our Toxites was very, very nice to us. He was once an erudite man of letters whom now I judge to be easily the best of men in his behavior and manner. I believe my Lord Ambassador is writing to you again. I hope you will learn much from his letter. I pray you, greet those noble brothers Anthony and Philip Werter. Farewell in Jesus Christ. Spires, October 20, 1552.

48 / To Johann Sturm (Giles I.cxci)
Greenwich, September 14, 1555

> Two years have elapsed, according to Ascham's own admission in this letter, since his last letter to Sturm. The last surviving letter antedates this one by almost three years, however, so at least one letter has been lost. We have confirmation in a letter from Sturm of July 22, 1553 (I. cliii), which alludes to comments by Ascham that do not appear in any existing letter.

The reason why I haven't written during this long interval of two years, most illustrious Johann Sturm, is not my lack of good will, nor my forgetfulness of you, nor my neglect of my duty towards you.

Neither have I lacked subject matter or means of sending you a letter. Not the revolutions in public life, but the difficulties of my private life and my own personal business have been my only hindrance. I mean my marriage, which you heard about, and which a turbulent fellow fought with all his might to make invalid.[1] But he was defeated by the verdict of the law and by the equity of my cause; the whole affair has been duly cleared up and settled to my satisfaction.

Therefore I will now gladly make good by frequent letters what has been lost by this excessively long intermission. And behold, very conveniently here is John Metellus,[2] a very learned man who admires you a great deal. He insists and urges me to write you. He is returning to Italy and plans to stop at Strasbourg just to greet you and meet with you. He came to England as a traveling companion and counsel to Antonio Agostino,[3] whom Pope Julius III sent as nuncio to our Queen last year. These two, Antonio Agostino and John Metellus, are the interlocutors in *De gloria*, a book which Jeronimo Osorio of Portugal wrote in a Ciceronian, that is, in a prudent and an eloquent, style.[4] That you welcome Metellus, so erudite a man and so devoted to you and loving of me, there is no need for me to ask, for I know

---

[1]See Ryan's account of "what was perhaps the most uncomfortably thrilling episode in Roger Ascham's life" (200-03), based on a letter from Ascham to his lawyer (I.clxii) rejecting the prior claims of a certain J.B. to his fiancée, Margaret Howe. See also Ascham's comments later in this letter about his wife and the date of their marriage.

[2]Metellus (Jean Matal), c. 1520-1597, was an erudite Frenchman who studied law in Bologna, where he met Agostino and Osorio, mentioned below. He accompanied Agostino on many diplomatic missions.

[3]Agostino, 1517-1586, was one Spain's most celebrated students of law and religion, having been educated at Alcala, Salamanca, and Bologna. He was reputed to be a man of great learning and judgment, and in response to Cardinal Pole's request, the Pope chose him as one well suited to advance the cause of the church of Rome in England during Mary's reign.

[4]Although in *The Schoolmaster* (III, 185, 204-05) Ascham would be critical of this renowned Bishop and Ciceronian stylist, he was at this time championing this man from Portugal: in November 1553 he offered a copy of *De gloria* (Florence, 1552) to Sir William Paget (see Letter 54), and a copy of *De nobilitate* (Florence, 1552) to Sir William Petre (see Letter 55); in April 1555 he would also offer the latter book to Cardinal Pole (see Letter 58). Osorio and Ascham even exchanged letters (II.xxix and xxxi; another is not printed by Giles: see Ryan 325).

that as a result of your kindness Metellus will write me long and grateful letters.

In conversation with Metellus you will learn the state of everything in England, including what kind of person my noble mistress Elizabeth is, with whom he had an audience through my efforts. How she excels in Greek, Latin, Italian, and French, indeed, how gifted she is with a knowledge of affairs and with a learned and intelligent judgment, he will tell you at length himself, so that you will surely know from Metellus' testimony that I never made anything up about any of her accomplishments. But you will hear these and other matters from Metellus himself.

Now a little about me and my affairs. How much I owe you, my Sturm, my dearest Johann Sturm, for that letter which you wrote to Paget on my behalf,[5] neither the present letter can declare nor my fortunes compensate. But, God willing, I shall make posterity understand that Sturm was a very dear friend, and Ascham did not forget. That which King Henry and King Edward formerly bestowed upon me has been not only wholly restored, but even doubled. I have also been appointed Latin secretary to the King and Queen. As Christ loves me, I would not exchange my position for any other way of life that might be offered me.

Stephen, Bishop of Winchester, Lord High Chancellor of England, has enfolded me in his favor and kindness, so that I cannot easily decide whether Paget was more ready to recommend me or Winchester to defend and honor me.[6] There were some who tried to impede the course of his good will for me on account of my religion, but they have gotten nowhere. And so I owe much to Winchester's kindness and owe it cheerfully. Not only I alone, but many others also have discovered his kindness. And I have often thought that I would discuss your excellent work on analysis with him. For I know that he favors the study of literature so much that I promise myself much from his generosity. If you wish it, and write me about your thoughts on it, I shall gladly, and I hope felicitously, try what I can do. There

---

[5] A letter of September 17, 1553 (I.clvii). Sturm also wrote a thank-you to Paget on June 23, 1554, for his assistance to Ascham (I.clxxii).

[6] See my introduction to Part Six concerning the work of Bishop Stephen Gardiner and Sir William Paget on Ascham's behalf during Mary's reign.

will be no problem with it, at least in my opinion. I give you my most heartfelt thanks for your letter to Paget, in which the testimony of your opinion of me was so pleasing that the pleasure which I take from your goodwill is more joyful to me than any advantage which proceeds from Paget's kindness. But I'll write at length about this some other time.

The Most Reverend Cardinal Pole is very kind, and I am inclined to think that no Italian can be compared with him for eloquence. He is very friendly towards me. During the summer when I had breakfast at his home, he started talking about the learned men of this age and mentioned you favorably. In the name of our love and my high opinion of you, I then spoke freely and fully about your analytical work on Aristotelian rhetoric, and he strongly endorsed the framework of your thought. After I had spoken of your method and your analytical ability, which can be seen not in terms of a carefully worked-out literary structure, but in terms of the natural connection of the subject matter, he openly and frankly declared that you had within you not only great learning and rare eloquence, but also moderation and good judgment.

Later he asked me whether I had ever seen anything of the books of Cicero's *Republic*. He said that he had once spent 2000 gold pieces to send a certain man to Poland to search out those lost books, which someone there had developed a hope of discovering. I immediately told him what you had once written to me about those books,[7] and he begged me to write to you to find out whether we know anything definite about these books.

I am very concerned about what might happen to the five books on rhetoric which the Werter brothers, as you indicate, have taken with them to Italy. I feel safer since I know that they are so friendly with you, but I am very eager to know what is happening to those books and how far you have progressed on the remainder of the task, and whether you have changed your mind about introducing me into the discussion, because I think that you did it out of love rather than prudence. But nothing I want more can befall me than that a witness

---

[7] In a brief letter of January 30, 1552 (I.cxxxvii), Sturm told Ascham that he had given some money to someone who promised to find these much-sought books, though he admits he is very skeptical about the prospects.

to the friendship between us will shine so brightly to the eyes of posterity.

Everything in the first two books is excellent (I have seen only these two),[8] but you surpass yourself when you digress, as you have in those fine passages about the brevity of life and the ways of spending time. Since I stayed three days in Strasbourg, it will be completely credible if we fall into various discussions about the Emperor's court, about war and peace, about the method of study, and do not consume all our time discussing the fine points of the art itself. Especially in Plato, but in Cicero also, the *digressions*, in my judgment, are better than *the actual topics*. But I am silly to write these things to you; at any rate you will consider it all part of the liberty we enjoy as friends.

As for my wife, about whom you wanted to know,[9] in features she does very much resemble her maternal aunt, the wife of Sir R. Walop.[10] I have just the wife Johann Sturm would want for Roger Ascham. Her name is Margaret, and the date of our wedding was the first of June, 1554, if there is any good luck in either her name or that day.

If you wish to know what I do at court, let me tell you that I never enjoyed more desirable leisure at the University than I do in the royal household. The Lady Elizabeth and I read together in Greek the orations of Aeschines and Demosthenes *On the Crown*. She first reads it to me, and at first glance she understands not only the propriety of the language and the speaker's meaning, but also the whole nature of the argument, the decrees of the people, the manners and the customs of the city: she is so intelligent you would be simply amazed. But

---

[8]In May 1553 Sturm wrote that he expected soon to be sending Ascham the second and third books of his *Aristotelian Dialogues* (I, 358), but the third was apparently not sent.

[9]In his *Oration on the Life and Death of Roger Ascham* Grant quotes from one of Sturm's letters, dated June 24, 1554, but now lost, in which Sturm asks whether Ascham's wife isn't the niece of the Walop whom he met near Calais years earlier (III, 333).

[10]Ryan (323) notes that the "R." is a scribal error; the Walop in question is Sir John Walop, once an ambassador for Henry VIII at Paris and then a commander of English troops at Guînes, near Calais.

our Metellus can explain this better than I can: he says that it did him more good to see her than to see England.

If any friend of yours, my dear Sturm, has any business to be expedited in England, either with her Majesty or with the Lord Chancellor, write to me, and your friend will see how much Ascham believes ought to be credited to his Sturm. For if I can ever do anything pleasing to you or helpful to your friends and you do not speak, order or demand, I shall consider you ungrateful.

But I am almost forgetting that matter about which I wanted to write to you in the first place. Cardinal Pole's book *On the Unity of the Church*, printed this year at Strasbourg, has reached his hands, and he himself showed it to me. There is here with the Cardinal a certain Venetian noble, Lord Priuli,[11] bishop-elect of Brescia, very learned in all sorts of literature, a complete gentleman, of whom Bembo and Sadoleto have made frequent mention in their letters. He asked me whether I did not think Vergerio's preface to Pole's book had been written by you.[12] I clearly indicated that not only was the style completely different from yours, but also that such a thing would never even enter your mind and heart. I wanted you to know this.

If I were not in the grip of a tertian fever, I should extend this letter until it compensated for the two-year hiatus in our correspondence. But you will pardon its brevity, for your good will is passing in review through my thoughts. And I think that all your letters are far too short.

Greet all our countrymen and that man of great integrity, Mr. Christopher Mont, for whose sake I will do whatever I can in England, and he will find me a loving friend. There is at Strasbourg a certain young Englishman, Thomas Lakin,[13] who has long been my friend; greet him, I pray, and befriend him for my sake. Greet Mr.

---

[11]After they became acquainted during Pole's sojourn in Italy, Alvise Priuli remained Pole's faithful and constant companion on the Continent and in England, even serving as Pole's designated heir and the executor of his estate.

[12]Pole's book was printed against his will, with a hostile Protestant preface, and he was the victim of a major campaign to discredit him by Pier Paolo Vergerio, the younger. See Dermot Fenlon, *Heresy and Obedience in Tridentine Italy: Cardinal Pole and the Counter Reformation* (Cambridge: Cambridge UP, 1972) 258-69.

[13]A graduate of St. John's College, Cambridge (MA in 1551), and at this time among the Marian exiles in Strasbourg (see Garrett 214-15).

Sleidan, Mr. Erythraeus, and especially my most sweet Michael Toxi-tes,[14] whose long silence has amazed me.   If he doesn't have some-thing to write about, I want nothing more than information about the course of Johann's Sturm's studies and writings during the last two years.

I often think about the epithalamion you are going to send to England, and I eagerly await it, whether it is wearing a Roman toga, an Attic mantle, or a Doric vest.   Finally, I greet you and my wife greets yours.   Farewell, and write back.   Greenwich, September 14, 1555.

49 / To Johann Sturm   (Giles II.xxxiv)
London, April 11, 1562

> Ascham acknowledges that he has not written for three years, but in view of the date of the letter above, it is clear that at least one, and probably several letters have been lost.   Perhaps during Mary's reign, when there was an important community of English exiles living in Sturm's city, Ascham had alternative, and less risky means of communicating with friends there.   It is difficult to believe, however, that the accession of Elizabeth did not prompt an enthusiastic exchange of letters between Ascham and his Strasbourg correspondent, but what survives is chiefly this memorable letter, written some three and a half years into Elizabeth's reign.
> This letter, along with an English translation, also appears in *The Zur-ich Letters*, Second Series, ed. Hastings Robinson for The Parker Society (Cambridge, 1845).   The text was transcribed from the holograph in the Strasbourg Library, a manuscript which has since been destroyed by the fire of 1870.   Giles' claim that "this letter is printed more correctly from the Zurich letters" is misleading in that he creates a composite text which con-flates the letter as it appears in the sixteenth-century editions of Ascham's correspondence (which derive from copies Ascham kept) and the letter as it is found in the volume of the Parker Society.   For a full account of textual issues, including this one, we await some future editor, but here we might simply note that the textual divergences are, after all, only minor verbal and typographical ones, except for two sentences which appear in only one tex-tual tradition: one (about Plato's maxim on laws and men) does not appear in Robinson's edition of the letter as it was found in Strasbourg, and one (the one immediately following the quotation from *The Iliad*) does not ap-

---

[14]See Letter 43, note 1.

pear in the sixteenth-century editions. For the sake of consistency Giles is
followed here.

Why is it, my Sturm, that Michael Toxites,[1] our common friend and
beloved courier, has arrived from Strasbourg without letters from you?
Is Cooke[2] or Hales[3] or any Englishman more devoted to you or more
eager for your letters than I am? But I seem to hear you protest, "Ah,
my Ascham, do you complain about my silence, you who have not
written *a line* to me these three years?" And by golly, you speak the
truth, my dearest Johann Sturm. My whole way of expostulating with
you doesn't spring from my quick temper or reproachfulness, but it's
really a clever stratagem, devised on purpose: I was afraid that you,
as you rightly could, would get ahead of me in complaining about
taciturnity.

But now goodbye to all that, for I write truly and sincerely, my
Sturm. This long interval was not caused by own will, not by my
forgetfulness of you, not by my neglect of duty. Not because there
was nothing to write about nor a means of sending them have our
letters so long remained silent. But when you hear from me the true
reason, I shall move you not to anger or irritation against me, but to
sorrow and grief for me, whom I know you love. During these most
recent four years I have been so racked by continual fevers that one
scarcely left me before another followed upon it immediately. And
thus my whole state of health has been broken and crushed by these
recurring waves of fever, so that now my entire body is convulsed by
this hectic fever, for which the doctors promise alleviation sometime,
but never a complete cure. Now those who are my true friends--and
among them my most trusted friend John Hales--repeatedly chirp that
lugubrious line of Thetis to her son in Homer, "*Thou hast thy portion of
life for but a little while.*"[4] And although we read that the men *doomed
to speedy death* were the most distinguished, why should I, a man not
of pride, but of a humble spirit, have to suffer this? I absolutely re-

---

[1]See Letter 43, note 1.

[2]Sir Anthony Cooke, a distinguished courtier who took refuge in Strasbourg
during Mary's reign and returned to England upon the accession of Elizabeth.

[3]John Hales: see introduction to Letter 45.

[4]*Iliad* 1.416.

pudiate that kind of consolation, whether it come from the *poet* or the *historian*. When, however, I turn to our teacher of true and complete salvation, who declares that as much is added to the internal man as is taken from the external,[5] I do not give myself over to grief, but from my physical infirmities I draw new joys for a new life.

But more about this at another time, for I want at this time to begin a long discussion with you, although to tell the truth, at present there is but a minimum of leisure for accomplishing it. These days my most Serene Majesty pulls me away and fills all my time with writing so many letters.

Your most recent letter to me is dated January 15, 1560.[6] In this letter two main points, one concerning the Scottish negotiations, the other concerning the marriage of the Queen, moved me so that I gave it to the Queen herself to read. She sagaciously noticed your singular respect for her, and amiably acknowledged and commended it. Then concerning the Scottish matters of that day, she strongly endorsed your opinion, and even now she is delighted with you for your concern for us and ours. The passage about the marriage, I well remember, she carefully read three times, sweetly *smiling a little* thereupon, but bashfully and modestly remaining silent. And about her marriage, my dear Johann Sturm, I have nothing certain to write, nor does anyone else among us know what she will decide. It was not for nothing, my Sturm, but advisedly that I wrote in my first long letter to you that in her whole way of life she resembled Hippolyta and not Phaedra. At that time I was referring not to her physical beauty, but to the chastity of her mind, for by her own nature and not because of anyone's advice, she is averse to marriage and shies away from it. When I know something for certain, I shall write to you at the first opportunity. Meanwhile I have nothing for you other than hope about the Swedish King.[7]

I wish that you would write something to Mr. Cecil, for he is very sound in religion and very wise in statesmanship and, next to

---

[5]2 Cor. 4:16, adapted.

[6]This letter is not extant in Giles' edition.

[7]The Lutheran King Eric was long considered a contender for the hand of Elizabeth in marriage.

God and our Queen, a staunch supporter of learning and learned men, and very erudite himself in both languages.

As for our affairs, I know that you long to hear from me. I have nothing which in my view is better to write about than the Queen herself. I shall therefore tell you briefly what affairs of great moment she has undertaken with wisdom and successfully accomplished since she took the helm of government. Her first efforts were dedicated to God, for she has wondrously purified religion, which she found miserably polluted, accomplishing it with such moderation that the Papists themselves can not complain of harsh treatment. This peace established with God was followed by peace with all the neighboring heads of state, even though upon her accession to the throne she found this country involved in twin wars with Scotland and with France. Then while the forces of the Guise were threatening us with amazing things, she courageously and skillfully stood firm in Scotland so that now there exists between each kingdom and each ruler a peace as secure and a friendship as close as between two very quiet neighbors or very agreeable sisters.

After religion and then the state had been restored to such a desirable tranquillity, she turned her mind to a proper settlement of other domestic reforms within the realm. All the debased coins made entirely of bronze she caused to be changed to pure, unalloyed silver, an arduous and royal task which neither Edward nor Henry himself even dared to attempt. She has so well equipped an arsenal with carefully chosen weapons that no European prince, I'm sure, can show its equal. Likewise she has furnished and fortified the fleet with all kinds of equipment, increasing both the amount of supplies and the capabilities of the sailors, so that the resources of some wealthy kingdom might seem to have been expended on this one item.

These matters are public, and have to do with the whole realm. Let us glance at more personal matters, such as her studies and her character. She quickly forgets private injury, but she is strict in her devotion to public justice. She grants pardon to none for his crime, she extends to none the hope of impunity, and she flatly refuses anyone a license to offend. Finally, in her every action she always holds this precept of Plato before her eyes as the rule for the whole realm of England: laws are the lords of men, men are not the lords of the law. Moreover, least of all princes does she covet the possessions and the wealth of her subjects; she is frugal and sparing in ordering the use of her wealth on her own private pleasures, but for every public use, whether it is for the common good or for the public splendor of her domestic magnificence, she is generous and regal.

In another letter I have described to you the glories which she derives from herself, and the ornaments of her talent and learning. Here let me add this: neither at court, nor in the universities, nor among our leaders in church and state are there four Englishmen who understand Greek better than the Queen herself. When she reads Demosthenes or Aeschines, she often amazes me as I see how well she understands not only the force of the words, the structure of the sentence, the propriety of the language, the figures of speech, and the rhythmical and well-turned expression of the whole discourse, but also those matters which are of greater importance: the feeling and tone of the speaker, the focus of the argument, the ordinances and the interests of the people, the customs and mores of their city, and everything else in this vein. All the natives of England and many foreigners can testify to how well she knows other languages.

I was present one day when she replied at one time to three ambassadors, the Imperial, the French, and the Swedish, in three languages, one in Italian, another in French, and the third in Latin, speaking fluently without hesitation and readily without confusion about various matters as they cropped up in their conversation. So that you may see for yourself how elegantly she writes, I am enclosing in this letter a piece of paper on which the word *quemadmodum* is written in the Queen's own hand. The upper one is mine, the lower one is hers. Tell me in your next letter whether it was a happy sight and a welcome gift.

This much, then, about our most noble Queen, my most munificent mistress, very fond as well of Johann Sturm. And if you should ever come to England, you will hear from her own mouth, I think, that even in the presence of such a great monarch Roger Ascham was a friend who remembered Johann Sturm. I think you will read this account of our most excellent Queen, just as I certainly write it, with the greatest pleasure to us both.

If she should marry, she would not leave any place for more ample praise. Would that you, my Sturm, would bring to bear all that you have drawn from the best fountains of learning and eloquence, whether it is *reasoning* from Demosthenes or eloquence from Cicero, to persuade her in this matter. You cannot undertake a more honorable cause than that one, nor can I want anyone with more ability than you. We want her to choose whom she will; we do not want others to designate someone for her. We all expect a native rather than a foreigner. I do not want you to be ignorant of these things, if perhaps you want to write something sometime about this matter. For if she should add this one gift to all those mentioned above which she has already bestowed on this kingdom, no people could be happier than us.

And so much for her; I will write about our other affairs some other time. Now, my Sturm, I come to you. I rejoiced when I learned from your letter last year to John Hales that your book on *Aristotle's Rhetoric* had been completed. And I was thrilled when you added, "All of you are mentioned in the book, even Morison and Cheke." When I learned in conversation with our Toxites that the Werter brothers had taken all those books with them into Thuringia, I was not at all happy. They ought to take care lest they become more notorious for this misdeed than they are noted for their birth and learning. They do injury to you, to the pursuit of learning itself, and to the anxious expectation of many good men, and if I weren't writing about myself, I should say to me first of all. Although I was not the originator, I did at least encourage you to undertake those renowned labors, worthy of light and immortality, and most unworthy of shadows and some dirty little box. If those outstanding fruits of your talent should decay and perish because of the baseness and avarice of those young men, I myself shall certainly try. . . . But I shall restrain myself and not say anything too severe against them before I learn what you think about what they have done. And so if you love me, my Sturm, while I am still alive (for, as I wrote, my hectic fever threatens *an early death*), do not allow me to be defrauded of the very sweet fruits of those books. I had the first and the second book, but the first, which I lent to Walter Haddon, Master of the Court of Requests,[8] was lost through the carelessness of his servants. I have often enjoyed perusing these books; I have been expecting all the rest at recent fairs. Bring it about, I pray you, that our expectations, which

---

[8]Here I emend Giles' *librorum* and follow the obviously correct reading of the Parker Society edition, *libellorum*.

are linked to so much glory for yourself and so much value for all students, will not be disappointed for long.

I am very glad that you have written on behalf of Philip [Melanchthon] against Staphylus the sycophant, as you say in your letter to John Hales.[9] I gather from Staphylus' writings that he is not only a market-place Gnatho, but even a kind of Thraso, albeit an honorable one.[10] His folly and insolent arrogance are obvious enough from the subscription of his dedicatory letter to the Bishop of Eichstätt, where he says, "Friedrich Staphylus, counsel to his Majesty the Emperor, to your lordship . . . ," information which the people are no doubt anxious to know. I do not think that this is the printer's fault, but the brash impudence of Staphylus himself, for he writes the same thing about himself in the little book *Apologia against Philip*. His book for the Bishop of Eichstätt was written last year in German, translated into Latin, I believe, by a Carmelite friar, and printed at Cologne;[11] it's totally virulent and *diabolical*. I pray you, not by Sicilian muses, but by sacred learning itself, to allow your book against Staphylus to be published at the first opportunity.

I was flooded with a wonderful joy when I read in your published letter to our Cooke that you had written *On the Controversy over*

[9]Friedrich Staphylus, who as a young man was educated and sponsored by Luther and Melanchthon themselves, reverted to Catholicism and wrote a number of attacks on Protestant leaders, including *Defensio adversus P. Melanthonem* (editions of both 1559 and 1560) and a book written in German and dedicated to the Bishop of Eichstätt, *Christlicher gegen Bericht an der Gottseligen gemainen Layen . . .* (1561), both of which are mentioned below. As the last sentence in this paragraph suggests, Ascham assumes that Sturm's defense of Melanchthon occurs in some volume yet to be published. It is more likely the case that in his comments to Hales Sturm had in mind the Bucer volume mentioned in the next paragraph, and that Ascham's assumptions are wrong; in any case Sturm did not publish a book against Staphylus.

[10]Ascham's scorn, couched in terms of stock characters in Terence's plays, arises from Staphylus' reversion to the church of Rome.

[11]The German work was indeed translated into Latin and published at Cologne in 1562 (*Apologia D. F. Staphyli . . .*), but by a Carthusian, a certain "F.L. Surius." In 1565 it would also appear in English, translated by the recusant Thomas Stapleton and published in Antwerp.

the Lord's Supper,[12] a book minimally choleric, as you yourself say, but, as you hope, provocative.   I shall readily put my trust in you, my Sturm, for I know that your nature tends wholly toward quietness and peace, not toward irascibility and contention.   I also know your learning, by which you are wont to prove what you undertake and to overcome where you compete and where you judge your powers are to be exercised lawfully.   I have not felt a greater joy for many years than when our Toxites told me that you are extraordinarily devoted to the study of sacred learning.

The cause of religion has lost a great deal indeed through the deaths of Philip and of Martin Bucer.[13]   But it will certainly gain back more through Johann Sturm's entrance into the battle.   I pray to God the Father and to our Lord and Master Jesus Christ that you are summoned by his Spirit from the thickets of Parnassus and Helicon, and that you give yourself completely to that Spirit as it leads you to the most delightful pastures of Mount Zion, the fertile mountain.

And although I myself would gladly concede to you both a lodging place in Rome and an inn in Athens, so that at any time you might stop over up at either city you choose for reasons of pleasure and for the sake of reestablishing old friendships and relationships, I do desire, however, that the permanent residence and tabernacle not only of your life, but of all your studies, shall be eternally located in Jerusalem itself, the great city of God.   And I believe that you can point out that there are many brighter lights and bigger flashes of oratorical lightning in our own David, Isaiah, John, and Paul, than ever shone from all the Pindars, Platos, Demosthenes, and Ciceros.   I pray God, if it is right to make such a request, to grant me the use of this life so that sometime I may see the stings of your pen, either offered of your own accord or driven out of you by some kind of blow, against the drones of the popes who occupy the more secret cells and almost all the better nests in the very temple of God.

I fear, my Sturm, that I shall offend you more in this my present prolixity than in all my recent *continual silence and reticence,* although if

[12]Sturm edited a collection of Bucer's writings on the Lord's Supper in a volume entitled *Nova vetera quatuor eucharistica scripta* (Strasbourg, 1561), with a preface, apparently separately printed, to Sir Anthony Cooke.

[13]Melanchthon died on April 19, 1560, Bucer on March 1, 1551.

you want to divide this loquacity into various letters, it cannot be said but that I have written many letters to you just now. But you will, I hope, pardon my prolixity, which if it give rise to any offense, I pray you to avenge with a letter even more prolix.

I ask you, my Sturm, what do you think of Dionysius of Halicarnassus? I believe that he is the very Dionysius who taught in the home of Cicero and whom Cicero mentions frequently in his letters. Cicero praised his learning very highly, but did not feel the same way about his moral character. When you leave that one city and that one age of Philip and Alexander, I do not see any Greek (and I do not except Plutarch himself) with whom you can compare this Dionysius of Halicarnassus. I want to know whether you think there is something to my opinion, or whether it is entirely worthless. His little book to Tubero on his judgment of Thucydides' history gives me extraordinary pleasure.

My wife, because she knows that I love you, herself loves your wife, and sends as *a token* of her good will a gold ring in the form of an arrow, with the inscription, "Gift of a Faithful Friend." Toxites has the ring.

You will pardon my letter; our Toxites was in such a hurry that there was no time to copy it. Farewell in Jesus Christ. From my lodging in London, April 11, 1562. Your very devoted R. Ascham.

50 / To Johann Sturm   (Giles II.xxxviii)
London, October 20, 1562

Like the preceding letter this one appears, with an English translation, in *The Zurich Letters*, Second Series, ed. Hastings Robinson for The Parker Society. Robinson supplies a transcription of the holograph found in the Strasbourg Library, a manuscript which has since been lost in the fire of 1870. In this instance Giles again supplies a composite text of the Robinson transcription and the sixteenth-century text (see my introduction to Letter 49). Here too the divergences are only minor verbal and typographical ones, with two modest exceptions: the second and third sentences in the paragraph about a history of the Guise conspiracy are absent in the early editions, and the Robinson transcription gives a date of October 21 for the letter (rather than October 20, the date in the early editions). For the sake of consistency Giles is again followed here.

Without pursuing very far the question of the nature and the significance of these textual similarities and divergences, we might at least note that they suggest rather clearly that the copies Ascham kept of his letters--copies on which the early editions were based--were actually very good drafts, from which he made his final, fair copy.

Since we are united to each other by our shared interests, judgment, spirit, and feeling for learning, religion, the state, and a mutual friendship, I often desire and even deeply wish that those who belong to us may be held together in like manner by some distinctive bond, and by some incentive for nurturing the same love we have for each other. And therefore when my wife eight days ago made me a father for the third time, I named my little son Sturm Ascham in perpetual memory of our friendship. I pray to God, and shall continue to pray every day, that just as he bears some resemblance to you in name, he may also resemble you in learning and virtue.

Therefore I entrust him to you as your own, linked to you not by consanguinity nor by family, but by his very name and the wishes of his parents. In whatever ways it can be done, I commend him to your faithfulness and to your tutelage, so that if I should die, you will enfold him with that same kindness, benevolence, *and affection* which you were always accustomed in days gone by to bestow upon me, his father.[1] *About my early death* I wrote you last April that rather long letter sent via our Toxites, a letter copiously flowing with tears enough, and too much grief. I am very anxious to know whether that letter reached you.

I have also written to you through Henry Knolles,[2] our most serene Queen's envoy at this time to the German princes. He is very fond of you, and from him you will very conveniently learn the whole

---

[1]Ironically, it was not Ascham who went to an early grave, but his son Sturm, who died before his fifth birthday (see Letter 60). In a further irony, when Johann Sturm at last communicated his willingness to serve as the boy's godfather, he promised to send a portrait of himself "so that if I die before he sees me, he may still see something of me after I am gone" (letter of November 13, 1563 [II, 94]).

[2]Henry Knolles (Knollys), brother of the better-known courtier Sir Francis Knollys, served in several minor diplomatic roles during the reigns of Edward, Mary, and Elizabeth, including this effort to solicit Protestant aid for the Prince of Condé against the forces of the Duke of Guise.

state of affairs in England. Her most serene Majesty is both fully determined and most amply prepared in all respects to crush the power and the tyranny of the Guise and to take arms for the safety of a youthful king[3] and for the protection of an innocent people, without threatening any injury to that king or harm to that kingdom in any way. On this very day, I believe, our soldiers have invaded Normandy, which you will learn from rumor before this letter reaches you.

I wish, my Sturm, that you would write a separate history of this Guisian conspiracy. I am not unaware, as that friend of ours says in a similar case, that you are weighed down each day by the burdens of the weighty affairs you have undertaken. But I certainly am no less desirous of your glory than of my own advantage. The subject is an excellent one, worthy of your learning, abilities, zeal for pure religion, love for that people, affection for that cause itself, as well as your indignation against those authors of such impious tyranny and such beastly cruelty. I have very often read, and I shall always remember, that fine passage in a certain letter of yours to Erasmus, your Bishop of Strasbourg,[4] where you discuss the right way to write history. When I consider once more the ability which that passage proves you have, somehow I easily despise the other writers, and I implore our great and good God with prayers and petitions that sometime you take up such a task. This longing of mine has been eased a good deal by a report carried here from Germany that the princes there have given you the charge of completing with your pen the *omissions* of your John Sleidan.[5] I have strongly maintained to the Queen that this is the case. Please inform me whether it is so.

---

[3]The boy King Charles IX acceded to the throne of France upon the death of his brother Francis II in December 1560. After the massacre of the Protestant congregation at Vassy on March 1, 1562, war intensified between the Huguenots and the Catholic forces of the Duke of Guise, with important implications for all of Europe, including Scotland and England, since Mary Queen of Scots was the Guise's niece.

[4]In 1541 Sturm prefaced the first volume of his *Epistles of Cicero* with a letter to Erasmus of Limburg, once Sturm's student, later Bishop of Strasbourg.

[5]John Sleidan, the official historian of the Protestant league against Emperor Charles V, died in 1556, having completed 26 books of his *De statu religionis et respublicae Carolo Quinto Caesare commentarii* (see Letter 42, note 3). The rumor notwithstanding, Sturm did not continue Sleidan's project.

I am eager to know about your *Aristotelian Rhetoric* and about your books, both the one against Staphylus, and the one about the Lord's Supper.[6] I also want to know about the rest of your studies and activities.   Our Hales has gone to his country home; today I wrote him.   Cooke is also in the country.   Cecil, by his effort, talent, prudence, and constancy, nobly sustains the first verse of Horace's second book of epistles,[7] with great credit to himself, our nation's profit, and the welfare, I hope, of other nations.

As for myself, I have never, thank God, been in greater favor with our most serene Queen.   Every day she reads something with me in Greek or Latin.

My wife greets you and yours.   Farewell in Christ.   London, October 20, 1562.

[6]See Letter 49.

[7]"Since you alone carry the weight of so many great charges . . ." (*Epist.* 2.1.1).   Horace is addressing Augustus.

PART SIX: 1553-1568

"I shape myself to be a courtier"

In late 1552, as Ascham anticipated the conclusion of Morison's embassy to the court of Charles V, he began once more to "follow the manner of wayfaring men" (I, 342), pressing his suit in correspondence with Cecil, Cheke, Gardiner, and others. For a period of nearly two years Ascham's letters, many of them again written in English, are full of indecision, importunity, and uncertainty about his course of life. He would love, he poignantly confides to Cecil, to "creep home to Cambridge" (I, 343), but "the goodly crop of Mr. Cheke is almost clean carried from thence, and I in a manner alone of that time left a standing straggler[;] peradventure though my fruit be small, yet because the ground from whence it sprung was so good, I may yet be thought somewhat fit for seed, when all you the rest are taken up for better store" (I, 351). As a good Tudor humanist, he assures Cecil that he stands ready to "serve my prince and my country" (I, 355), but the "excellent wisdom" of Anthony Denny's warning haunts his mind: "The Court, Mr. Ascham, is a place so slippery, that duty never so well done, is not a staff stiff enough to stand by always very surely" (I, 350).

In the end, however, Ascham was realistic enough about the avenues of preferment to "shape [himself] to be a courtier" (I, 396). Each succeeding letter seems to bring with it new protestations of loyalty and humble readiness "to apply myself wholly to your will and purpose" (I, 349-50), and collectively these epistolary cultivations first of Cecil, later (after Mary's accession) of Gardiner, supply some of the best evidence available anywhere concerning the ways in which mid-Tudor humanism reflected, and essentially depended upon, court patronage and sponsorship.

Sometime in 1552, through the combined efforts of Cheke and Cecil, Ascham succeeded in securing an appointment as Latin secretary to Edward VI, but an unexplained "sudden frowning of fortune" (I, 342) put a stop to the matter late in the year. Ironically, however, Edward's death on July 6, 1553, and the accession of Queen Mary, with all the tempests attendant upon her determination to reverse the course of religion in England, did not undo him. Years of dependency and of experience in the wayfaring life made it easier for him to pledge himself to those in authority, and it is only mildly surprising, therefore, to find Ascham in the new circumstances again returning to his old conservative Catholic patron, Stephen Gardiner, Mary's Lord Chancellor. Only in the context of the client-patron relationship can one comprehend that remarkable moment within the letters assembled here when within the space of a few months Ascham uses identical language to profess fealty to Edward's most talented Protestant minister and Mary's most capable Catholic servant (see Letters 51B and 53). Thus to Cecil Ascham could write, "Most glad I am that it pleaseth you I may be yours; and as sure I am I shall cease to be mine own, when I shall leave to labor to be otherwise" (I, 328). And to the new Catholic Chancellor Ascham made virtually the same profession, dissembling his Protestantism in a desperate bid for confirmation of an appointment to the same post under Mary: "I offer myself, with will, word, and work, with heart and hand, always to wait upon your lordship's state and honour. . . . I owe . . . mine all and me whole only to your lordship" (I, 406-7). There were those, he wrote to Sturm, who "tried to impede the course of [Gardiner's] good will for me on account of my religion, but they have gotten nowhere" (Letter 48). In May 1554 he at last received his letter patent.

Neither was Ascham to become the victim of any other court tempest when Elizabeth succeeded her sister on November 17, 1558. His estrangement from his royal lady had long been resolved, and he continued, seemingly unaffected by the storms of religion, to serve the new monarch, as he had the former, in his post as Latin secretary until his death in December 1568.

The first editor of Ascham's correspondence sought to create the impression of an indefatigable secretary; during the three days following Philip and Mary's marriage, according to Grant's memorable account, Ascham wrote 47 letters to various potentates and princes, "of whom the lowest in rank were cardinals" (III, 332). The feat seems less impressive, however, when we consider that many of these letters were formulaic, and were worked out by Ascham's assistants.[1]   No doubt his chief delight as secretary were not these official obligations, but the privileged moments when he and Queen Elizabeth read Greek or Latin together; such a moment is invoked at the outset of *The Schoolmaster*, for example: "After dinner, I went up to read with the queen's Majesty.   We read then together in the Greek tongue, as I well remember, that noble oration of Demosthenes against Aeschines" (III, 81).   Even Ascham's friends commented on his neglect of his correspondence during these years (see Ryan 242), and aside from occasional letters to Sturm, most of the letters which survive from the Marian and Elizabethan periods were official letters, or ones written for a fee on behalf of others.   They deal mainly with the routine business of state: the conduct of foreign merchants, appeals for redress for lost ships, introductions soliciting courtesies for a traveller, etc.   None is of sufficient interest to be included here.

---

[1]The role of assistants may be inferred from scattered notations and from the handwriting in the registers and letterbooks preserved in the following manuscripts: British Museum Additional MS. 35840 (the letter file 1554-1558), BM Lansdowne MS. 98 (part of the Burghley papers, not in Ascham's hand), and BM Royal MS. 13. B. I (the register from 1558 to 1568, some in Ascham's hand, some probably made by scribes). It should also be noted that a good number of these letters do not appear in Giles' edition.

51A / To Sir William Cecil (Giles I.cxlix)

Brussels, July 7, 1553

Almost as soon as Emperor Charles V began to retreat before the advance of the German Protestant princes allied against him, Ascham began his own campaign to find new avenues of preferment. This letter is the fifth in a fascinating series of appeals for the support of Principal Secretary Sir William Cecil, who over the course of Ascham's life would prove his most reliable patron. (The first four letters within this series were written in English and therefore do not appear here, though they are included in Giles: I.cxxxix, cxl, cxliii, cxlv.)

The first of these expressions of loyalty was written in July 1552, nearly a year before this one. By November of that year Ascham was writing to thank Cecil for "obtaining the suit made for me to the king's majesty" (I, 341), that is, an appointment as Latin Secretary to King Edward. But while he was writing, he says, Weston the courier "bringeth me word what stop is in the matter" (I, 342), and for unexplained reasons the patent was after all not issued. In the present letter Ascham continues to allude with gratitude to the office Cecil had secured for him months earlier, but clearly the "stop" has not been removed, and Ascham the client here continues to cultivate his patron.

This letter has heretofore been considered to be one letter within a curious pair of letters (here Letters 51A and 51B) which have essentially the same opening and closing, but which differ in the middle. In the first, dated July 7, 1553, Ascham offers Cecil two coins as tokens of his loyalty and affection, pausing as he does so to recount his conversation with a fellow coin collector. In the second, dated two days later, a more formal, elaborated affirmation of loyalty and affection replaces all mention of these coins.

Closer analysis of these "two letters," however, suggests that in fact they are simply two states of the same letter, one representing a good draft which Ascham retained (51A), and the other the final, fair copy, that is, the letter actually sent (51B). More specifically, version A appears in the sixteenth-century editions, and was therefore based on Ascham's own papers supplied to the editor (see my general Introduction, as well as the introduction to Letters 49 and 50), while version B represents the letter in its final form, for it is transcribed from Ascham's autograph preserved in British Museum Lansdowne MS. 3, a collection of Cecil's original manuscripts from 1552-1559. Clearly Ascham changed his mind about sending the coins, and when he penned the fair copy two days after completing his draft, he substantially reworked it. There are several possible explanations for his having done so: perhaps in the interval he learned more about King Edward's illness, for only the second version alludes to it; perhaps he decided to try a different strategy of clientage and to save the coins for another occasion; perhaps the draft did not meet his rhetorical standards.

With great pleasure, most accomplished sir, I learned from your letter to Mr. Morison[1] how much favor you have shown me; by your kindness you have obligated me to you forever. My hope is very much set on that which you offer, and the outcome which I await will be very agreeable, but by far the most pleasant is your good will, which is so generous in affording the best for me that it outruns all my ability to offer thanks. Therefore, since I can scarcely return any thanks to you, and since those things which I have for you are very scanty, I shall betake myself, outstripped in wealth and destitute of eloquence, to the only remaining way I have of compensating you. I shall follow you with my good will, devotion, and unending observance; as a declaration thereof I am sending you two bright hostages, two famous Caesars, the one a bronze god, the other a golden devil. Fearing neither, I have enclosed both in this letter, so that they may present themselves to you in person.

The gold piece will please you less, for what has the worst of princes to do with the best of men? But since the metal is very pure, and the workmanship very skillful, perhaps you will enjoy looking at the tyranny and enormity which still appear in that countenance and in the very jaws, as Suetonius so cleverly describes them.[2]

The bronze coin is very remarkable, so much so that I have nothing within my humble means more precious to offer to so great a man, so much my patron. Last month I visited Don Diego de Mendoza,[3] a man very devoted to learning and very knowledgeable about all of antiquity. He showed me a great number of coins, gave me some, and inquired whether I had others. I pulled out this bronze one,

---

[1]Cecil's letter is unknown; cf. Ambassador Morison's letter to Cecil of October 7, 1552, as reported in *Calendar of State Papers, Foreign Series, Edward VI* 223: "Cecil has given life to dead spirits that lay in Mr. Ascham. They begin to shine, and will be able to wax hotly, if Weston [the courier] might bring his patent sealed." Morison also alludes to Cecil's good offices in letters of November 28, 1552 (*CSP* 230-31) and of February 20, 1553 (*CSP* 248).

[2]In *Lives of the Twelve Caesars*; Ascham's coin is apparently from Nero's reign.

[3]Don Diego, of the noble Hurtado family in Spain, was a noted diplomat and humanist, active at the court of the Emperor, envoy to the Council of Trent, ambassador to Venice, among many other accomplishments. The picaresque *Lazarillo de Tormes* is often ascribed to him.

which I had with me.   Having examined it, he turned to me.   "Do you know what coin this is?" he asked.

"Augustus Caesar," I replied.

"Right," he answered.   "But never in history has a coin more remarkable than this come into our hands.   You read in Titus Livy[4] that the temple of Janus was closed twice when world peace was established, first in the reign of Numa, later during the time of Augustus, in the year Christ chose to be born.   The Senate and the Roman people, ignorant of God's providence, attributed this universal peace to Augustus' providence, and honored him as god and father, striking this coin which shows the temple of Janus closed and which bears the word *providentia*."

He asked me where I had found it.   I told him in a small town on the Rhine.   "That's reasonable," he replied, "for a little later Drusus and Tiberius destroyed all that area in war."

I offered him the piece as a gift, since I saw he was so taken with it, but he preferred not to accept it, adding that it was worthy of being offered to his Majesty when I returned to England.

But I am going on too long about such an unimportant matter, especially to such a man as you.   I am remembering your kindness, but I have imprudently forgotten your authority and the tasks which pull you away.   You will receive with this letter a map of Mirandula showing most of Lombardy and the very long winding course of the Po River.   I think you already have one,[5] but why not put these maps up in two different locations?   If I had not experienced your kindness and singular good will for me, I should never have dared to send you such trifling gifts or such an empty letter.   Farewell, most accomplished sir.   Brussels, July 7, 1553.

[4]See his history of Rome, 1.19.

[5]In September 1552 Ascham had sent Cecil much the same map (see I, 330), not to mention another full map of Europe in November 1552 (see I, 344).

51B / To Sir William Cecil   (Giles, "additional letter," I, 457-58)
Brussels, July 9, 1553

See Letter 51A above.

From the letter which you sent to Mr. Morison, most accomplished sir,
I learned with great pleasure how much favor you have shown me; by
your kindness you have obligated me to you forever. My hope is
very much set on that which you offer, and the outcome which I
await will be very agreeable, but by far the most pleasant is the good
will you have now pledged, which is so generous and which flies so
much like a bird sent out to afford the best for me that it outruns not
only my hope of being equal to it through any service of my own, but
also all my ability to offer you sufficient thanks. Therefore, since I
can scarcely return any thanks to you, and since those things which I
now have for you are very scanty, I shall betake myself, outstripped
in wealth and destitute of eloquence, to the only remaining way I
have of compensating you. I shall follow you with my good will,
devotion, and unending observance.

It is not currently the fashion, most accomplished sir, nor is it
the custom of men in your position thus to stoop to familiarity with
men in my rank. Nay, it belongs not to humanity, but to some divine
nature to be so ready, to be so determined to benefit all men, even
those whose service is not able to earn in advance or compensate later
for your so extraordinary kindness. This is the point I was making at
the outset when I said that I certainly have a firm hope of being offered something, and also await an agreeable outcome, but your good
will is by far the most pleasant. In my opinion, none of the assistance
rendered to me apart from this outcome can equal the kind of good
will lodged within you.

However, to speak frankly, I rejoice not so much in your good
will toward me as in your renowned good disposition, nay, I rejoice
not so much in your good disposition as in the happiness of all England, whose general, literary, and Christian welfare you daily labor to
assist, promote, and enlarge by your wise counsel, excellent learning,
and ardent devotion.

But while I am eager to congratulate my country and show myself grateful to you from my heart, I am afraid lest I grow intemperate
and foolish. I certainly want to write you a letter of thanks, but in

these times and among such rumors I cannot write you a joyful one. Even when I am cheerful, my letter does not want to be cheerful, and when I lament, it too, as you see, is dressed in mourning. But I shall employ my mind and hand to write a letter more cheerful in tone and dress as soon as we shall receive a more cheerful message concerning the health of the one in whom the health of our time, our people, and our affairs is contained.[1]

I am sending you a map of Mirandula, showing most of Lombardy and the long winding course of the Po River. I think you already have one, but why not put them up in two different locations? But I am going on too long about such an unimportant matter, especially to such a man as you. I am remembering your kindness, but I am unwisely forgetting your authority and the tasks which pull you away. If I had not experienced your singular good will for me, I should never have dared to send you such trifling gifts or such an empty letter. Farewell, most accomplished sir. Brussels, July 9, 1553.

52 / To Sir John Cheke   (Giles I.cl)
Brussels, July 7, 1553

> The letter opens with Ascham's congratulations to Cheke, who in June 1553 was not only sworn to the Privy Council, but also named the third Principal Secretary. Later, as he turns to his own affairs, Ascham speaks about what is now usually called his *Report of Germany*. This informal eye-witness account of affairs in Germany from 1550 to 1553 was never finished, however, and it apparently was not published until 1570, some two years after Ascham's death.

I was very pleased with the messenger, most accomplished sir, who brought word that you have been chosen for the Privy Council. But since this honor was long owed to your learning, wisdom, and integrity, by the will, consensus, and vote of all men, I do not congratulate you alone. Indeed, I do not so much applaud you as I do those who in my judgment deserve credit for their wisdom in electing you, a

---

[1]Ascham alludes to the illness of Edward VI. Ironically, though Ascham had not yet heard, the King was in fact already dead, having died on July 6.

credit which is greater than your own share of happiness in rising to this position of honor. And so I congratulate all Britain. First and certainly foremost, I congratulate our good Prince, because his boyhood enjoyed you as his most excellent teacher, and now his youth, his mature manhood, and henceforth his old age will have you for many years as his wisest and most faithful councillor. We freely attribute your wisdom to your outstanding erudition, your faithfulness to your famous probity and esteemed prudence, and we assign both to the supreme happiness of our King and Kingdom. But whatever there is of the immortal we credit altogether to God's grace, through which he wished to make you a blessing to our Prince and the whole of England. For I rejoice very much in our political, literary, and Christian life, three areas which always stood so much in your care that now everyone's domestic tranquillity, the leisure desired for learning, and the peaceful calm of pure religion will henceforth rest very much upon your special authority, your excellent learning, and your burning zeal for God. Certainly I heartily congratulate Cambridge, which bore you, and principally the College of St. John, which taught you. The one had you as its best alumnus, the other as its most flourishing pupil, and both now see you as their best and most powerful patron. Then finally in the last place, I congratulate myself, unless there seems to be too much self-love in it. Even then, I congratulate myself, and do so eagerly, for this reason: some other time I may prefer to have some of my work and my respect reveal my very heart, but now I wish my words to be the indication of my devotion and good will.

This congratulating, making both native Englishmen and foreigners around here joyful and eager to vie with you for honor, increases my own joy. So do my conversations with Thomas Hoby,[1] with whom I very frequently discuss your probity and his singular respect for you. This young man shows very clearly in whose literary work-

---

[1] Young Thomas Hoby, 1530-1566, had been a student in St. John's College, Cambridge, and would become known for his translation for Castiglione's *Book of the Courtier*. In *The Schoolmaster* Ascham terms him "a worthy gentleman who was many ways well furnished with learning, and very expert in knowledge of divers tongues" (III, 141). His older half-brother, Sir Philip Hoby, 1505-1558, was a noted soldier, diplomat, and courtier during the reigns of Henry VIII and Edward VI. In particular, Sir Philip served as the English ambassador to Charles V before and after Morison's term of service; in July, as Ascham writes, he and Morison were serving jointly at the Emperor's court.

shop he has served his apprenticeship. His brother, Sir Philip, a man of great experience, employs him and only him in all matters to be dealt with in the court of the Emperor. In this capacity he conducts himself so well, so diligently, thoughtfully, and quietly that the seeds which you sowed in him as a lad at Cambridge are not only sprouting now with some promise, but are already flowering and maturing remarkably in him as a young man. He is so promising that in my judgment you would do well if you were to let him know that you are not only watching him with pleasure in his course, but also that you are encouraging him with some applause as he runs so well, for no stimulus to virtue is more apt than a joyous, hearty commendation coming from a distinguished man. Therefore bind this young man of yours wholly to yourself, or at least arouse him to greater aspirations by greeting him in your letters to others.

Sometimes my heart is heavy because I have written many letters to you, but cannot know whether they have reached you. In truth, you can think little of the old, the obscure, the worn out, and the silent ones, those *past their prime*; however, you ought not ignore those more remarkable youths born into the light, growing into excellence, and surging to a bright fortune--although certainly you do not ignore me, whom you remember so well and with such love in your letter to Mr. Morison.[2] I send you letters less often now because I fear to write about worthless or trivial matters, especially to so great a man. I am afraid, in addition, that my letters may be excessive or untimely, since I do not in any way wish to seem either troublesome or foolish.

Last month I did write to you, however, by Mr. Chamberlain's servant.[3] I am glad if my letter has reached you on account of two old coins which I enclosed within the letter, one of C. Caesar, the other of P. Clodius. Your last letter[4] was delivered to me at Augsburg last year. It was certainly very welcome, but it was not as delightful as your others usually are. I considered it very friendly, but at that time I thought it was certainly somewhat sharp, and it stung for a while. I believe this happened because I read nothing from you of

[2]Not extant.

[3]Sir Thomas Chamberlain was the English representative in Brussels at the court of Mary, Regent of Flanders.

[4]Not extant.

which I do not ponder every single word, and I weigh every single sentence in order to ferret out your innermost thought. The more I make of what you say, the more anxious I always am about what you think of me in everything. But the scruple which a foolish fear had raised, a better judgment has cast out, and I have not wanted to make the mistake of in any way giving more weight to my own lightly considered opinion than to your very well-known generosity. And you will forgive this fear in me, your very loving friend, and be liberal in your kindness, which permits me to utter freely even the foolish things I think.

If you want to know what I am doing here, I will tell you that I am now writing about the real reasons why Parma, Salerno, Brandenburg, and Saxony have deserted the Emperor. I am also compiling a narrative of each day's events as they occurred in the Emperor's court, from the flight out of Innsbruck to the failure of the siege at Metz, during which period there were great confusions of alliances, dissensions, plunderings, wars, various changes of fortune, and very serious disruptions, all these disasters compounded by *ingratitude*, treachery, perfidy, lust, avarice, ambition, tyranny, and *enmity toward God*, as liberty was driven out, the law violated, religion besmirched, and God himself scorned. Concerning these matters I aim for truth, and I am not looking for embellishment. I am writing in English, only for myself and my puzzled associates, so that together we may while away next winter's nights with pleasant conversations and recollections of these events. There was a time, most accomplished Cheke, when I could have given such material a tolerable polish in Latin, but the stream of pure diction which flowed to me from the fountains which you diverted so plentifully to me and very successfully to many others, has now wholly dried up, and my pen, which the whetstone of your excellent talent and learning once sharpened for me, is now altogether blunted, in the harsh and desperate state of my poor fortune in my poorer studies. But I had not meant to deplore my own fortune, but to rejoice in yours. I will have a better opportunity to do so at home in conversation with you face to face.

We hope that our return draws near with each passing day; more and more I wish you could speed that time. This fuss I am making is not over a foolish longing for home or a fickle distaste for foreign affairs, since I take great pleasure in the company of well-versed men and derive much profit from my experience in very important affairs, in addition to the enjoyment of a good conscience in faithfully and steadily discharging the task you gave me.

Johann Sturm recently wrote to me and asked if you might learn from my letters that he is your most devoted and loving friend.[5] But the more he loves me and the better he thinks of me, the more timidly and sparingly do I do what he asks. So I refer you to the judgment of those two fine men, Christopher Mont and John Hales, who credit Sturm with the greatest excellence in learning, and even more in kindness, wisdom, experience, counsel, judgment, and religion. He does not, I believe, seek any gain from your fortune, but hungers most for the sweetness of your good will, since he is very well fixed for money. But I should be terribly sorry if a Frenchman or a Pole should steal away from our good Prince the glory of Sturm's distinguished work *On the Analysis* of both languages.

I am enclosing a gold coin of Antonius Pius in this letter. Happy was that century on account of the purity of its gold and the quality of its workmanship, but happier far on account of its good ruler.[6] I am delighted by these ancient artifacts, not only because they give a reliable record of antiquity, but because they come closest to the nature of eternity itself; for coins alone, especially gold ones, cannot be ruined by long periods of time, although time consumes everything else.

Farewell, most accomplished sir, and love me as you are wont, because I shall never consider any kindness greater or more welcome to me than your good will. Brussels, July 7, 1553.

53 / To Bishop Stephen Gardiner (Giles I.clviii)
[Cambridge?], October 8, 1553

During the last year of King Edward's life Ascham had carefully cultivated Sir William Cecil (see introduction to Letters 51A and 51B), and in the new circumstances following the accession of Mary on July 19, 1553, Ascham quickly launched an equally vigorous new campaign with Lord Chancellor

[5]See Sturm's letter of May 9, 1553 (I, 358).

[6]Emperor Titus Antonius, surnamed Pius (died AD 161), was known for his benevolence and virtue.

Gardiner in particular, but also with the Queen's ministers William Paget and William Petre (see Letters 54 and 57). Ascham had been promised the position of Latin Secretary under Edward (see I, 399), and his efforts were clearly bent on obtaining the same post in the new reign, though in this letter, just as he had in his series of letters to Cecil, he offers to consider rendering further service abroad or returning to Cambridge, where he still officially retained academic offices and where he may have spent some time as he awaited a new appointment (there is a record of his presence in Cambridge on September 28, 1553: see Ryan 194-95).

This letter to the Queen's conservative Chancellor, who for years had been the powerful antagonist of Ascham's circle of Protestant Athenians, is the first surviving letter written after Ascham's return to England around the first of September, 1553, nearly three years after he had left. It is also the first of the letters we have from him in Mary's reign. There were others, perhaps many more; in this one Ascham himself mentions previous letters, now lost, written in English to Gardiner. Certainly a number of letters to Gardiner, again mostly in English, follow upon this one, and complete the account suggested here of Ascham's campaign for patronage: see Giles I.clix, clxiv, clxvii, clxx, clxxv, as well as Letter 55 below. In the end his campaign was successful: Gardiner played a crucial role in having his annuity for *Toxophilus* renewed and increased (I, 412; II, 154); the patent for the secretaryship was at last sealed on May 7, 1554, a seemingly interminable delay which severely strained Ascham's resources (see Ryan 196-99).

None of Ascham's letters has more to say about his famous ability to accommodate his strong support of Edwardian Protestantism to the new conservative, Catholic realities of Mary's reign, and to shift with such apparent ease from soliciting the patronage of his old Protestant friend from college days, William Cecil, to appealing to the Cambridge humanists' old adversary in religion and Greek studies, the Bishop of Winchester. One of the most striking features of this letter is that it incorporates whole passages from the letters written three months earlier to Sir William Cecil (Letters 51A and 51B) and to Sir John Cheke (Letter 52). With only slight changes (Ascham praises Cheke's "zeal for God," for example, but Gardiner's "zeal for the country") the same tributes, the same professions of loyalty, the same rhetoric, and the same arguments are used. As would-be client, therefore, Ascham does not simply shift with the times, but even says the very same thing to two fundamentally different patrons.

The death of our good Prince Edward was certainly a matter of life to him, and to me it is truly sorrowful and utterly calamitous for my prospects, good bishop. Thus while my mind has been afflicted with grief, and my fortune has been severely encumbered and impeded by cares and poverty and isolation, I was not happy, but completely mournful, as I offered you my recent letters written in English, not very elegant, but altogether sorrowful. But truly since you not only read with such gentleness those same letters, barbarous in language, rude in composition, troublesome and wordy, importune and insistent, but also showed them to other persons, I have not wanted to get involved in anything except arousing both head and hand to offer to your grace these new letters, speaking in a more joyful voice, clothed in neater garments, and composed in more pleasing manner. For I have understood from the speech of others and from your own countenance and voice how well you remember my requests, and how readily inclined toward me you are, so that you have bound me forever to yourself by your kindness. It is so far from my mind to wish to free myself from this bond that I shall forever labor with all effort, faith, obligation, and observance to entangle myself more tightly in those very fetters. And although my hope is very much set on that which you offer me, and the outcome which I await will be very agreeable, nevertheless your good will in committing yourself to protecting me is by far the most pleasant of all. Your good will is so generous and flies so much like a bird to afford the best for me that it outruns not only my hope of being equal to it through any service of my own, but all my ability to offer thanks. And since the thanks which I can return to you for your favor are very scanty, and even the greatest ones which I now possess are in my judgment not worthy enough, therefore I, outstripped in wealth and derelict and destitute of eloquence, shall surely follow you with grateful good will in turn, with ready service, and with unending observance, and thus betake myself to the only remaining way I have of compensating you.

It is not currently the fashion, most famous bishop, nor is it the custom of men in your position and of your dignity thus to stoop to familiarity with men of my rank. Nay, it belongs not to humanity, but to some divine nature to be so ready, to be so determined to benefit all men, even those whose service is not able to earn in advance or compensate later for your so extraordinary kindness. This is the point I was making earlier when I said that I certainly have a firm hope of being offered something, and also await an agreeable outcome, but your good will is by far the most pleasant of all. Certainly none of your kindness can be more pleasing to me than your good will.

However, to speak frankly, I rejoice not so much in your good will toward me as in your renowned good disposition toward kindness, nay, I rejoice not so much in your good disposition as in the happiness of all England, whose public life in Parliament and whose literary life in the University, both long unsettled in many ways and long afflicted with various miseries, you now try very hard to aid with your counsel and to promote by your erudition. Their welfare always stood so much in your care that now at last hope shines upon everyone's domestic tranquillity, the leisure desired for learning, and the peaceful calm of the entire state, which are going to rest very much upon your special authority, your excellent learning, and your burning zeal for the country.

And since our most prudent ruler has entrusted and commended the care of these important matters solely to your equity, learning, and direction, I myself rejoice not a little that these three requests of mine are of the sort that whether it be leisure to study at the University or the position as secretary at court or a job of traveling in foreign countries, I shall be appointed by your grace and favor, and that all the plans of my life must be completely devoted to these matters which your wisdom oversees and regulates.

For if it is your decision to grant me leisure at the University, which is my first choice, all that leisure, I say, will not lie languid and inert, but will stand guard, quietly and eagerly, so that language and learning, of which you are now the high priest, will be cultivated and will flourish somewhat to my own benefit, more to the profit of others, but most of all to your own glory.

But if I am sent abroad either to improve my learning or to serve my country, my goodness, how frequent and long will be the letters I write you, suited to each audience, appropriate to the subject matter, organized and structured according to time and place, with everything completely reliable, careful, and considered. I can also bring some experience to this task, for recently I have been involved in the attack of Maurice[1] and the French wars, during which there were great confusions of alliances, dissensions, plunderings, wars, various changes of fortune, and very serious disruptions. With my own eyes I saw to what extent *ingratitude*, treachery, perfidy, lust, ambition, and *enmity toward God* compounded and confounded these disasters. There was a time, most erudite bishop, when I could have given such

---

[1]Maurice of Saxony led the German Protestant princes in forcing Emperor Charles V to retreat into the Low Countries.

material a tolerable polish in Latin, but the stream of pure diction which I drew from the best fountains of both languages has now wholly dried up, and my pen, which a hope lodged in King Edward somewhat sharpened for me, is now altogether blunted, in my harsh-- and if it were not for you--nearly desperate poverty and isolation. But in truth, if the gentle wind of your grace and favor for me will breathe upon me, as I hope, I shall so awaken myself to new hopes, and so attune myself to your feeling and will that you will never regret having bestowed this blessing upon me.

My third request was that I should be appointed to write Latin letters for her Majesty, an office which King Edward graciously assigned to me. To this task I can bring not so much art or wit as loyalty and diligence, and no little experience of head and hand in a similar post.

If under the guidance of your wise governance, these three requests cannot merit commendation, at least they can escape reproach. Thus whether I make my living at the University, at the court, or abroad, I and all the plans of my life rest in your pleasure, favor, and influence. And I have decided to repeat these three petitions of mine in this letter not to show that you are unmindful of my business, but that I myself have not forgotten. This I want to entreat earnestly of your kindness, so that I may know whether you wish to establish me at the University, at court, or abroad, and meanwhile I may prepare myself for that station of life, for having assumed obligations too weighty for me, I fear that I cannot sustain them for long. The pension which Henry VIII generously bestowed upon me and which Edward VI kindly confirmed, I have no doubt that our most noble Queen will confirm as well. And so I have taken the trouble to have letters patent, as they are called, written, so that by your grace and influence they may be sealed according to custom by the hand and seal of the Queen's Majesty.

May our Lord Jesus Christ forever keep you the most equitable judge, the most liberal patron, and the most learned bishop of the republic of learning and of Christianity. October 8, 1553.

54 / To Sir William Paget   (Giles I.clxi)
London, November 14, 1553

The record of William Paget's favors to Ascham goes back to 1544, when like a *deus ex machina* he came to the rescue of the naive young scholar from Cambridge (see Letter 8); in the following year Paget was one of those who helped Ascham secure an annuity from Henry VIII as a reward for *Toxophilus* (see I, 398). Both of these kindnesses appear to be in Ascham's mind in this letter. During the later years of the reign of Henry VIII and during much of the reign of Edward VI Paget held positions of prominence and authority, but in April 1552 his fortunes took a sharp turn, as Northumberland ordered him imprisoned, stripped of his offices, degraded from the Order of the Garter, and assessed a heavy fine. Later in the year he was released from many of these penalties; the last of his fines was forgiven in April 1553. Ascham also alludes to both of these turns at the outset of this letter.

    The letter anticipates by about two weeks Queen Mary's official renewal of Ascham's annuity for *Toxophilus*. In fact, her patent did not simply renew the favor, but it actually doubled the amount specified by Henry VIII.[1] Although the patent is dated December 1, 1553, Ascham appears here to know that Paget has insured its issuance; he also seems to know that the amount will be doubled. Elsewhere Ascham credits Lord Chancellor Gardiner with this happy doubling of the amount, which was also accomplished through Ascham's own "pretty subtlety" (see II, 154 and I, 412), but this letter indicates that Paget also had a role, just as he had in the issuance of the first patent under Henry.

    Ascham offers Paget a volume *De gloria* (Florence, 1552) by Jeronimo Osorio da Fonseca, a renowned Portuguese bishop and Ciceronian prose stylist. In *The Schoolmaster* (III, 185, 204-05) Ascham would be critical of his stylistic excesses, in part because Osorio also tangled with Ascham's fellow Cantabrigian Walter Haddon in a protracted quarrel over the Protestant religion under Queen Elizabeth: see Lawrence Ryan, "The Haddon-Osorio Controversy (1563-1583)," *Church History* 22 (1953) 142-54. At this point, however, Ascham is actively championing Osorio's work. Besides this gift to Paget, he will offer a copy of *De nobilitate* (Florence, 1552) to Sir William Petre (see Letter 57); in April 1555 he will also offer the latter book to Cardinal Pole (see Letter 58). In later years Osorio and Ascham also exchanged letters (II.xxix and xxxi; another is not printed by Giles: see Ryan 325).

---

[1]See Ryan 197, and *Calendar of Patent Rolls, Philip and Mary, 1553-1554* (London, 1937) I, 278.

An amazing necessity of keeping my silence was imposed upon me in both your fortunes, most honorable lord, since during your spoliation I could not show my sorrow without offense, nor could I congratulate you during your recuperation without suspicion of flattery. At last my desire to congratulate you did win out, and I wrote a letter to you from Brussels. I had composed it in anticipation of my old office and in the rush of my new joy, but out of a sense of shame I kept it and suppressed it, lest I seem to you to pursue not the business of the job, but a display of my learning, not your good will, but my own profit, not the proper sense of timeliness, but the emotion of the moment. But since in recent days you have determined not only to preserve and continue your former favors bestowed upon me, but even to increase and double them through your efforts, and have done so in such a way as to make your good will much more welcome because of your kindness than any favor of yours would be because of some profit within it, I did not want to act in such a way that I could be considered powerless to compensate you or averse even to showing an interest or a gesture of thanks.

Therefore I want right now to be most grateful to you, and want to be so forever. But since I can not return any thanks to you at all, or at any rate terribly meager ones, and since now the greatest thanks I have for you are unworthy and unequal to your favors, I have assigned this part of the task to my dear Sturm and Nannius,[2] who, I hope, will show themselves no less happy and grateful to you as my fortunes are firmed up and established than they previously were concerned about me--and perhaps troublesome to you--when my prospects were dubious and entangled. Indeed, I must write to these men. But now I shall write gladly, not because of a duty I owe to them, but because of the subject given to me through you. To be sure, I owe them both much; indeed, I shall make much of their devotion and their judgment in writing to you on my behalf, their devotion springing from their great love and their judgment from their great wisdom. But I shall write to them about you, not to you. I usually say openly that you were born under a certain fatal sign, you who alone have the desire and the habit of getting involved in my affairs; now, however,

---

[2]Both Sturm and the Belgian humanist Peter Nannius had recently written Paget in support of Ascham's appeals for support. See I.clv (Nannius' letter of August 18, 1553) and I.clvi and clvii (Sturm's letters of September 17, 1553).

since your efforts are united with the Lord Chancellor's in assisting me, I shall no longer keep your glories separate; through the wisdom, kindness, and guidance of both of you my human and material welfare and that of virtually everyone else is established.

At this time I want to offer you this little book *On Glory*, a gift very fitting for you. For if glory is nothing else than the uncorrupted voice of those who judge correctly and the combined praise of good men concerning someone's excellent virtue and outstanding probity, I am offering nothing else in this book than that which all men eagerly bestow upon you in their conversation and in their judgment.

But in a universal chorus of praise for your intellect, learning, experience, industry, counsel, wisdom, moderation, abstinence, and most courteous urbanity of manner, no virtue of yours sparkles more brightly than that which, since it belongs to human beings in particular, is called *humanitas*. This virtue takes its name from *homo*, but the attribute itself is certainly given by God, to whose goodness it seems especially to relate. And when I have seen you always naturally inclined to deal kindly with everyone, I have always considered this excellence of yours to belong not to humanity, but to a certain divine nature. Since therefore you have a natural willingness and the power of your office and the means of doing good even during these times, continue, most honorable sir, to do eternally what you always have done, that is, to help by your favor as many as you can and to deserve the best from everyone. And although in this course of glory you have no one other than you yourself with whom you ought to compete or whom you can surpass with more glory, hasten onwards to enhance this palm of praise, snatched away from others, by conquering even yourself.

But to what end do I say this? I did not wish to assume the role of one who urges, but to take the part of one who congratulates. I have decided to follow not the counsel of an adviser, but the office of a praiser, although this sweetest verse of the most pleasant of poets has always pleased me:

> He who exhorts you to do what you are already doing
> Praises you by his exhortations and by his advice
> shows his approval of your actions.[3]

[3]Ovid, *Tristia* 5.14.45-46.

Nevertheless, I would not have dared to write you in this manner if I were not promoting your honor and glory to the extent that I am in debt to your goodness.

But enough of this about you. About Osorio, the author of this book, I really think that no one after those happy times of M. T. Cicero has ever lived who has written anything with purer or more decorous diction or with greater eloquence than this man, who has here embellished and polished this topic of glory. For he is so prudent in his choice of words and so skilled in framing his sentences, so apt and modest in metaphor, so abundant and felicitous in antithesis, so proper and pure, so clear and perspicacious, everywhere urbane but not fastidious, always dignified without affection, so fluent without redundancy, so surging without roaring, so full without turgidity, so perfect in every mode that nothing can be added or taken away, at least in my opinion. I do not see why Italy in her Bembo and Sadoleto, France in her Longueil and Périon, or Germany in her Erasmus and Johann Sturm can boast more now than Portugal can in her special Osorio.

If as you read your judgment agrees with my opinion, I shall be very glad, for I think you will enjoy this book of Osorio, which contains and manifests monuments of his genius and learning no greater than the ornaments of your life and virtue, nor more credit to his eloquence than commendation of your wisdom. Farewell, most honorable lord, and love me as you do, and preserve me. London, November 14, 1553.

55 / To Bishop Stephen Gardiner   (Giles I.clxv)
London, January 1, 1554

This letter accompanies Ascham's New Year's gift to Queen Mary's Lord Chancellor, the Bishop of Winchester; it constitutes another venture within Ascham's sustained campaign to win the patronage of leading figures within Mary's court (see introduction to Letter 53). Ascham's gold coin of the empress Helena Augusta was a particularly apt and flattering present for a conservative Catholic bishop: this is the Helena who later became St. Helena, mother of Constantine the Great, and legendary discoverer of the true Cross. Modern scholars allow that she may have been born in Trier, and that Constantine resided there for some years, but Ascham here follows medieval legend and confusion in believing that she and Constantine were buried in Trier.

I write to you often indeed, most generous bishop, and always gladly, but this time I do so timidly and very anxiously, lest my letter seem troublesome if it bring some work to you, or lest in the midst of your extensive range of public responsibilities it seem unnecessary if it contains nothing. For at a time "when you alone carry the weight of so many great charges,"[1] if I should write about any little thing, I could easily seem excessive, and if about nothing, I could easily appear foolish. But since I have too often chosen to be unmannerly rather than to be considered much too ungracious, this time I have decided it is better to seem to have had no reason for busying you rather than to have completely ignored your great kindness toward me.

But at this time I do write somewhat more confidently than usual, because I have resolved not to increase the throng of things you attend to, but to refresh the sweet memory of your kindness toward me. In my last letter, written in English,[2] I tried to do this, but fearing that the billows of the storm of work by which you were almost swamped hour after hour had swallowed up my letter, I wish now to take up the same task, but this time sparingly and briefly, focussing not on the context, but on the thing itself, scanty though it is, and yet carefully considered and well-suited to what I seek.

In my last letter I very tightly bound myself, that is, my whole duty, devotion, loyalty, and observance, to your wish and will and command, just as though it were a legal obligation. In this letter I want to make some kind of down-payment, as it were, on my promise. I am speaking of this gold coin, which I offer to you with a grateful heart, to be sure, but also as a very auspicious token. Stamped on one side is the best woman in the memory of mankind, Helena Augusta; on the other side is the sweetest motto of the happiest of princes from the happiest of times: *Securitas Republicae.*[3] Oh woman worthy of a world empire, whose heart and soul were fixed

---

[1]Horace, *Epistles* 2.1.1.

[2]Probably Giles I.clxiv, which is undated.

[3]*Securitas*, security, when personified, was the tutelary goddess of the Roman state.

on nothing but the security of the state! This is the Helena who gained very great glory from her search for the Cross, a glory made even greater by her calming of the disasters which befell the Cross, disasters by which the name of Christian has been too often so cruelly and savagely attacked. Therefore, most learned Bishop, with a grateful heart and as an auspicious token take this coin not so much as a remarkable monument of those times, but as a tangible and visible comment on your efforts and on your devotion to and counsel for the state. I have enjoyed this memento for a long while because of its material, workmanship, person, age, *and its lifelikeness.* I have also treasured it because of the place where it was found and because of the friend who gave it to me. And now I delight in it and find it very appropriate because of you, the person to whom I give it. You will not spurn this gift, I think, just because it is small, but will rather embrace the judgment of that divine poet because of his humanity and approve it because of his learning who so often praises and recommends *small things but precious ones* as the general rule of benevolence.

Last year when I was at Trier, I happened to meet the most reverend Elector's secretary, who had been my very good friend and associate at the Emperor's court in Augsburg.[4] I asked him a great many questions about Trier, once a celebrated academy, now a ruined city, which I knew to be a noble city from the testimony of St. Jerome, who went there to study. I asked many questions also about Helena and Constantine the Great, who are buried in that city and of whose presence there are still traces. I understand that many monuments are honored and preserved there. After he had told me and shown me each of these things one by one, he suddenly pulled out this coin and give it to me; he wanted it to be a *remembrance* of that city, those rulers, and his own good will and affection for me. If I had had anything in hand which I cherish more, I would have given if to you, to whom I owe the greatest debt of gratitude.

When I saw that this coin portrayed a woman and a queen, one who not only brought the cross of Christ back to light but also restored the state to security, I had in mind to offer it to our most illustrious Queen Mary in a short letter, for in their respective countries

___

[4]Hubert Thomas Leodius, secretary to Elector Frederick II of Heidelberg, and an avid antiquary and historian (see Letter 38).

they occupy a similar rank in the kingdom, and they are equal in holiness of life and in their determination to establish justice. But I readily changed my mind, fearing that I would seem too imprudent and too forward, and have thought of you, for whom, I think, this coin is a very suitable gift, seeing our interests and our desire to work for the good of the state are the same. Thus as you admire another's glory in this little coin, you will also recognize your own, which you have achieved according to the judgment of all good men by virtue of your nature, learning, goodness, and kindness. But I had rather you enjoy it in the quiet contemplation of these matters rather than through my overt proclamation. I am going on too long to such an important man, especially in so insignificant a matter.

Sir William Petre says he will meet you shortly, I believe, in reference to my appointment to a court office. But since this matter is not at this time more mine than yours, by whose favor and influence I was summoned from the leisure of learning to the bustle of the court, I hope the same considerations will be given to your good will and to my advantage. That is, I hope your goodness will never cease from affording the best for me until the thing is done and my affairs are duly settled. In this hope I come more confidently to court, where, if my hand and heart can serve your needs, I shall be ready to devote myself and all my own to your wish, your will, and your command. The Lord Jesus preserve your highness forever. London, January 1, 1554.

56 / To Mary Clarke   (Giles I.clxvi)
           [London], January 15, 1554

> Ascham's offer to assist Lady Mary's pursuit of learning is remarkable because it again underlines the range of those whose patronage he actively seeks. As Margaret Roper's daughter and Thomas More's granddaughter, and a lady-in-waiting at the court of Queen Mary, Mary Clarke was a prominent symbol of recusancy. Ironically, as we learn in this letter, even in Ascham's salad Protestant days at Cambridge he had had some contact with this family, and the More tradition of learned women is Ascham's focus here, not religion. In his life of More, Nicholas Harpsfield also testifies to Clarke's learning, and credits her with excellent translations from both Greek and Latin.

Although Ascham's patent for the position of Latin secretary would be delayed until May 7, 1554 (see introduction to Letter 53), he writes here as though he has already taken up the work at court.

Most illustrious lady, your remarkable love of virtue and cultivation of learning, united with your great talent and industry, certainly deserve great credit in and of themselves, and still greater credit because you are a woman, and greatest credit of all because you dwell at court, where others of your sex are usually occupied with things other than learning, and delighted with things other than virtue. Your double credit is further increased by that two-fold model of virtue and learning which you have prudently set before yourself and followed faithfully. This court supplies you with one, your family with the other. I mean our illustrious Queen Mary and your noble grandfather Thomas More, thanks to whom, though he was just one man, foreigners consider all England to be the nobler. From this our ruler you have obtained your commitment to virtue, from your grandfather your genius for learning, and from both your great excellence in both areas. Since therefore the two leaders whom I have mentioned have started you auspiciously on the course of virtue and learning, so that with respect to virtue a woman seems to be winning a signal victory over men, and with respect to learning the court seems to be triumphing over the university, I am certainly moved by the greatest admiration for you, and I want in this letter not to urge you to take on new work, but I want to applaud your enjoyment of your share of the credit. Perhaps I am such an unknown that I am acting too boldly, but I feel completely free to approach you since you are so noble; because of your reputation I am very confident, for I judge that with the troop of such divine virtues within you, you cannot be lacking kindness.

This decision to write to you did not arise wholly from my admiration for you, but somewhat from my own desire and mostly from a consideration of my office. For I am the one who was invited some years ago from the University of Cambridge to the home of your relative Mr. Giles Alington[1] by your mother Margaret Roper, a woman most worthy of her great father and of such a daughter as you. She asked me to teach you and her other children Greek and Latin, but at

---

[1]Alington married Alice Middleton, the daughter by a previous marriage of Thomas More's second wife, "Lady Alice."

that time I would not allow myself under any circumstances to be wrenched from the University. Now I gladly renew with you this very pleasant memory of your mother's request. Now that I am at court, I would offer you, if not the fulfillment of that request, at least some attempt at it, were it not that through your own efforts you excel in this very learning, and have plenty of help, where there is need, from those two most learned men Cole and Christopherson,[2] so that you have no need of my help, unless they are not always present for you to call on and you want to use me sometimes--and if you like, even to misuse me.

I write this to you not because I have talent, for it is meager, but because of my good will, which is very great, and because of the opportunity, long wished for and now granted me. For by the good will, favor, and influence of his highness, Bishop Stephen of Winchester, I have been called from the university to serve our most illustrious Queen at court. I shall serve in a post which allows me to follow the same way of life that I followed in my studies at the university, for my job is to write Latin letters for the Queen. I hope I will fill that office, if not with genius and talent, at least with some credit, loyalty, and diligence, and without great reproach.

But as I use this occasion to congratulate you and let you know of this opportunity and of my desire to do you a favor, I fear that I shall make myself too troublesome by my importunity. I was carried along farther than I had planned by a certain admiration and love of your virtue. For I would deservedly have seemed boorish if I did not honor you, who are so famous as an ornament of your sex and of the court, and uncivil, if I did not devote myself to you.

Therefore I wish, if not to help along your noble intention of obtaining true glory through the pursuit of virtue and the cultivation of learning, at least to honor it with my congratulation and to encourage it with my applause. But if at some point you need me or mine to help with that which you are accomplishing by your own accord

---

[2]Henry Cole was educated at Oxford, with a doctorate in civil law; he was a man of notable learning, and a staunch Catholic who was much involved in religious controversy during Mary's reign. John Christopherson, an alumnus of St. John's College, Cambridge, was also a devout Catholic, serving as Queen Mary's chaplain and confessor and as Master of Trinity College; near the end of her reign he was named the Bishop of Chichester.

and by your own native ability intent on the loftiest thoughts, something which you are undertaking with the example of your prince and your parent, and which you are learning in accord with the advice of the most learned men, I shall freely make myself ready for your service, your will, and your wish.   Farewell, most accomplished lady. January 15, 1554.

57 / To Sir William Petre   (Giles I.clxxxviii)
                [London, January-February, 1554]

> Giles mistakenly conjectures that this letter, similar in many ways to one written to Cardinal Pole on April 7, 1555 (Letter 58), was therefore written about the same time. It can be more accurately dated, however, from Ascham's own comment about having completed five months of living in expensive London. He is referring to the time elapsed since he returned to England, a reference that puts this letter near the first of February (Ascham and Ambassador Morison arrived at court at Richmond on September 3, 1553). Some corroboration can be found in a sentence in an English letter of January 18, 1554, to Lord Chancellor Gardiner, where Ascham describes his expenses in exactly the way he describes them in this letter: "I that have spent since Bartholomew tide forty pounds cannot live a whole year on twenty, and yet I have been as ware in expences and as bare in apparel as any man could be" (I, 406; St. Bartholomew's Day is August 24, about the time Ascham landed again on English shores). In early 1554 Ascham was still awaiting his patent for the position of Latin secretary; it was not issued until May 7, 1554 (see introduction to Letter 53). Among his resources was the annuity of 20 pounds for *Toxophilus*, which had been renewed on December 1, 1553. Apparently Petre, one of the most durable of all Tudor administrators, and one of Mary's secretaries himself, had also secured him an advance of half of the stipend for the Latin secretary's position (I, 388, 405, 408), though the date cannot be determined. In any case, this letter occurs in the context of two previous letters to Petre, one undated and in Latin (I.clx), the other in English and dated December 25, 1553 (I.clxiii).
>
>   Ascham again offers his patron a volume written by the Portuguese Bishop Jeronimo Osorio (see introduction to letter 54), this time a work on civic and Christian nobility: *De nobilitate civili libri II. Eiusdem de nobilitate Christiana libri III* (Florence, 1552). Later he offers the same volume to Cardinal Pole, using the same rhetoric as well (see Letter 58).

It is a matter of fame, most illustrious sir, to be born of noble parents or to be connected to an ancient family, but the man who, together with such good qualities, achieves wealth and intellectual distinction so that he is not only adorned with the gifts of nature, but also fortified by the resources of fortune, truly has ready access to a high and exalted place of honor. But although all these advantages for the most part lead to glory if they have to do with virtue and to toil if they have to do with riches, those individuals are acting much more wisely who do not only advance by means of outside influence, but endeavor to grow toward excellence through learning and to rise to glory through virtue and reach the pinnacle of honor by their own efforts, not by those of their ancestors.

But since you yourself, most illustrious sir, have wisely entered upon and happily followed the correct path of true nobility, guided by virtue and learning and accompanied by nature and fortune, I am persuaded to offer you this book *On Civic and Christian Nobility.* I thought that you would heartily welcome the author of this book because of his subject and enjoy him very much because of the way he deals with it, for he writes about the things you are involved in and does the kind of writing which you excel in. Both of you seem to have the same idea, he in writing this book and you in working out a way of life. For the book shows and reveals not only the thoughts and ideas of your mind, but also your actions and way of life, and thus it shows you to yourself, as though in a polished mirror. You will see also how advantageous it has always been for all the people to be obedient to the rule of the prince or to surrender themselves to the governance and counsel of the wise. On the other hand, the furor of the masses and Cataline passions threaten all kingdoms and public affairs with not only dreadful peril but devastating ruin. He explains this intelligently, fully, methodically, and eloquently. With a sharp, biting style he attacks the madness, the mores, and the behavior of the lower class, who are more noted for vice than the nobility are for virtue, and who often show their country the appearance of liberty while menacing her with the flames of fury and a license for evil. In addition, he explains in this book the frequent disorders injustice brings to public life, and the unexpected disruptions wrought by impiety, as well as the joyful and lasting happiness which comes from keeping divine and human law, and an infinite number of other memorable matters wherein your thoughts, ideas, and daily concerns are occupied and over which you in your wisdom keep watch. Thus I hope the book will not only be one you enjoy reading, but also one you want to put into practice.

In discussing this renowned subject, he displays a quality and a power of eloquence which in my opinion no one since the days of Augustus Caesar has employed with more purity or distinction. For he is so skilled in choosing words, so polished in framing sentences, so proper and pure, so clear and perspicacious, so apt and modest in metaphor, so abundant and felicitous in antithesis, everywhere urbane but not fastidious, always dignified without affection, so fluent without redundancy, so surging without roaring, so full without turgidity, so perfect in every rhythm that nothing can be added or taken away, at least in my opinion. Nay, so distinguished an artist is he that Italy can not boast more in Sadoleto, nor France in Longueil, nor Germany in Johann Sturm than Spain now in Osorio. This stream of eloquence is the more salubrious because it does not overrun and flood his pages with inane and anile levities and rambling thoughts; instead, the whole book arises from and gently flows toward proclaiming the true glory of Christ and contending for the definite immortality of the soul.

Although the true excellence of the author's eloquence and wisdom is evenly distributed throughout the various books, it especially sparkles and shines in the last book, which he wrote particularly against the Florentine Nicolo Machiavelli. Always with great wit, but often not with a healthy way of thinking, Machiavelli seems to many good men to disparage impudently the religion of the Lord Jesus Christ, and to mock impiously.

Thus you will find this Osorio welcome because of the subject of his book, pleasant because of his eloquence, and very pious because of his principles. He shows himself to be a serious philosopher by his topic itself, a skillful orator by his handling of it, and a true Christian by his devotion to religion. With this reputation he ought henceforth to be very dear to you and sought after, since the book seems to contain and manifest monuments of his genius no greater than ornaments of your virtue, nor more credit to his eloquence than commendation of your wisdom.

But enough about you and Osorio. About myself there is nothing to say except this: since all my hope depends on your goodness alone, as it kindly offers and sweetly promises itself to me, I have ordered this book never to intrude itself into your presence as an untimely beggar, but to come before you only as a shy and modest petitioner for me and my business.　But if now, most prudent sir, either because of my Lord of Winchester's, or Lord Paget's, or Sir William Cecil's opinion of me, or because of some modest example of my ability which is now available to you from my private letters to you or from my public ones for her Royal Majesty, you think me not utterly unfit to hold the office of secretary, I shall gladly keep myself at your complete disposal to obey your will and command.　But if you feel otherwise, I would consider it a favor if you would let me know, lest I nurse my hope too long here and waste my time, and every day get myself deeper into debt and become more of a burden on my friends for daily expenses.

　　For how can I sustain life in London, not to mention life at court, for a whole year on twenty pounds when in the past five months of spare and restricted living I have spent forty pounds? Thus just as I have firmly resolved to nurture and preserve an unending remembrance of your kindness to me through my eternal devotion, service, and respect, so I am also somewhat afraid that I cannot hold out for long, waiting here for you to put your kindness into practice.

　　But this care concerns and worries me less when I realize that it is not that I and my fortunes have entrusted ourselves to you out of necessity, but that we have gladly and kindly been sustained by you, to whose goodness, by common agreement, so much credit must be given that I have very little doubt but that in the hope of that work for which you called me to the courtly life, you will make me more eager for every service through its ripe fruit, so that in proportion as I now receive the pleasure of your much desired good will toward me, I shall shortly perceive the great value of your welcome kindness. May you meet the hope I have placed in you in the following way: first, in consideration of my will or desire, at whatever pace you choose; second, in consideration of my need, with whatever speediness you can; finally, in consideration of your own wisdom and goodness, at whatever time you decide is most suitable.　Farewell.

58 / To Cardinal Reginald Pole   (Giles I.clxxxix)
London, April 7, 1555

This represents the third time Ascham offers Jeronimo Osorio's *De nobilitate civili et Christiana* to a potential patron: around February 1, 1554, he gave a copy to Sir William Petre (see introduction to Letter 57); on March 12, 1555, he dedicated a copy to Bishop Cuthbert Tunstall (see Ryan 208 and 325); here he offers the volume to the distinguished Cardinal Pole, who in March 1556 would become Mary's Archbishop of Canterbury. The language of these three dedications, it should be noted, is almost identical, as Ascham again follows his practice of re-using material from his copybooks.

Some years later Ascham sent a copy of this letter to Osorio himself, who graciously acknowledged it in a response to Ascham (II, 53-54).[1] The editor of Osorio's collected works (*Opera omnia*, 1592) choose to include it as well, garbling the author's name as "R. Ascanius."

The copy of the book Ascham gave to Pole, with Ascham's autograph inscriptions on the flyleaves, is preserved in the library of St. John's College, Cambridge. Giles' text of the letter is derived, with only slight typographical errors, from John E. B. Mayor's transcription of it in *Antiquarian Communications, Proceedings of the Cambridge Antiquarian Society* 1 (Cambridge, 1859).

It is a matter of fame, most illustrious Cardinal Pole, to be born of noble parents or to be connected to an ancient family, but the man who, together with such good qualities, achieves wealth and intellectual distinction so that he is not only fortified by the resources of fortune, but also adorned with the gifts of nature, truly has ready access to a high and exalted place of honor. But although all these advantages for the most part lead to glory if they have to do with nobility and to toil if they have to do with riches, those individuals are acting much more wisely who do not only advance by means of outside influence, but endeavor to grow toward excellence through learning and to rise to glory through virtue and reach the pinnacle of honor by their own efforts, not by those of their ancestors.

But since you yourself, most noble sir, have wisely entered upon and happily followed the correct path of true nobility, guided by virtue and learning and accompanied by nature and fortune, I am persuaded to offer you this book *On Civic and Christian Nobility*. I think that you will heartily welcome the author of this book because of his

[1]Giles erroneously gives the date as 1561: see Ryan 325.

subject and enjoy him very much because of the way he deals with it, for he writes about the things you are involved in and does the kind of writing which you yourself do. Both of you seem to have the same idea, he in writing this book and you in working out a way of life. For the book shows and reveals not only the thoughts and ideas of your mind, but also your actions and way of life, and thus it shows you to yourself, as though in a polished mirror. For he teaches how advantageous it has always been for all the people to be obedient to the rule of the prince or to surrender themselves to the governance and counsel of the wise. On the other hand, the furor of the masses and Cataline passions threaten all kingdoms and public affairs with not only dreadful peril but devastating ruin. He explains this intelligently, fully, methodically, and eloquently. In addition, he explains in this book the frequent disorders injustice brings to kingdoms and public life, and the unexpected disruptions wrought by impiety, as well as the joyful and lasting happiness which comes from keeping divine and human law, and an infinite number of other memorable matters wherein your thoughts, ideas, and daily concerns are occupied and over which you in your wisdom keep watch. Thus I hope the book will not only be one you enjoy reading, but also one you want to put into practice.

In discussing this renowned subject, he displays a quality and a power of eloquence which in my opinion no one since the days of Augustus Caesar has employed with more purity or distinction. For he is so skilled in choosing words, so polished in framing sentences, so proper and pure, so clear and perspicacious, so apt and modest in metaphor, so abundant and felicitous in antithesis, everywhere urbane but not fastidious, always dignified without affection, so fluent without redundancy, so surging without roaring, so full without turgidity, so perfect in every rhythm that nothing can be added or taken away, at least in my opinion. Nay, so distinguished an artist is he that Italy can not boast more in Sadoleto, nor France in Longueil, nor Germany in Johann Sturm than Spain now in Osorio. This stream of eloquence is the more salubrious because it does not overrun and flood his pages with inane and anile levities and rambling thoughts; instead, the whole book arises from and gently flows toward proclaiming the true glory of Christ and contending for the definite immortality of the soul.

Although the true excellence of the author's eloquence and wisdom is evenly distributed throughout the various books, it is especially abundant in the last book, which he wrote particularly against the Florentine Nicolo Machiavelli. Always with great wit, as you know, but often not with a healthy way of thinking, Machiavelli seems to many good men to disparage impudently the religion of the Lord Jesus Christ, and to mock impiously.

Thus you will find this Osorio welcome because of the subject of his book, pleasant because of his eloquence, and very pious because of his principles. He shows himself to be a serious philosopher by his topic itself, a skillful orator by his handling of it, and a true Christian by his devotion to religion.

But enough about Osorio, whom I have ordered never to intrude impolitely into your presence, but to step forward only now and then, prudently, when in my name and in my absence he is not to be the bird-catcher of profit and privilege, but the witness of my devotion and good will, with which I now honor your reverend lordship, and which I shall observe forever. May God have your reverend lordship ever in his keeping. London, April 7, 1555.

59 / To Valentine Erythraeus   (Giles II.vi)
[London], April, 1559

Erythraeus is frequently mentioned in the Sturm-Ascham correspondence, for he was a teacher in Sturm's school for some 29 years, as well as a frequent editor and assistant in Sturm's scholarly projects and publications. This letter has particular reference to what was undoubtedly the most notable of these contributions: his organization of Sturm's works on rhetoric and logic into schematic, tabular form. Sturm led off with an extraordinarily popular manual on rhetoric, which took the form of dialogues commenting on Cicero's beloved little catechism on rhetoric: *In partitiones oratorias Ciceronis dialogi duo* (Strasbourg, 1539; enlarged to *dialogi quatuor*, 1545). Erythraeus then presented his synoptic analysis of these dialogues in SCHEMATISMOI, *hoc est Tabulae quaedam Partitionum oratoriarum Ciceronis et quatuor dialogorum in easdem Joa. Sturmii* (Strasbourg, 1547, with a preface by Sturm). Similarly, Sturm wrote an exceedingly popular manual on logic, *Partitionum dialecticarum libri duo* (Strasbourg, 1539, enlarged to *libri quatuor* in 1543), and Erythraeus published a schematic analysis of it in two publications, the first on the Sturm's Books I-II, the second on Books III-IV: SCHEMATISMOI DIALEKTIKOI. *Tabulae duorum librorum Partitionum dialecticarum Joannis Sturmii* (Strasbourg, 1551), and DIAGRAMMATA, *hoc est Tabulae tertii et quarti libri Partitionum dialec-*

ticarum Joannis Sturmii (Strasbourg, 1555). For Ascham as educator, these were valuable pedagogical innovations, performing some of the functions of Ramus' reforms without his extreme restructuring of the two arts of discourse.

Johann Sturm's preeminence in intellect, learning, and good judgment has always seemed to me to shine forth so much, most learned Erythraeus, that he should be ranked not among the men of our own age, but among the number of those leaders and preceptors in both languages in every city whom God has raised up for the great profit and maximum admiration of all posterity. The consensus of the learned credits this excellent man with shining the bright light of his genius on us, very ably teaching us how to organize and differentiate the arts of logic and rhetoric. The whole scholarly world owes just as much to you, my Erythraeus, because with your renowned devotion, industry, talent, and judgment you have constructed the most perfect *schematic diagrams* of the elements of discourse.

And thus when I by chance happened to mention and praise your work to that most honorable young man Matthew Negelin,[1] and he at once declared to me your singular learning and your very charming manner and gentility, I could scarcely believe how suddenly an eternal love for you was kindled within me by the extraordinary power of your probity, a power that shone out amazingly, as if in a kind of mirror, in Negelin's conversation and in his very pleasant remembrance of you.

Certainly everyone here thinks so well of your work that we desire nothing more strongly than that you undertake the same kind of thing with Aristotle's *Rhetoric for Theodectes*, with its brilliant commentary by Johann Sturm. Matthew Negelin showed me how industriously and artfully you have illustrated the rules of rhetoric with examples of oratory; there is nothing which sheds more light on literature or has more usefulness for learning. That passage in Cicero's *Parts of Rhetoric* about translating and changing wording was explained so well by Johann Sturm through his brilliant use of examples that I

---

[1]Negelin was one of those who moved back and forth between England and Strasbourg; a native of Ulm, Germany, he studied at Strasbourg, and then followed Bucer to England in 1549. When he returned to Germany the next year, he served as secretary to the Protestant historian of Germany, Johann Sleidan.

readily prefer those three pages of his to the entire commentaries of others. I wish they would cut short their other work, and while paying careful attention and choosing judiciously, be as ample and full as needed in supplying examples, wherein they are too sparing and too stingy. Anyone who links a precept with an apt example explains it to great advantage.

But you do not need my exhortation to do this, unless perhaps you adhere to the thinking of that most pleasant of poets, who says,

> He who exhorts you to do what you are already doing
> Praises you by his exhortations and by his advice
> shows his approval of your actions.[2]

Because I am writing so boldly, I am not much concerned that you will find me lacking in prudence; at this time good will has been my sole consideration. No sordid hint of money animates this establishment of our friendship, but merely the commendation of learning and kindness. Either your silence will show you reject this viewpoint, or your letter will freely announce your willingness to respond in love. Farewell in Christ. April, 1559.

---

[2]Ovid, *Tristia* 5.14.45-46.

PART SEVEN: A "little book" on Imitation

Until the nineteenth century, when Giles arranged the letters chrono-
logically, Ascham's final letter to Sturm, chiefly about imitation, stood
at the head of every edition of his letters.   "The letter on imitation
moved me to the extent that I put his last letter first," explained Ascham's first editor, Edward Grant, whose judgment on this score has
never been challenged (III, 301).   Interestingly enough, in length too
this last letter of Ascham's life was his greatest; near its end he himself confesses that it has become "a little book."   Thus both its size
and its substance have won this letter a special place in any volume
of Ascham's correspondence.
     Ostensibly Ascham's "little book" gives some account of his Eng-
lish *Schoolmaster* to his German friend.   The letter is not, however, a
mere digest of what Ascham had been writing.   In general, it can be
said not only to recount, but also to extend *The Schoolmaster*, filling the
gap left when Ascham died before completing that work.   More particularly, the letter elaborates on what for Ascham was the most important of all pedagogical issues, the question of imitation.   The issue
had engaged him for years.   It lay at the heart of his pedagogy, dominated his reading, and explained what he valued most in Sturm's
scholarship.   The "doctrine of imitation," as Ascham himself says, will
"bring forth more learning and breed up truer judgment, than any
other exercise that can be used" (III, 216).
     The Schoolmaster breaks off in the midst of Ascham's review of
those who constitute "the best authors" for "right imitation" (III, 213-
14), a review that clearly was going to culminate in a discussion of
Cicero.   Thus this letter functions as Ascham's fullest declaration of his
Ciceronianism, and plunges him squarely into what he himself calls "a
great controversy" concerning how to follow these "best authors":
"here riseth amongst proud and envious wits a great controversy:
whether one, or many, are to be followed; and if one, who is that
one" (III, 213).   It was in reference to the discourse of Ciceronianism
that humanists took their stand, declared their loyalties, and professed

their humanistic creed.[1] And it is above all this letter that won Ascham his dubious place on Francis Bacon's famous roster of distempered Ciceronians.

At the center of these Ciceronian controversies was Christophe de Longueil (Longolius), 1488-1522, whose life and work became a symbol to both Italian and transalpine humanists alike, and who therefore figures prominently in this letter.[2] Longueil was born in Brabant, but he was educated largely in France and developed French loyalties, until around 1517, when he established himself in Italy and was welcomed into the distinguished literary circle of Pietro Bembo and Jacopo Sadoleto, the leading Ciceronians of the time. Soon he made a name for himself as the purest and finest of Ciceronians, and was invited to Rome to receive honorary citizenship in that city. After riding out the fierce tempests blown up by some native Italians' jealousy over this honor for a Northerner, he died prematurely at age 33 in the house of Reginald Pole in Padua, who, according to the generally accepted view, wrote Longueil's life and assisted with the preparation of a posthumous collection of his work.

It was not Pole, however, but Erasmus who played the key role in making Longueil the focal point and the symbol of the Ciceronian controversies. In 1528 his landmark dialogue Ciceronianus highlighted the ideological issues, intensified the debate, and further exposed Longueil as the center of controversy. In its wake the ideological purists were forced to defend themselves, and there was a strong new impe-

---

[1]The history of Ciceronianism remains to be written. Altogether inadequate is Izora Scott, Controversies over the Imitation of Cicero, Columbia Teachers College Contributions to Education No. 35 (New York: Columbia Teachers College, 1910). Within Erasmus scholarship, Pierre Mesnard's introduction and notes to Ciceronianus in the Amsterdam edition (see pt. 1, vol. 2 [1971], of Erasmus, Opera omnia [Amsterdam: North-Holland, 1969-]) and Betty I. Knott's introduction and notes on the same work in the Toronto edition of Erasmus in English (see Collected Works of Erasmus 28, Literary and Educational Writings 6, ed. A.H.T. Levi [Toronto: U of Toronto P, 1986]) are very helpful. Also immensely valuable is Emile V. Telle, ed. L'Erasmianus sive Ciceronianus d'Etienne Dolet (1535), Travaux d'Humanisme et Renaissance 138 (Geneva: Droz, 1974). On Ciceronianism in England, see J.W. Binns, "Ciceronianism in Sixteenth Century England: The Latin Debate," Lias 7 (1980), 199-203; and Alvin Vos, "'Good Matter and Good Utterance': The Character of English Ciceronianism," Studies in English Literature 1500-1900 19 (1979), 3-18.

[2]On Longueil, see Théophile Simar, Christophe de Longueil, humaniste, 1488-1522 (Louvain, 1911).

tus for humanists to chart their position of the map of humanism. Much of Ascham's letter, therefore, represents his own efforts to explain and defend his alignment or position on the ideological map. More than any of his other letters, this one contains many references to developments within Italian humanism; it represents Ascham's most sustained effort to address one of the most sensitive questions of his time.

60 / To Johann Sturm   (Giles II.xcix)

[London, late 1568]

This letter may never have been sent, for it seems unfinished; Ascham's other letters always open and close with graces that this one lacks. It is also undated. The *terminus ad quem* is the date of Ascham's death, December 30, 1568, which followed the onset of his final illness by exactly one week (see III, 340-42). That he had written at least portions of this letter months earlier follows from his allusion near the end of the letter to Queen Elizabeth's summer progress. Ironically, this is his very first indication to Sturm that he is writing *The Schoolmaster*, a project he had been working on intermittently for some five years. The opening section about money for the family of Gerhard Sevenus, a deceased instructor in Sturm's school, responds to specific concerns within Sturm's letter of July 26, 1568 (II.xcv), but this section seems to have been added to pages already written about education, imitation, and the world of learning.

I shall gladly and conscientiously do what you ask me to do on behalf of Sevenus,[1] and I really hope I am going to accomplish something. For when those who have full capability and full confidence promise something, there can be no doubt but that what they promise will be done. There was some truth in it when he wrote to our friend Mont that I intended to send money before I wrote to you, for I had rather send it than promise it. I desired not to string you along with a mere promise, but to satisfy you to some degree by actually presenting you some money. The reason why little has yet been done is plain: those who really want, as I hope, to contribute to this *gift*, and those who, I know, easily could contribute, and those who by rights ought in fairness to contribute--they all have been rather distant.

I understand that our bishops have been very well received everywhere in Germany during these hard times, but especially in Strasbourg. They will come in large numbers to the assembly of Parliament, when it meets. But meanwhile, although I shall not lose any time or overlook anyone in promoting this cause, if after all the Bish-

---

[1]Gerhard Finck, called Sevenus from the place of his birth in the Low Countries, was one of the first members of the faculty in Sturm's school. Upon Sevenus' death, Sturm undertook the support of his wife and children (see II, 167-68; cf. Christopher Mont's similar appeal to Ascham, II, 124).

op of London,[2] a very good and influential man in our midst, will join me in my assiduous efforts in this process of solicitation, I am sure you can expect something rather ample. And you know how wisely Homer expresses all this: *"When two go together . . ."*[3] Therefore urge the man on by your letters to undertake this pious duty along with me. But why do I say "urge"? Only remind him, and I promise that you will not need to drag him along reluctantly, but he will already be coming along as you guide him, and will do what the ingenious poet wisely teaches:

> He who exhorts you to do what you are already doing
> Praises you by his own exhortations and by his advice
> shows his approval of your actions.[4]

So much for this matter at this time.

I am pleased and delighted, my Sturm, that you are writing *On Oratorical Imitation*, dictating it to your students at this time.[5] You ask whether it will please me! Send it, I pray you; send what is dictated as soon as possible, for you promised it, and I want nothing more eagerly, and for nothing have I waited longer than its actual appearance. You want to know my judgment in advance. I do not presume so much, my Sturm, nor do I volunteer my advice.

Nevertheless, concerning the method of imitation, I shall certainly, and perhaps too audaciously, reveal at length what I think, which is inconsequential, and what I long to know, which is very great. Thinking about it, I continually realize the truth of the dictum, "Friends have everything in common." As I see it, they share not so much the mutual rewards of favor and fortune, but the same interests of the mind and heart, and our shared interests are as much a matter of knowledge and learning as of kindness and obligation. You write about imitation, and I have been doing some thinking about the same

---

[2]Edmund Grindal.

[3]"When two go together, one discerns before the other how much profit may be had" (*Iliad* 10.224).

[4]Ovid, *Tristia* 5.14.45-46.

[5]Unfortunately for Ascham, Sturm did not publish *De imitatione oratoria*, one of his major works, until 1574.

topic. Your treatment of it is polished, for educated men; mine is rough, for the uneducated, who are yet but boys.

Here is what I am thinking. I have but two sons, Giles and Dudley, for Sturm certainly lives, but he lives where he shall never die. Although I cannot promise my sons a bright, shining fortune, I want to leave them some appreciation of sure knowledge. Therefore I am preparing a *Schoolmaster* for them, not one hired at the markets for a handsome fee, but one sketched out here at home by my own rough pen. He takes shape in two small books; the first in large part is *ethical*, the second has to do with method. And because my *Schoolmaster* was not brought over from Greece or Italy, but was born on this barbarous island, and because he was reared within my household, he speaks in a barbarous tongue, that is, in English. For his speech is aptly going to be nearer and nearer to the everyday speech of our people, and I am writing to our countrymen, not to aliens, to Englishmen, not to foreigners. In addition, with this service I shall in some part have discharged the debt I in fairness owe to my country and to learning if by this interest of mine some interest can also be awakened in parents to support learning liberally and in their children to pursue it eagerly.

But this *Schoolmaster* of mine is not Cantabrigian, but Windsorian, of the court, not of the university. For that reason he may not exhibit the more flashy sort of learning, but he makes clear his usefulness, however modest, as much as he can. But I myself am not so inimical to our language but that I feel it highly capable of all the adornments of both speech and thought, and this subject matter is not so dry and thin but that it could even in English be *written in a flowery style* if it fell to an artisan like our Cheke was, or like Smith and Haddon, who are yet among us.[6] But if there is anything good in this little book, my Sturm, it all is to be credited to you, for I have taken pains that what I write should be wholly Sturmian. Indeed, I wish that my sons should pass through this little vestibule cobbled together in a rough way by their father and enter into that famous Gymnasium of Sturm, with all its refined workmanship. Still, something in this *schoolhouse*

[6]Thomas Smith, formerly Regius Professor of Civil Law at Cambridge, soon to become one of Elizabeth's Principal Secretaries; Walter Haddon, Elizabeth's Master of Requests, and also formerly Regius Professor of Civil Law (he succeeded Smith in 1551 when the latter was called to court).

will stand out and show itself to be a lasting testimony of my indubitable, lasting love for and high opinion of you.

My *Schoolmaster*, therefore, will be satisfied if he builds in the right way and constructs the stairs, as it were, for an easy ascent to those rather exalted doors which duly open into the Sturmian Academy. The steps are these: first, translation from one language to another. I do not mean the simple explication of a foreign language, which the schoolmaster does in his lecture every day in school, but a double method, a kind of reciprocation between two languages, one being translated into the other, the Greek, of course, being translated into Latin, and that same Latin back into Greek, always with careful preparation and precision in written work, putting it in a proper rather than an inappropriate style. This is the way I understand that especially useful and wise method of Crassus in the first book of *De oratore*,[7] and of the younger Pliny in his seventh letter to Fuscus. One can scarcely believe to what level of excellence in Latin and Greek I myself have brought our Queen Elizabeth in just a short time by this method of double translation, her composition always being compared with the original.

Then follow the remaining steps: paraphrase, metaphrase, epitome, imitation, annotation, composition, and declamation. Up these steps my *Schoolmaster* rather cautiously and timidly conducts his pupils, at times with outstretched hand, for these steps are somewhat slippery, and it would be easy to fall if one did not exercise caution and good judgment.

But where am I being carried? Certainly I am too rash: I wanted to show you only the face of my *Schoolmaster*, but I am not only revealing and describing his other limbs, but with neither prudence nor modesty I am even uttering his inner thoughts and feelings.

But why should I not tell you everything plainly and openly? Listen, then, to what I have also decided to say about imitation. My *Schoolmaster* goes on rather long about imitation. He confesses that he has eagerly read almost all the ancient and modern authors who have written on imitation, and he approves of many, but he admires no one except Sturm alone. There are, to be sure, some who ought to be imitated, but how the very method of imitation is to be formulated, only

[7]Cicero, *De oratore* 1.34.155.

Sturm teaches. And therefore if you had joined an abundance of examples to the perfect rules which you set forth very fully in your books *A Learned Nobility* and *The Lost Art of Eloquence*,[8] I do not see what more could be asked. For just as in one's philosophy of life and morals, so also in the philosophy of learning and education, examples are far more beneficial than rules. Indeed, in the arts or crafts within which one becomes accomplished through imitation alone, rules have no place, or at least a very small one, since in those areas examples have sole sway. Painters, sculptors, and writers understand this principle very well, and prove it decisively.

Some systems of thought require that I include orators in this group, and Quintilian is the authority who explains how this goes. He says that Cicero--and Cicero himself did not remain silent on this point--expresses the pleasantness of Isocrates, the abundance of Plato, and the power of Demosthenes,[9] and everyone can see when it comes to imitation whether or not his expression occupies its own niche. Nevertheless, simply to determine and to show where Cicero does this is a mundane and common task, requiring only average diligence. This is the way Périon, Vettori, Estienne, and others dealt with Cicero,[10] and the way Macrobius, Hessus, and recently Fulvio Orsini, the most diligent of all, treated Virgil;[11] in such fashion even Clement of

---

[8]*Nobilitas literata* (Strasbourg, 1549) and *De amissa dicendi ratione* (Strasbourg, 1538).

[9]*Institutio oratoria* 10.1.108. Cf. *The Schoolmaster* (III, 227).

[10]Cf. the parallel passage in *The Schoolmaster* (III, 228): "Some men already in our days have put to their helping hands to this work of Imitation: as Perionius, Hen. Stephanus *in dictionario Ciceroniano*, and Pet. Victorius most praiseworthy of all, in that his learned work containing twenty-five books *de Vario Lectione*; in which books be joined diligently together the best authors of both the tongues, where one doth seem to imitate another." Ascham alludes to the following: *De optimo genere interpretandi* (Paris, 1540), by Joachim Périon, a French Benedictine scholar whom Ascham had once criticized for translating Aristotle into Ciceronian Latin (see Letter 39); *De varia lectione libri xxv* (Florence, 1553), by Pietro Vettori, Professor at Florence and probably the greatest Italian scholar of his day (see also Letter 39); and *Ciceronianum lexicon Graeco-Latinum* (Paris, 1557), a collection of passages from Greek authors along with Cicero's imitations of them, by Henri Estienne II (Stephanus), the renowned French scholar and printer.

[11]Cf. the parallel passage in *The Schoolmaster* (III, 215): "For Macrobius's gatherings for the Aeneis out of Homer, and Eobanus Hessus' more diligent gatherings for the Bucolics out of Theocritus, as they be not fully taken out of the

Alexandria in the fifth of his *Miscellanies* carefully dealt with the ancient Greek writers.[12] They are still like day-laborers and porters who carry material and thus undoubtedly work hard, but who deserve a small wage and not a great deal of praise.

To teach clearly and completely how Cicero imitates Demosthenes or Plato takes, I confess, singular learning, very good judgment, and a rare excellence. Still, this excellence is but the proper mark of a teacher. I want something else, I require more. We need an artisan and an architect who knows how by an artful method to bring the parts together, to polish the rough spots, and to build up the entire structure. I am firmly of the opinion that it should be done like this: on one side I want a passage from Demosthenes to be brought forward, on the other one from Cicero. Then I want the artisan to show me what in the two authors is either the same or very similar. Next, I want to be shown what was added in the one and why, and what was omitted and for what reason. Finally, I want to be shown what was changed, and with what artfulness, whether it has to do with the choice of the words or with the shape of the thought or with the arrangement of the clauses or with the method of argumentation. And I will not be content with one or two examples, but I am looking for many of them, varied in kind, drawn from Plato, from Isocrates, from Demosthenes, and from Aristotle in his books of rhetoric.

I allow my *Schoolmaster* to be sparing in laying down rules, provided that he shows himself liberal and generous not only with offering examples, which takes effort and diligence, but also with analyzing them, which takes learning and good judgment. I demand a volume

whole heap, but . . . only to point out, and nakedly to join together their sentences, with no further declaring the manner and way how the one doth follow the other, were but a cold help to the increase of learning." Macrobius, the fifth-century Roman philosopher, wrote of Virgil's debt to Homer in Book 5 of his *Saturnalia;* German poet Helius Eobanus Hessus, 1488-1540, better known for his Latin translations the Psalms and of *The Iliad*, published his lecture notes on Virgil at Erfurt, 1509, with an enlarged edition in Hagenau, 1529. Fulvio Orsini (Ursinus), 1529-1600, an erudite Roman cleric and librarian to Allesandro Cardinal Farnese, published *Virgilius collatione scriptorum Graecorum illustratus* (Antwerp, 1568).

[12]Clement of Alexander was not only one of the early Greek Church Fathers (first-second century), but also a noted scholar of Greek literature. On his journey to Germany Ascham saw the first edition of Clement's *Stromata*, a work that sought to reconcile the Christian faith with Greek learning (see Letter 35).

of examples, a page of rules. It will not bother me if he follows the same plan or approach when he compares Caesar with Xenophon, Sallust with Thucydides, Livy with Polybius, Virgil with Homer, Horace with Pindar, as well as Seneca with Sophocles and Euripides--unless perhaps it would be better to do what those skilled writers do who wish to write perfectly, for they attach themselves firmly to the one most perfect example, and cling to it. They do not willingly allow themselves to be pulled toward various models or to be led astray by bad ones. If I should want to write a poem, I could not find anyone more divine than Virgil, more learned than Horace. But for rhetoric I want Cicero himself--if not him alone, certainly him in preference to others. And I must have Cicero the imitator as my model, not the imitator of Cicero.

At any rate I have embraced uniquely an imitation of Cicero, but I mean the kind of imitation, first in rank and foremost in value, with which Cicero himself followed the Greeks, not that with which Lactantius[13] once, or Omphalius[14] recently, or, much more successfully, certain Italians, Frenchmen, Portuguese, and Englishmen have followed Cicero. Whoever has been not only a diligent observer, but also one skilled in learning and prudent in judgment, observing what path Cicero himself travelled and what steps he took when he followed, equalled, or outstripped the Greeks; and whoever notices wisely in which passages and by what method our model equalled the Greeks themselves and very often surpassed them--he is just the one who will come safely and by the right road to the imitation of Cicero himself. For the one who intelligently observes how Cicero followed others will most successfully see how Cicero himself is to be followed. And therefore I cannot approve of the thinking of Bartolomeo Ricci of Ferrara, although he is a learned man. Although he has written about the correct method of imitation, so that when you leave Sturm out, Ricci in my opinion is to be preferred to all others (for all his teachings are Sturmian, drawn and derived from your fountains), nevertheless he prefers to offer examples of Longueil's imitation of Cicero rather that of Cicero's imitation of Plato, and to advance examples of Virgil's im-

[13]The "Christian Cicero" of the third century.

[14]Jacob Omphalius, 1550-1567, was a German humanist whose career centered around his professorship of law at Cologne.

itation of Catullus rather than of Homer. Of course he has done this well, but it is not the best; it has some value, but not outstanding merit; he has achieved some modest success, but not full perfection.[15]

If indeed I should desire to become another Cicero (and certainly that is hardly a sinful thought), whom should I sooner consult for advice than Cicero himself concerning whether to do so, and how to do so? And if I should wish to go straight to that point which Cicero once reached so successfully, what better road could I travel than to follow the very footsteps of Cicero himself? Right in Rome he had the Gracchi, Crassus, and Antonius, all of them rare models for imitation, but he sought other models elsewhere. He drank in the propriety of the Roman language together with his mother's milk at Rome, in its purest age, from the most delightful flower of Latinity. But that divine Latin speech of his, not recognized by his ancestors, but so admired by his descendants, he acquired from another place, augmenting and nourishing it in a manner different from Latin practice and Latin institutions. For his speech was not born in Italy, but was imported into Italy from the discipline of the Greeks. Cicero was not satisfied that his tongue should be pure and ornate in its native propriety until his mind had made intelligent use of the erudition of the Greeks and their learning. Thus it came to pass that out of all the other Romans who lived before Cicero or during his time or around his time, the rhetoric of Cicero alone became so admirably resplendent, tinctured not only by the pure color of the vernacular, but also richly imbued with a kind of rare and transmarine shading.

Thus since the Latin language, in those happiest of times, in Rome itself, in the hands of Cicero himself, did not achieve full perfection without drawing on Greek, why should anyone seek from Latin alone what Cicero himself did not find without the aid of Greek? And since we are neither more blessed with talent nor more intelligent in our thinking than Cicero himself was, why do we rashly hope to attain what he could not? Why do we blindly strive to march upon that road which he was unwilling to tread, especially since we consider him to be the only one to be followed, or at least the one we

---

[15]On Ricci, see Ascham's parallel discussion in *The Schoolmaster* (III, 223-25), commenting particularly on Ricci's book *De imitatione libri tres* (Venice, 1545). Ricci, 1490-1569, was known for his supervision of the education of the d'Este children in Ferrara.

prefer to others, as though he were our supreme leader. And in the field of literature, if we accept Cicero's judgment above all, why should we repudiate his counsel? Since we confess that he always spoke intelligently about this matter, why should we not frankly admit that he also acted rightly in the matter? Unless perhaps it seems to some that Cicero himself, wise as he is in judgment, is really a useless guide and an absurd model!

Thus just as we clearly know what Cicero often wisely decreed and always consistently taught in this matter, so let us follow willingly what he himself very successfully accomplished. As an example to others, therefore, Cicero wisely joined together those languages which he considered useful to himself. Far be it from us to separate ourselves from those languages, for it would be crude ignorance, or to repudiate one of them, for it would be foolish haughtiness. For to flourish in the one without the other and to achieve some real excellence happens about as easily and as often as a bird flies swiftly with one wing or a man runs fast with one leg. For I have read, listened to, or heard about only one or two individuals out of all the centuries of history whom I can mention as having achieved great excellence in Latin eloquence without the aid of Greek. But however fair it is that we admire those men, we cannot safely imitate them. I esteem them and gladly congratulate them on their rare success. But I am not the one to start advising others that they can hope for equal excellence or follow the same approach, if for no other reason, then certainly for this one: Cicero himself either wisely did not want to go down this road or he did not dare to make a vain attempt at it with the multitudes. As someone says, "Cicero was right. Before him there was no one to imitate except the Greeks. But now we have Cicero himself, who certainly should be compared with the Greeks in general as well as with individual Greeks; the glory of his eloquence is as great as that of anyone who ever lived. Why therefore should I not take Cicero alone as a model for imitation, setting aside the various Greeks?"

There is something to what you say. For I myself set Cicero principally to be imitated, but in a safe way, according to the correct method, in his own rank and in his own place. And I will openly explain my reasoning about why and how I want it to be this way. First, if I should desire to become another Cicero, as I said before, what approach would be better than the approach Cicero himself took to make himself Cicero? That this way is certain, known, and workable, the best witness is Cicero himself. And so when our feet are planted firmly and correctly on that very road which Cicero took ahead of us, and we have full knowledge of all his secret retreats and various detours and sharp corners, then at last we shall be safely and happily building our road to Cicero, with Minerva herself as our guide. If in this fashion, as I said before, the more distinguished examples, many in number and varied in kind, are selected from Cicero where he imitated the best of the Greeks, and are carefully pointed out by a distinguished master, not simply as certain people do, but as Sturm teaches, they will be learnedly treated.

This is the right way, in my definite opinion, to proceed toward the imitation of Cicero: not the way Ricci shows that Longueil has done (that is, as he himself believes, with an excellent approach; as I believe, very laudably; as many feel, in a mediocre and tolerable way; as Erasmus and Paolo Manuzio judge, foolishly, childishly, and coldly),[16] but according to the method for imitating Cicero which is taught by Sturm, who teaches the rules perfectly in his book *A Learned Nobility*, and who points out the examples extraordinarily well in his *Explanation of "Pro Quinctio."*[17]

And here that remarkable passage in *Pro Quinctio* fittingly comes to mind: "*Etenim si veritate amicitia, fide societas . . .*"[18] Twice, my Sturm, you have imitated this sentence with wonderful artfulness, first in *The Lost Art of Eloquence*,[19] later in *Explanation of "Pro Quinctio."*[20] In

---

[16]For a brief summary of the complex relationships between Erasmus and Christophe de Longueil, see Betty I. Knott's introduction to her translation of Erasmus' *Ciceronianus*; cf. pp. 430-435 for Erasmus' own discussion of Longueil. Concerning Manuzio's opinion of Longueil, see Ascham's more extensive discussion below.

[17]*Nobilitas literata* was published in 1549; Sturm incorporated his analysis of Cicero's oration *Pro Quinctio* into his *Lost Art of Eloquence*: *De amissa dicendi ratione . . . Explicata est . . . et . . . interposita Ciceronis oratio . . . pro Quintio* (Strasbourg, 1538). Sturm also contributed to a separate commentary on this oration which was published in 1551.

[18]Cicero, *Pro Quinctio* 26: "Even if friendship is maintained by faith, partnership by good faith . . . ."

[19]See *De amissa dicendi ratione* 103-04.

[20]On the important role of the rather Gorgian rhetoric of *Pro Quinctio* in Sturm's and Ascham's thinking, see Alvin Vos, "The Formation of Roger Ascham's Prose Style," *Studies in Philology* 71 (1974), 344-70.

both places you very elegantly imitated the same rhetorical structure, with differing content, to be sure, and with varied treatment. My *Schoolmaster* timidly and modestly petitions me to ask you to allow him by your good leave to make use in his little commentary of your remarkable two-fold imitation of that one passage from Cicero, and I promise on his behalf that he will honor you as he does so with a loving mention of your name.

But to what end, my Sturm, do we work so hard for imitation when those are not wanting who wish to seem learned and prudent, but who believe imitation to be nothing or consider it to have no value at all or who confuse the whole issue rashly or who entirely repudiate imitation, whatever it is, whosoever it is, as servile and puerile? But they are indolent and ignorant, fleeing from work, not knowing art. When in their poor judgment they attribute everything to nature, they after all despoil her of her own best resources by their perverse way of thinking, and in their great temerity and extreme ignorance, they pull apart things which always ought to be united. Whoever engages in literary studies by chance and not by choice, on a whim and not with care, creates a divorce between art and nature. Such people feel the same way about that elegant part of eloquence which has to do with oratorical rhythm; they either wish it not to exist, or they think the whole business is absurd. And they believe that the ear has no commerce with the artistic and intelligent judgment of the mind. Ironically, some through ignorance do not know this aspect of learning, or they scorn it out of pride, but those who are the leaders in all aspects of learning--Aristotle, Demetrius, Halicarnassus, Hermogenes, Cicero, Quintilian, Sturm--have refined it so much by their great interest in it that there is nothing else on which they seem to have worked as carefully.

But let us leave the former sort to their ignorant indolence and their proud folly, and let us cherish and follow these others, who, although they were gifted by nature, always wanted their natural gifts to be developed by education so that they might be considered to be no more assisted by their natural gifts than fortified by the resources of the arts, and no more blessed by their natural talents than made wise by their good judgments.

And when I reflect upon the discourse about imitation, I am often overcome with a heavy sorrow over those lost books of Dionysius of Halicarnassus, which he wrote very learnedly and at great length concerning both oratorical and historical imitation. He himself puts these books ahead of all his other books in that commentary in which he wisely and learnedly and fully explained his opinion about the whole history of Thucydides: what within it can be imitated safely and what should be warily avoided. But meanwhile all learned men owe a great deal to Andreas Dudith of Pannonia and then to your Paolo Manuzio, because recently the one very learnedly translated this erudite commentary into Latin (I have not seen the Greek), and the other printed it very beautifully.[21] For in that book Dionysius has so carefully organized and so clearly outlined all the virtues and vices of Thucydides that whatever is in him, whether it be in the selection of the words or the form and construction of the sentences or the evaluation and treatment of the material, is plainly and fully shown by Halicarnassus, whether it was written as a commendation of Thucydides' excellence or as a criticism to keep others from the same mistakes. For Dionysius' diligence in organizing details, his learning in thinking them through, and his judgment in evaluating them are so great that if Thucydides himself should come to life again, I do not believe that he could know himself better or analyze himself either more correctly or more fairly. And I do not believe that a better, more learned study of historical imitation has yet been written.

As often as I read this commentary (which I gladly do rather often), I am drawn to the conclusion that I fully believe that no one in either Greece or Rome has ever approached the writing of history with greater ability than Dionysius of Halicarnassus, especially if to the great excellence of his diligence, learning, and judgment there had been added, through the kindness of Augustus, the whole great treasure of Varro's library.[22] If perhaps you have been occupied with

---

[21]Dudith (or Dudito), 1533-1589, travelled from his native Hungary to study in Italy, where he become friends with leading Italian humanists, including Paolo Manuzio, who continued the famous Aldine Press founded by his father Aldo. He also became part of Cardinal Pole's Italian circle, at one point attending the Cardinal on a papal embassy to England; still later he entered a career in the church. *On Thucydides* was one of a number of treatises to come down from Dionysius of Halicarnassus, a Greek living in Rome during the first century B.C.; Manuzio published Dudith's translation in 1560.

[22]Varro, a prolific and immensely learned writer of the first century B.C. in Rome, was employed by Caesar to superintend the collection and arrangement of a great library for public use. By the time Dionysius of Halicarnassus had come

other things, my Sturm, and have not read this work of Halicarnassus on Thucydides, I pray you to read it. And write too whether your feeling coincides with my opinion of the book or not. In the same book he indicates that he wrote a book on the imitation of Demosthenes which took the same approach, and another book on civil philosophy. Would that these books were extant, for in my mind I already anticipate that books written by such a great man would have been full of learned and wise instruction about procedures in civil law.

These reflections about imitation and my earlier mention of Christophe de Longueil, who himself wanted to be an eminent imitator of Cicero, and who seemed to others to be one, move me somewhat to disclose to you what I myself think of his ability and of his reputation. Those who think well of Longueil get no argument from me, although both at home and abroad I have some whom I put ahead of him. Budé in a certain letter to Erasmus too sharply attacks his friend, who does not deserve this ungrateful disparagement.[23] Erasmus rails openly at him, and argues that he absurdly, furtively, slavishly, and childishly does nothing more than stitch together patches from Cicero. I think Erasmus wrote out of irritation rather than with a cool head, for I know that just after Longueil died, Erasmus credited him not with some special eloquence, but with a supremely excellent eloquence.[24]

I am more amazed, to be sure, at what came into Paolo Manuzio's mind, a great gentleman by nature, according to what I hear, and a very well educated man, according to what I observe, for when in a published letter to Stephen Sauli,[25] he sharply attacked Longueil, it was an attack of the living on the dead, the good on someone not bad, the

to Rome (29 B.C.), however, Varro had been caught up in political conflicts, and most of his magnificent library had been destroyed.

[23]In a letter of April 22, 1527, William Budé, the glory of French learning, complains to Erasmus that Longueil renounced his French heritage: see P.S. Allen, *Opus epistolarum Erasmi* (Oxford, 1906-1958), #1812.

[24]See Allen #1675 and #1706.

[25]Stephen Sauli, born into a wealthy family in Genoa, became a member of the learned Paduan circle which included Longueil, Reginald Pole, and renowned Italian humanists. Manuzio's harsh comments occur in a letter of 1553 to Sauli, a letter that Manuzio included in the numerous (and ever-growing) editions of his own letters.

erudite on someone not unlearned, an Italian on someone who was the delight of Italians. I do not know why he thought that way; I know he certainly was not kind enough, and I doubt very much that he used sound judgment. For he says that Longueil's thought is thin, his vocabulary is not rich, his Latinity is impoverished--in a word, that he does not amount to anything. Manuzio looks for good judgment in Longueil, and he finds folly.

How much more temperate, humane, and sagacious you once were, my Sturm, in writing to the Duke of Jülich.[26] There, after you had given your very sober judgment of Erasmus and Longueil and their entire controversy, you deprived neither of his glory, but frankly gave each his due. And on that same point, as Manuzio labors so mightily to overthrow Longueil, in my opinion he himself slips somewhat. For he announces with great fanfare that he has his own excellent method for enriching Latin, a method, as he himself writes, which is used by only a few others, namely that he customarily takes choice passages from Cicero and adorns them in different words, selected as carefully as possible. But does he not indisputably show that he prefers with Carbo to be led astray into errors than to travel the right road with Crassus?[27] And does he not set the opinion of Quintilian ahead of the judgment of Cicero? For Crassus and Cicero do not only fight this battle with a greater authority, but they win the war with their better method. It is useless to be guided by bad judgment in chasing after worse ideas when good judgment has already laid out the best ones, and it is useless to seize rashly on commonplaces when the most select wisdom is already in hand.

I am glad that my *Schoolmaster* speaks English, lest when he dissents so freely in this matter from Manuzio, he should offend such a great man. However, he does not name Manuzio, for when he dissents from someone, he does so silently, and when he praises, he does so openly. Still, if Manuzio himself should read this letter, there is no

---

[26]See *M.T. Ciceronis orationum volumina tria* . . ., ed. by Sturm (Strasbourg, 1540, with numerous later editions); a letter from Sturm to William, Duke of Jülich, constitutes the preface to the first volume of this collection.

[27]Gaius Papirius Carbo was an orator of some note, but unprincipled in political life; Lucius Crassus was one of the great orators of his day, and Cicero's spokesman in the dialogue of *De oratore*. In 119 B.C. Crassus brought charges against Carbo, who then took his own life as he saw the case going against him.

reason why he should be offended. For no one knows better than he does that the muses are both candid and wise, and patiently endure some differences of opinion between lovers of literature, and sometimes they themselves sow these differences with some profit. But they always ban any intellectual discord and do not allow it for long. And so I wish your Paolo Manuzio to be mine also; I shall not allow you to love him more than I do. And although you are nearer to him by virtue of geography, I certainly shall not permit you to be joined more closely to him when it comes to being devoted to him out of good will and to actually offering him a service.

I have the same thoughts about other very famous men in Italy: Pietro Vettori;[28] Giovita Rapicio, who wrote learnedly and elegantly about oratorical rhythms;[29] Carlo Sigonio;[30] Giovanni Battista Pigna of Ferrara;[31] and Pietro Angeli Bargeo of Pisa.[32] For one must be considered ignorant if he does not clearly see, and jealous if he does not

[28]See note 10 above.

[29]Rapicio (Jovita Rapicius), 1476-1553, pursued a career as an educator in Venice, Bergamo, and other cities in Italy, and counted Cardinal Pole, Bembo, and other distinguished humanists among his friends. The first four books of the work to which Ascham refers, De numero oratorio, were dedicated to Pole.

[30]Sigonio (Carolus Sigonius), 1524?-1584, was one of the most prolific and widely learned humanists of his day; he was an orator, historian, and scholar of classical antiquity, as well as translator of Aristotle, commentator on Cicero, and editor of Livy. In the course of his life he was a professor at Venice, Padua, and Bologna. Many of his research projects focussed on Greek and Roman chronology, law, and political institutions. Below Ascham seems to have in mind his parallel publications on Athenian and Hebrew culture: De republica Atheniensium libri V and De republica Hebraeorum libri VII.

[31]Pigna, 1530-1575, was a gifted scholar who at age 20 became Professor of Rhetoric at Ferrara. There he was also secretary to the well-known Duke of Ferrara, Alfonso II d'Este. He was a major figure in the literary criticism of the Italian Renaissance, and his long and detailed commentary on Horace's "golden" Ars Poetica (published in 1561), which Ascham mentions below, was only one of his efforts to formulate and extend classical literary ideals.

[32]Pietro Angeli (Angelio), 1517-1596, called himself Bargaeus after Barga, the town of his birth, in Tuscany. After traveling and serving as a soldier, he developed himself as poet and scholar of classical learning, and served as professor in several Italian universities over the course of his life. He was best known for his Cynegeticon, a Latin poem on hunting in two books, begun during his student days and finally published in 1561. Ascham alludes to it below, as well as to other fruits of his scholarship.

frankly acknowledge, how much all educated men owe to Carlo Sigonio for having explained both republics in both cities. The rare learning and the profound judgment with which Battista Pigna explained Horace's golden *Art of Poetry* at great length has moved me with a great desire of seeing the study he wrote which takes the same approach to Aristotle's three books of rhetoric. As he himself writes, he has taken examples of all kinds from the leading Greek and Latin orators and from writers on politics, ethics, and history, and joined them to the best rules of the art of rhetoric, bequeathed by the master of learning. Although I have yet to see it with my own eyes, in my mind I have already anticipated with great pleasure what an excellent piece of work this is.

Battista Pigna wrote, as he himself testifies, another book called *Sophoclean Questions*, in which he discussed at length the whole doctrine of tragedy, the faults of Seneca, and the virtues of the Greek tragedians. I have no less a desire of seeing his book, my Sturm, since Sophocles and Euripides, in my opinion, can be compared with Plato and Xenophon in their explanation of civic discourse, especially what pertains to the morals, deliberations, institutions, and experiences of those who spend their lives in the splendor of court.

Pietro Angeli Bargeo of Pisa has turned *hunting* into divine poetry, and he excels no less in eloquence. He has written, as I gather from his own writing and from Manuzio's comments, very learned commentaries on Demetrius' erudite little book *On Style*. And I should very much like to know whether this book and those which I have mentioned by Giovanni Battista Pigna have already been published or are forthcoming. As you are a gentleman, my Sturm, please find out as soon as possible through a letter to Paolo Manuzio, who knows best of all. And what he answers, write me speedily, for nothing will make me more grateful. To the shade of Longueil, I wish eternal happiness, who gave me this occasion for requesting this from you. To you, my Sturm, I give tremendous thanks because you are writing *On Oratorical Imitation*, and because you promise to send me what has been dictated. Send it, therefore, and send it speedily, so that my *Schoolmaster*, who now is nearly naked and obviously unattractive, may borrow from it some more elegant garb and thus, being clothed somewhat more tastefully and looking more distinguished, may go forth in public with more confidence.

Meanwhile I want to know from you whether in this context imitation ought to be construed loosely enough to encompass even that exercise which we call metaphrase.[33] Plato, however, calls it *mimesis* in the third book of the *Republic*, where Socrates himself very elegantly gives a free prose rendering of the poetic speech of Chryses priest.[34] I do not see why it is not called imitation, since in that passage I observe certain things skillfully drawn from the source and many things ingeniously altered. I am of the same mind about Lucretius, a poet very adept at Latin, who with a different technique turned Thucydides' famous account of the plague into erudite and elegant poetry.[35]

But what are you doing, my Ascham, I hear you say, that you write me not a letter, but a little book? What I am doing, I am doing willingly and with enjoyment, my Sturm, especially during this sweet respite and free time at home away from all court responsibilities, while the Queen, according to her custom at this season, is now far away from the city devoting herself not to the service of Pallas in the sanctuary of the muses (which she does during the rest of the year), but to the service of Diana in the woods.[36]

This long-windedness of mine certainly does not trouble me, and I hope it will not be at all unwelcome to you. For since it did not weary me to write it, I am not very fearful that you will be loathe to read it. And if I accomplish nothing else, at least I shall accomplish this: you will know for certain that during this long silence of mine my love for you has not diminished in the least. May you understand in addition that I still think the same way about our pursuit of learning--though my ability is not equal to yours, of course--as I did when, with Dr. Bucer's encouragement, I first sent you that long letter, which you then as a dear friend wanted to be a public witness to our love for each other.

---

[33]Turning verse into prose, or vice versa: see the parallel passage in *The Schoolmaster* (III, 192-99); Plato's metaphrase of Homer is discussed there as well as here.

[34]*Republic* 3.393, where Socrates comments on *Iliad* 1.8ff.

[35]Lucretius, *De rerum natura* 6.1138-286, following Thucydides 2.47-52.

[36]Ascham alludes to Elizabeth's summer progress: see Ryan 330.

But now all the fruit of our university leisure, which seemed to you then of some importance, languishes because of the daily business at court, and each day, like wine going flat, it gradually declines, so that I plainly fear that it will seem in your judgment to have, in a word, withered. And so your sweet and very amiable expostulation with me is altogether appropriate, as you call me, jocularly of course, but too truthfully, an indolent fellow, and as you lovingly demand that we renew our interrupted correspondence of many years, and greet and console each other with frequent letters between us.

In truth I have nothing to say about my taciturnity of long duration, nor do I urgently seek indulgence, or seek any excuse at all. Although I could offer a reasonable and probable excuse, I do not want to avail myself of one, lest it should trouble me and not make you glad. But may you not triumph in this my sluggish silence. Although I myself freely commend you highly for writing dutifully, and give no credit to myself, nevertheless I can compete with you on equal terms. You can cite the large number of your letters, I the magnitude of my one; you the variety of the pages, I this volume; you the weight of thought, I the pile of words; you the erudite brevity, I the rough loquacity; you the frequent declaration of love, I the unending study of good will. Thus do we both strive, but I am certainly not going to get worked up over whether you surpass me or I surpass you.

BIOGRAPHICAL REGISTER

John Astley (Ashley)   (d. c 1595)

Astley was a cousin to Princess Elizabeth through the Boleyns, and came to court when Anne was Henry VIII's queen. In time he was given a confidential position in the household of the Princess. There he became friends with William Grindal, the Princess' tutor, through whom he then met Ascham, who had tutored Grindal at Cambridge. Their friendship developed during the period Ascham himself served as tutor to the Princess. In a letter to Ascham of 1552 Astley recalls fondly "our friendly fellowship together at Cheston [Cheshunt], Chelsey, and here at Hatfield, her Grace's house," as well as "our pleasant studies in reading together Aristotle's Rhetoric, Cicero, and Livy. . ." (III, 3). Around 1546 Astley married Elizabeth's governess, Kate Champernowne. (He was thus brother-in-law to Anthony Denny, who married Kate's sister Joan.) Ascham's *Report of Germany* takes the form of a report to Astley, responding to the latter's request for news from Ascham about the "great stirs in those parts" (III, 4). During Mary's reign Astley was among the Protestant exiles in Frankfort. Upon the accession of Elizabeth he was named master of the royal jewel house, and his wife chief gentlewoman of the privy chamber. Accompanying the Queen on her visit to Cambridge, he was awarded an MA in 1564. Recounting the occasion for writing *The Schoolmaster*, Ascham notes Astley's presence at Cecil's memorable dinner party in Windsor (III, 78).

Charles Blount   (1516-1544)

Member of a distinguished family, Charles was the son of William, fourth Lord Mountjoy; he succeeded his father as fifth Lord Mountjoy in 1534. William served in the court, and like his father Charles was a prominent aristocratic patron of learning with strong ties to the leading figures in the group of Erasmian humanists active in the generation previous to Ascham's. His father had been Erasmus' pupil as well as his principal English patron; to him the famous humanist dedicated his *Adages* and numerous other works. Erasmus also took an interest in the education of Charles, therefore, and upon his father's death Charles received the dedications of new editions of the *Adages*. He was also honored by Vives in *De ratione studii* (1523).

Richard Brandisby

The date of Brandisby's birth is not known; he received his BA in 1521, and his MA in 1526, having been elected a fellow of St. John's in 1523. As fellow students at Cambridge, Ascham and Brandisby became good friends. Years later, during Ascham's travels on the Continent with the English ambassador to the Emperor, they eagerly--but unsuccessfully--sought each other out. Apparently Brandisby had left England for religious reasons; he matriculated at the University of Louvain in 1538. Like other friends such as Thomas Watson and John Seton, he was a strong supporter of Rome. At Louvain he worked with the noted Belgian humanist Peter Nannius, and helped to introduce him to prominent Englishmen, including William Paget, Ambassador Nicolas Wotton, Bishops Edmund Bonner and Stephen Gardiner, and Ascham himself. In his dedication of an edition of Cicero's Verrine Orations to Wotton, Nannius praised Brandisby as his virtual alter ego, comparing their friendship to that of Castor and Pollux. Brandisby probably returned to England during Mary's reign.

Henry Brandon   (1535-1551)   Charles Brandon   (1537?-1551)

These promising boys belonged to the Suffolk clan, and were heirs of its dukedom. Both were handsome and precocious, and their proficiency in learning impressed all who knew them. Their father, Charles, was a favorite of Henry VIII, from whom he received his dukedom and many other honors; he had been married to the King's sister Mary Tudor (died June 1533). His next wife, Katherine, was the boys' mother; as baroness Willoughby she was first the Duke's ward and then his child bride (September 1533). She was one of Queen Catherine Parr's aristocratic associates in the patronage of Protestant humanism, and later patronized the great Protestant preacher Hugh Latimer. When the boys' father died in 1545, she saw to it that they received a humanistic and strongly Protestant education. For a time they were educated with Prince Edward in the royal nursery school, and Ascham first met them at court when he came to visit his friend John Cheke, the Prince's teacher. In 1550 they went up to Cambridge, where they studied with the prominent Protestant theologian Martin Bucer. Ascham, who was known for his fine handwriting, gave them lessons in penmanship, and also taught Charles some Greek. Only a year after they came to the University they died on the same day of the "sweating sickness," a loss widely lamented by the foremost humanists of the day. Thomas Wilson, their tutor, edited a volume of commemorative verses upon their deaths, and gives an account of them in his *Arte of Rhetorique*.

Martin Bucer   (1491-1551)

Bucer was the leader of the Reformation in Strasbourg before he came to England in 1549 upon repeated invitations from Archbishop Cranmer. He was one of two major Reformers brought over from the Continent during the reign of Edward VI (Peter Martyr Vermigli went to Oxford). Bucer was born in Alsace and educated at Heidelberg; in 1523 he moved to Strasbourg, where the strength of his preaching and his intellectual dominance made that city one of the leading centers of Protestantism. Calvin learned much from him during a sojourn at Strasbourg. A senior figure among the Continental reformers, Bucer followed a path of reconciliation between competing Protestant theologies, especially between Lutheran and Zwinglian views of the Lord's Supper. Bucer's arrival in England constituted a strong boost to the cause of Protestantism at midcentury. Ascham first met him during the latter's residence with the Archbishop in London; in Cambridge their talk was often of Bucer's close friend Johann Sturm. It was Bucer who encouraged Ascham to write Sturm the April 1550 letter which marks the beginning of their lifelong epistolary friendship. Bucer assisted Cranmer in the revision of the Anglican Book of Common Prayer, and wrote his major theological work, *De regno Christi*, while he was teaching at Cambridge as the Regius Professor of Divinity. Bucer died less than two years after his arrival, on February 28, 1551. Sir John Cheke edited a memorial volume of epigrams and orations (London, 1551). The strength of Bucer's impact can be seen in the fact that upon her accession Queen Mary ordered his bones exhumed and his remains excommunicated with bell, book, and candle. When Ascham learned that Bucer had died, he wrote to Sturm that he had lost a dear, saintly friend from whom he had learned much concerning the right course of learning, religion, and the state.

William Cecil   (1520-1598)

Cecil entered St. John's College, Cambridge, at the age of 15; Ascham declares in *The Schoolmaster* that "in the fairest spring that ever was there of learning," Cecil was "one of the forwardest young plants in all that worthy college of St. John's" (III, 238). Ironically, he left Cambridge for Gray's Inn without taking a degree; nevertheless, his six years at Cambridge formed the basis of the strong, life-long friendships he would maintain with Ascham, Cheke, and all the leaders of the Cambridge circle. His loyalty to the University is also reflected in the fact that Queen Elizabeth named him its Chancellor in 1559, a position he occupied until his death almost 40 years later. "In the temperate and quiet shade of his wisdom," according to Ascham, *"religio* for sincerity, *literae* for order and advancement, *res publica* for happy and quiet government, have . . . specially reposed themselves" (III, 238). He entered government service during the reign of Edward VI, moving up under Protector Somerset, and then under the Duke of Northumberland into a variety of increasingly important posts, until in 1550 he became a Principal Secretary to the Privy Council. He was knighted the following year. During the reign of Mary he largely withdrew from government service, spending some of his time abroad in various capacities. Upon Elizabeth's accession he came into his own as one of the most capable and trustworthy men of his time. Once more he became Principal Secretary, an office he held until 1572, when he was appointed Lord Treasurer, the post he held until his death. A prudent, judicious, and cautious man, he was Elizabeth's most trusted and faithful counsellor. She created him Lord Burghley in 1571. His first wife was John Cheke's sister Mary, his second Mildred Cooke, one of four extraordinary daughters of Anthony Cooke. The husbands of all four of these learned women were friends, part of Ascham's Cambridge circle.

John Cheke   (1514-1557)

In *The Schoolmaster* Ascham terms Cheke "my dearest friend, and teacher of all the little poor learning I have" (III, 240); he was, to cite one more tribute, the "best master that ever I had or heard in learning" (III, 264). With respect to learning, Ascham agreed wholeheartedly with his dear friend: "he that will dwell in these few books only[:] first, in God's holy Bible, and then join with it Tully in Latin, Plato, Aristotle, Xenophon, Isocrates and Demosthenes in Greek, must needs prove an excellent man" (III, 228). Although he left no major literary work, he was honored in his day, especially by Protestants, as the chief glory of English learning. He entered St. John's College at 12 years of age. His talent quickly became apparent to all, and he was much admired as a student and as a tutor. In his quietly charismatic way he was an inspiration to Ascham and a whole circle of friends who went on to fame and distinction. Congregating around him, they heard him "read privately in his chamber all Homer, Sophocles, and Euripides, Herodotus, Thucydides, Xenophon, Isocrates, and Plato" (II, 67-68), and the alliances formed during this period at Cambridge shaped the subsequent careers of many of them. In 1540 King Henry VIII named Cheke the first Regius Professor of Greek at the University. His and Thomas Smith's efforts to reform the pronunciation of Greek brought them into conflict with the conservative Chancellor of the University, Stephen Gardiner, and inflamed the ardor of the Cambridge circle to advance the cause of Protestant learning. As the most renowned teacher in England Cheke was called to London in 1544 to tutor Prince Edward and others in Queen Catherine Parr's reorganized "royal nursery." During the reign of Edward VI Somerset and Northumberland were strong patrons of Cambridge men; Cheke, Ascham, Cecil, and Thomas Smith, for example, acquired roles in government. Cheke in particular received a number of royal favors, and rose to become one of the Principal Secretaries. In October 1551 he and his friend Cecil were knighted. His sister Mary was Cecil's first wife. When Edward died,

Cheke entangled himself in Northumberland's scheme to enthrone Jane Grey, and was imprisoned for a year in the Tower. Upon his release he sought refuge in Strasbourg and other centers of English exiles. In May 1556 he was lured to Brussels, kidnapped, and hauled to London, where he publicly recanted. Shamed and humiliated by this forced betrayal of his friends and the reformed religion, he died within a year.

Mary Clarke   (d. 1572)

Mary was one of five children of William and Margaret More Roper, and a granddaughter of Sir Thomas More. In his life of More, Nicholas Harpsfield describes her as "very well experted in the latine and greeke tonges; she hath very hansomely and learnedly translated out of the greeke into the englishe all the ecclesiaticall storye of Eusebius," although, he continued, "she suppresseth it, and keepeth it from the print." She also translated her grandfather's *Treatise on the Passion* from the Latin, a translation "so elegantly and eloquently penned," according to Harpsfield, "that a man would thinke it were originally written in the saide englishe tonge." She served as a lady in waiting to Queen Mary. Her first husband was Stephen Clarke, whom she outlived. She then married James Bassett, a gentleman of the chamber to Queen Mary, and for many years a servant of Bishop Stephen Gardiner. Interestingly, although she was a member of a Catholic recusant family, Margaret Roper invited Ascham around 1544 to leave Cambridge and teach Mary and her brothers. Ascham declined, but about ten years later he offered to assist her studies while she was at Mary's court.

Anthony Cooke   (1504-1576)

Cooke was a man of much learning in Latin, Greek, poetry, history, and mathematics; he was probably educated privately. Like Cheke and later Ascham he was during the late 1540s an instructor in Queen Catherine Parr's royal nursery school. He was the father of a notable family of daughters, at least four of whom were women of intellectual distinction, learned in Greek and Latin. Each of the four married leading servants of the Queen: Mildred was the second wife of William Cecil; Anne married Nicolas Bacon, Elizabeth's first Lord Keeper; Elizabeth married Sir Thomas Hoby, and Catherine married Henry Killigrew. All four sons-in-law were Cambridge men, and through these marriages Cooke was well-connected to Cecil and his network of friends. He was knighted at the beginning of Edward's reign. With other Protestant friends such as John Cheke and Richard Morison he sought refuge in Strasbourg during Mary's reign. There he got to know Ascham's friend Sturm, with whom he corresponded after his return to England at the outset of Elizabeth's reign.

Thomas Cranmer   (1489-1556)

Cranmer was educated at Cambridge; he received his BA in 1511, his MA in 1514, and a doctorate of theology in 1526. From about 1520 onwards he was a leading member of the "Little Germany" group who gathered at the White Horse tavern to discuss Lutheranism and the new learning. He was drawn, somewhat reluctantly, into government service during the reign of Henry VIII when the King found support in Cranmer's viewpoint on the "great matter" of the divorce from Queen Katherine. He served the King on various embassies, and was recalled to England and named Archbishop of Canterbury in 1533. The King and his Chancellor Cromwell found Cranmer a dependable and loyal man, and turned to him to advance the King's cause with favorable declarations concerning his marriages, and to guide the English church into the Anglican mode. In 1537 he stood godfather to Prince Edward, and during the last days of Henry's reign he was named in the king's will to serve on the Council appointed to govern during Edward VI's minority. During Edward's reign Cranmer played a leading role in transforming the English church along Protestant lines, particularly in the preparation of Edward's first Book of Common Prayer (1549) as well as the second, somewhat more Protestant one (1552). In Queen Mary's reign he was arrested, imprisoned, and convicted of treason and heresy; like Nicholas Ridley and Hugh Latimer he was burned at the stake in Oxford, his strength and courage in death serving as a powerful inspiration to the cause of Protestantism in England.

Anthony Denny   (1501-1549)

Like his father, a chief baron of the Exchequer, Denny was a trusted associate of Henry VIII. As a boy he was a pupil of William Lily, the noted master of St. Paul's School. There is an unbroken tradition that he attended Cambridge, but recent research has called it into question. In any case he developed close ties with Ascham's Cambridge circle; he was also the leader in protecting St. John's interests in its property at Sedbergh, Yorkshire. Strongly Protestant, and noted for his interest in classical learning, Denny was closely associated with the Parr family and with Cheke in the education of Prince Edward and others in the "royal nursery school." At court he was one of the King's favorites, first serving at the King's remembrancer and groom of the stole. He was knighted at Boulogne in 1544. During much of the last year of Henry's life he superintended the use of the manual stamp by which the King's signature could be affixed to documents. As chief gentleman of the Privy Chamber, he also controlled access to the King during his last months, and attended at the deathbed of King Henry. Denny was also a member of the Privy Council, an executor of Henry VIII's will, and a member of the council appointed to govern during the minority of Edward VI. He was married to Joan Champernowne, a lady of great beauty and accomplishments. Lady Denny was sister to Kate Astley, governess to Princess Elizabeth. Thus when the scandal of Thomas Seymour's unseemly familiarity with the Princess broke, she was packed off to Denny's country house in Cheshunt.

John Dudley   (1502?-1553)

Son of Edmund Dudley, Henry VII's minister, John Dudley was brought to court by Henry VIII. He served the King ably as a soldier, and was enriched by the spoils of the monasteries. He was named Viscount Lisle in 1542, appointed to the Privy Council in 1543, created Earl of Warwick in 1547, and named as one of Henry's executors. During Edward's reign (October 1549) he engineered a coup d'etat against the Lord Protector Somerset and established himself as ruler of England. With motives that were heavily political, he became a vigorous supporter of the Reformation and a patron of the New Learning. He was created Duke of Northumberland in 1551. When he foresaw the death of King Edward, he sought to block Mary's accession to the throne by arranging the marriage of his weak son Guildford to Jane Grey; upon Edward's death (July 1553) he proclaimed his daughter-in-law the new monarch. The plot failed miserably, and Northumberland himself fell and was executed.

Valentine Erythraeus   (1521-1576)

Along with Michael Toxites and John Sleidan, Erythraeus was one of Sturm's learned humanist associates at Strasbourg. He began as a pupil of Sturm in Strasbourg, and then went to Wittenberg, where he came under the influence of Luther and Melanchthon. He returned to Strasbourg to become Professor of Rhetoric, a position he held for 29 years. A philologist and schoolteacher, he wrote books on grammar, elocution, and letter-writing. He also edited some of the work of Sturm. A year before his unexpected death, he accepted an appointment as rector of the newly established gymnasium at Nürnberg.

Barnaby Fitzpatrick   (1535?-1581)

As a young boy Fitzpatrick was sent to court as a pledge of his Irish father's loyalty to Henry VIII. There he became a favorite school friend of Prince Edward during their years together in Queen Catherine Parr's royal nursery school. Thomas Fuller's *Church-History of Britain* (1655) is the authority for the legend that Fitzpatrick was Edward's "proxy of correction," but this "whipping-boy story" is discounted by more reliable sources. Both boys were pupils of John Cheke, who introduced Ascham to them during his visits to London. When Edward succeeded to the throne, Fitzpatrick served in the King's privy chamber, and when he was abroad completing his education in the French court, the boy King wrote numerous affectionate letters to his friend. Fitzpatrick served many years in Ireland. For his loyalty he was knighted in 1566 by Philip Sidney's father.

Stephen Gardiner   (c 1497-1555)

Gardiner was a very capable Cambridge man, more conservative in both religion and learning than Ascham and his circle of Cambridge friends, but one to whom Ascham, surprisingly, kept open the lines of access. Gardiner was educated at Trinity Hall, Cambridge, graduating as a doctor of civil and canon law in 1521 and 1522 respectively, after which he joined the faculties in these fields. Through the offices of the Duke of Norfolk, he attracted the attention of Cardinal Wolsey in 1523. He rose rapidly in government service, serving on numerous embassies to France and the papal court. In 1529 he became the King's principal secretary. He was rewarded handsomely for his activities in the divorce proceedings of Henry VIII, and was consecrated Bishop of Winchester in 1531. His book *De vera obedientia* (1535) was a particularly competent defense of the Royal Supremacy. After the fall of his rival Thomas Cromwell in 1540, Gardiner became the most influential man at court, as well as the Chancellor of Cambridge University. His vigorous opposition to Protestantism and to the reformed pronunciation of Greek championed by Thomas Smith and John Cheke brought him into direct clash with some of Ascham's most cherished ideals. Nevertheless, Ascham ironically found in Gardiner a patron who advanced his cause in the presentation of *Toxophilus* (1545), to the King at Greenwich, a favor which neither Ascham nor Gardiner ever forgot. Gardiner was imprisoned during much of Edward VI's reign, and was deprived of his chancellorship of Cambridge, his mastership of Trinity Hall, and his bishopric of Winchester. All of these offices were restored to him upon Mary's accession, however, and he became, in addition, her Lord Chancellor. Although he led Mary's efforts to return the Church of England to the Bishop of Rome, Ascham carefully cultivated Gardiner during this period, and once again turned successfully to him for patronage.

Jane Grey   (1537-1554)

Lady Jane Grey was the daughter of Henry Grey, Marquis of Dorset (later Duke of Suffolk), and Frances, the daughter of Mary Tudor and granddaughter of Henry VII. Her lineage made her vulnerable to becoming a pawn in political struggles. She was brought up in the household of Catherine Parr, the sixth wife of Henry VIII; by the age of seven she was being tutored in Latin, Greek, and modern languages. Under the Parrs' influence she also was also decidedly Protestant in religion. After the death of Henry VIII, the Dowager Queen Catherine married into the Seymour family, and Edward Seymour, Duke of Somerset and King Edward's Lord Protector, sought to arrange a marriage of Jane to her cousin the King. When that failed and Thomas, the Protector's brother, was executed for treason in 1549, Jane was sent back to live with her parents, though by then she was betrothed to the Protector's son Edward. Despite this betrothal, the new power behind the boy King, John Dudley, Duke of Northumberland, married her off to his youngest son Guildford when he foresaw the King's death. This plan to subvert the Tudor succession by making her the Queen of England failed miserably; a "nine-days' queen" and a victim of her father-in-law's scheme, Jane was imprisoned and executed the following year at the age of 16. After her death she quickly became a symbol of Protestant heroism and learning. In *The Schoolmaster* Ascham gives a memorable account of coming upon this "noble and worthy lady" as she was reading Plato's *Phaedo* in Greek "with as much delight as some gentleman would read a merry tale in Bocase." The others in the household were hunting in the park, but she asserted, Ascham reports, that "all their sport in the Park is but a shadow to that pleasure that I find in Plato" (III, 117-19).

William Grindal   (d. 1548)

Grindal was another St. John's man, strongly Protestant like his friends Ascham and Cheke. Ascham was Grindal's tutor, and Grindal his favorite pupil. For nearly seven years they studied together, and shared the same room. Ascham ranks him among the best of his circle in Greek scholarship as well as in character (see the tribute in Letter 42). Grindal was admitted a fellow of St. John's in March 1543. Soon after Cheke went to court in July 1544, he secured Grindal's appointment as tutor to Princess Elizabeth. The presence of his two dear friends at court gave Ascham an excuse to visit London, where he met and then corresponded with the Princess herself, as well as such associates as Lady Jane Grey, Anne Parr, and Katherine Astley. When Grindal died of the plague in January 1548, Ascham succeeded him as Elizabeth's tutor.

Walter Haddon   (1516-1571)

In *The Schoolmaster* Ascham terms Haddon one of his "two dearest friends," and alludes to him as "one of the best scholars in deed of all our time" (III, 203; 81). He was a graduate of Eton and of King's College, Cambridge, receiving a doctorate of law in 1549. In 1551 he succeeded his friend Thomas Smith as the Regius Professor of Civil Law at Cambridge. Other academic posts included Vice-Chancellor of Cambridge, Master of Trinity Hall, and President of Magdalen College, Oxford. He also held numerous posts in the governments of Queens Mary and Elizabeth. As Master of Requests, for example, he was present in 1563 at William Cecil's famous dinner party in Windsor Castle, which is memorialized in the Introduction to *The Schoolmaster*. A prominent member of Ascham's Cambridge circle, he was reputed second to none in the Elizabethan period as eloquent Latinist, though he did not know Greek. A collection of his orations, epistles, and poems published four years before his death by Thomas Hatcher was popular in its day. He served the cause of the English Reformation, particularly in a protracted epistolary controversy with Jeronimo Osorio da Fonseca, the learned Portuguese Bishop.

Robert Holgate   (1481?-1555)

Holgate was generally a reformist clergyman, but a rather cautious and bureaucratic one. The details of his education are not known, although he may have studied at Cambridge University. Thomas Cromwell and Thomas Cranmer arranged to have him appointed as Bishop of Llandaff in 1537. In the following year he was named President of the Council of the North, a York-based, secular position of importance in view of Cromwell's efforts to advance the King's interests in the North on the heels of the uprising known as The Pilgrimage of Grace. In 1545 he was ordained as Archbishop of York, and through a series of exchanges with the King having to do with control of properties and revenues arising out of the dissolution of the monasteries, he emerged as "the wealthiest prelate in England," to quote the *DNB*. During the reign of Edward he lost his Presidency of the Council over a dispute with John Dudley, afterwards Duke of Northumberland. Under Mary he was also deprived of his Archbishopric for being married; his goods too were confiscated, and he was imprisoned in the Tower. He was released in 1555, but died in the same year.

William Ireland   (d. 1571)

Ireland, along with Edward Raven, with whom Ascham often mentions him, was one of Ascham's younger pupils. He and Raven seem to have replaced William Grindal as the objects of Ascham's special affection after Grindal's death in January 1548. He received his BA in 1544, and was admitted as a fellow of St. John's in 1547. The following year he commenced MA. He went abroad during the reign of Mary, and when he returned from exile upon the accession of Elizabeth, he served as a rector in country parishes.

Edward Lee   (1482?-1544)

Lee is now best known for his bitter controversies with Erasmus, and as the prelate against whom Thomas More directed a memorable defense of humanism. Well-born and ambitious, he graduated BA from Oxford and MA from Cambridge; twelve years later he matriculated in 1516 at Louvain because he wanted to learn Greek. While he was still young and inexpert in Greek, Lee began to offer Erasmus notes and suggestions for revision of his *Novum instrumentum*. When Erasmus failed to accept them, the relationship grew hostile, eventually exposing Lee to the ridicule of the humanist community. Petty differences and personal animosities generated a whole series of invectives, especially from 1518 to 1520. Lee went on, however, to ecclesiastical power and diplomatic influence. He served Henry VIII as ambassador and as royal almoner. In 1531 he became Archbishop of York, in which capacity he became a minor patron of Ascham.

Hubert Thomas Leodius   (c 1495-c 1555)

Hubert Thomas adopted his last appellation as a contraction of *Leodensis*, "of Liège," the city of his birth. He journeyed to Heidelberg to take up university studies, and there came to the attention of Frederick II, Elector Palatine of the Rhine, whom he served as secretary and councillor until his death. His biography of the Count, in 14 books, was his chief publication, but he also had an antiquarian interest in the city of Heidelberg, as well as other parts of Germany. He travelled widely and was something of a diplomat, meeting many of the great European princes of his day.

Richard Morison   (d. 1556)

Morison was one of the more colorful and engaging personalities of his time. His early years are obscure. He received his BA in 1528 from Wolsey's Cardinal College, Oxford, but afterwards he also spent some time in Cambridge. Around 1532 he went to Italy to study Greek, and for a time lived in Reginald Pole's household in Venice. In 1535 or 1536 Henry's new Chancellor Thomas Cromwell recruited Morison for government service. He soon proved an exuberant propagandist, with a colorful style. After Cromwell's fall, he held a variety of positions in the governments of both Henry VIII and Edward VI. His strong Protestantism and his interest in learning formed the basis of his ties to such prominent court Cantabrigians as Smith, Cheke, and particularly Cecil, of whom he was a close friend. By June 1550 he had been knighted. With Ascham as his secretary, he served from 1550 to 1553 as King Edward's ambassador to the court of Emperor Charles V. The liveliness and wit of his letters and dispatches won him the sobriquet "merry Morison." He joined other English exiles in Strasbourg during Mary's reign and died there.

Jeronimo Osorio   (1506-1580)

As Bishop of Silva in Portugal, Osorio was noted for his learning, his rhetorical skill, and his defense of Catholicism. He was educated at Salamanca, Paris, and Rome, and became an eminent Ciceronian, with a reputation throughout Europe as an elegant stylist. One measure of his stature is Francis Bacon's famous censure of him in *The Advancement of Learning*; his "flowing and watery vein," no less than Ascham's own Ciceronianism, Bacon termed a "distemper of learning" in which men idly pursue "words more than matter." Osorio's epistle to Queen Elizabeth (1563) urging her return to the true Catholic religion sparked a protracted epistolary controversy with Ascham's friend Walter Haddon. In its wake Ascham apparently became critical of the Ciceronian he once admired, acknowledging in *The Schoolmaster* that at one time "there hath passed privately betwixt him and me, sure tokens of much good will and friendly opinion" (i.e., an exchange of letters: see II.xxix and xxxi), but arguing as well that Osorio "overreached" himself stylistically in his "over-rank railing against poor Luther, and the truth of God's doctrine" (III, 185, 204).

William Paget   (c 1505-1563)

An able government servant who held high office under Henry VIII, Edward VI, and Mary, Paget was cautious and flexible in religion; in politics he was no less flexible and opportunistic in shifting with the tide of power. In the title of S. R. Gammon's modern biography, he was "statesman and schemer." He was educated at St. Paul's School, London, and Trinity Hall, Cambridge, where he came to the attention of the Master, Stephen Gardiner. He entered the service of Henry VIII as a protege of Gardiner, advancing through a number of offices, including clerkship of the Privy Council, until he became one of the two Principal Secretaries in 1543. He was knighted the following year. During King Henry's last years Paget was one of his closest and most trusted advisers. When young Edward VI was king, he had various roles in Somerset's Protectorate, and was raised to the peerage in 1549 as Baron Paget of Beaudesert. With the fall of Somerset he too was arrested and imprisoned in the Tower; conflicts with Northumberland resulted in his being degraded from the Order of the Garter, stripped of his offices, and assessed a huge fine. Only in 1553 was he readmitted to the Council and his last fines forgiven. When Edward died, he quickly turned from Lady Jane Grey, the nine-days' Queen, to support Mary, and he became one of her chief councillors, promoting her marriage to Philip of

Spain. He was not included within the government organized by Elizabeth upon her succession in 1558.

Anne Parr   (1514?-1551)

Like her brother William, the future Earl of Essex and Marquis of Northampton, and her sister Catherine, who became Henry VIII's last Queen, Anne was well educated by her widowed mother. She was an apt pupil with a strong love of learning. As a young girl she was placed in the Queen's household; she served for many years as one of the "waiting gentlewomen." Henry named her one of the "King's wards." In 1537 she assisted at Prince Edward's christening. She was married to Sir William Herbert, whose fortunes rose dramatically when Henry VIII married Catherine in 1543. Herbert was created Earl of Pembroke by King Edward VI.

Catherine Parr   (1512-1548)

Catherine was a woman of learning and Protestant piety. She was the leader of a circle of aristocratic women who patronized the kind of humanism dear to Ascham and his circle, and supported the cause of religious reform during the last years of Henry VIII. Daughter of Sir Thomas Parr, she was a member of a distinguished family. Her widowed mother designed an ambitious program of education for Catherine, her brother William, the future Earl of Essex and Marquis of Northampton, and her sister Anne, who would serve in Queen Jane Seymour's court and become wife of William Herbert, Earl of Pembroke. In July 1543 Catherine became the sixth wife of Henry VIII (she herself had twice been widowed), and by December of that year she had brought all three of Henry's children together in the same household. With her ability to promote harmony and domesticity and learning she reorganized the royal nursery, bringing the best scholars of Cambridge to court to tutor the two younger royal children and others from influential and well-connected noble families. After the death of Henry VIII she married Thomas Seymour, the younger brother of the Lord Protector. The Princess Elizabeth was in her charge. She was the author of various devotional works, including *The Lamentacion of a Sinner* (1547), for which William Cecil wrote the preface.

William Parr   (1513-1571)

A brother of Catherine, who became the sixth wife of Henry VIII in 1543, William Parr in part derived his prominence and his titles of Earl of Essex and Marquis of Northampton from his relationship to the Queen. However, his birth and talent were themselves contributory to his success. He was the son of Sir Thomas Parr of Kendal, a prominent courtier early in the reign of Henry VIII. After Thomas' death, his wife devoted her income and her energies to an ambitious program of education for William and his sisters Catherine and Anne. William also studied at Cambridge for a time, and was on friendly terms with many of the members of Ascham's Cambridge circle. Parr was knighted in 1537. In March 1543 he was named a member of the Privy Council. Five months after his sister married the King, he was named the Earl of Essex. When Henry VIII died, Parr became a prominent supporter of Protector Somerset. He was soon created Marquis of Northampton. Again he was named to the Privy Council, and was active in a variety of embassies and deputations during the reign of Edward VI. For his support of the succession of Lady Jane Grey, Queen Mary had him committed to the Tower, and he was stripped of his titles and offices. Although he was pardoned, his fortunes did not revive, and he was not restored to his rank and offices until the accession of Queen Elizabeth, in whose reign he was also named for the third time to the Privy Council. William Cecil, Elizabeth's chief minister, termed Parr one of his "best pillars." Like his sister Catherine, William Parr was Protestant, and a patron of learning.

William Petre   (c 1505-1572)

Petre accomplished the remarkable feat of serving four successive monarchs as secretary. Neither partisan in religion nor strongly ideological in politics, he was a steady, undemonstrative minister who managed never to become entangled in serious political trouble. He was an Oxford man, earning a doctorate in civil law, perhaps in 1533. It was at Oxford that he came to the attention of Thomas Cromwell, though perhaps he also had the support of the Boleyn family. As a clerk, and then master in Chancery, he was active in the Cromwell's program for the dissolution of the monasteries. In 1544 he was named of the two Principal Secretaries, joining Sir William Paget. At the same time he was sworn to the Privy Council, and knighted. He continued in the post of Secretary of State under Edward VI, and survived the fall of Somerset relatively unscathed. Queen Mary also continued him as a secretary and member of her Council, although near the end of her reign he resigned for unknown reasons. With the accession of Elizabeth he was back in the government, working closely with William Cecil, and serving as acting secretary in his absence. He was in attendance at Cecil's memorable dinner party at Windsor in 1563 when Ascham got the idea for his *Schoolmaster*. In the preface Ascham notes coolly that Petre was "somewhat severe of nature," and records his conservative opinion that "the rod only was the sword, that must keep the school in obedience, and the scholar in good order" (III, 79).

Reginald Pole   (1500-1558)

In his youth Pole enjoyed the generous support of King Henry VIII, his cousin, who sponsored him for six years of humanistic studies at Padua after he had received his BA at Oxford in 1515 under the tutelage of William Latimer. At Padua Pole became close friends with some of Europe's leading humanists. Upon his return to England he resisted being drawn into the debates over the King's "great matter," for he found himself completely unable to support the divorce and the reconstitution of the church. To escape Henry's hostility he returned in 1532 to Padua, where a large number of students and scholars found a welcome in his household, including Italian churchmen of note. His treatise *On the Unity of the Church* appeared in 1536; it was a vigorous rejection of the divorce, and a defense of the Catholic faith. In the same year he was named a Cardinal of the church; his connections with prominent churchmen were such that in 1549 he narrowly missed election to the papacy. He was active in the Council of Trent. With the accession of Mary the way was cleared for him to return to England as papal legate. In March 1556 he was consecrated Archbishop of Canterbury. Two years later he fell ill, and he died on the same day as his Queen.

Edward Raven   (d. 1558)

Raven, along with William Ireland, with whom Ascham often mentions him, was one of Ascham's younger pupils. He and Ireland seem to have replaced William Grindal as the objects of Ascham's special affection after Grindal's death in January 1548. Raven received his BA in 1546, and was admitted fellow of St. John's on the same day as Ireland in 1547. He commenced MA in 1549, and was elected a senior fellow in 1551. Unlike Ireland, he apparently did not go abroad during Mary's reign, but acceded to Catholicism. He died shortly before Elizabeth came to the throne.

John Redman   (1499-1551)

In *The Schoolmaster* Ascham names Cheke and Redman as "two gentlemen of worthy memory" whose "example of excellency in learning, of godliness in living, of diligence in studying, of counsel in exhorting, of good order in all things, did breed up so many learned men in that one college of St. John's at one time, as I believe the whole university of Louvain in many years was never able to afford" (III, 142). See also Ascham's extended tribute in Letter 43, where he explains that Redman spent some time at Oxford before studying languages and divinity at Paris. When he returned to England about 1520, Redman was joined to St. John's, where he had a special influence on Ascham, Smith, and Cheke, all about 15 years his junior. In 1537 he was awarded a doctorate in divinity, his fourth degree from Cambridge, and in the following year he was appointed Lady Margaret Professor of Divinity. In his lectures he supported Smith's and Cheke's reforms in the pronunciation of Greek. He was the first of the distinguished Masters of Trinity College to come from St. John's (III, 235). He was known for his skill in divinity, and although he differed slightly from Protestants of Ascham's stripe on the question of justification by faith alone, he worked with Cranmer and others in articulating a Protestant theology. He was awarded numerous preferments within the church, and served on several ecclesiastical commissions during the reigns of Henry VIII and Edward VI. He was buried in Westminster Abbey.

John Seton　　　(1498-1567)

Another St. John's man, Seton was a friend of Ascham, but not a member of his circle, for Seton was a member of the recusant tradition of humanism stemming from St. John Fisher, who as the executor of the affairs of the Lady Margaret was instrumental in the founding of the College. In fact, Seton was chaplain to Fisher, and attended him in the Tower as he faced martyrdom for refusing to accede to Henry's reforms. In 1554 the University also turned to Seton to champion the Catholic cause, sending him to Oxford to dispute with Cranmer, Ridley, and Latimer, who would become martyrs to the Protestant cause. He also served as chaplain to Bishop Stephen Gardiner, and later in life was restricted and imprisoned for being "settled in papistry." His most important contribution to learning was a work on logic, Dialectica (1545), which became a standard treatise on the subject in England.

Edward Seymour　　　(1500?-1552)

First Earl of Hertford and first Duke of Somerset, Seymour profited extraordinarily from being brother to Henry's Queen Jane Seymour and uncle to King Edward VI. As a young boy he was introduced at court by his father, who had been knighted by Henry VII. He served first as a page, and later entered Cardinal Wolsey's service. In 1523 he was knighted for valor in war in France. When Henry fell in love with Seymour's sister Jane, the family fortunes rose spectacularly: after the King married Jane in 1536, he was created Viscount Beauchamp; after she gave birth to Prince Edward, he was made Earl of Hertford. In the same year he was sworn to the Privy Council. Lucrative grants of land and offices also came his way, including the positions of Lord Admiral and then Lord Chamberlain. During the last years of Henry VIII he was very active in diplomatic and military service, and became a leader of the party of Reform. When Henry died in January 1547, Seymour was well-situated to take control. As Lord Protector of the realm, the traditional assignment of the King's eldest uncle during a minority, he acted as king in all but name. Soon he was created Duke of Somerset. In collaboration with Archbishop Cranmer he led efforts to reform church doctrine and ritual, to reduce the church's authority over freedom of conscience, and to enlarge the range of religious freedoms to read, preach, and publish. As a result of the unrest generated by his obvious ambition and his inability to implement his policies smoothly, he was overthrown in October 1549, and imprisoned in the Tower. Two of his secretaries, Thomas Smith and William Cecil, Ascham's friends from Cambridge, went to the Tower with their patron. After a few months he made up with his rival and the leader of the revolution, John Dudley, Earl of Warwick and later Duke of Northumberland. Although he was pardoned and reinstated on the Council, new intrigues brought about his ultimate downfall in October 1551. His execution on trumped-up charges early in 1552 touched many, and soon gave rise to his title in legend as "the good Duke."

John Sleidan (Jean Phillipson or Philippson)   (c. 1506-1556)

Sleidan was one of Sturm's learned humanist associates in Strasbourg, and one of the leading figures of the German Reformation. In his day he was highly regarded as an historian. He was born in Sleidan, Luxembourg, and his friendship with Sturm dates back to their student days in Paris. With Sturm's encouragement he settled in Strasbourg in 1544, and came under the influence of the city's great reformer Martin Bucer. During the Schmalkaldic War, he spent some time in England under the patronage of King Edward VI, but he returned to Strasbourg, where he was appointed Professor in 1554. He was especially noted for his meticulous history of the Reformation, entitled *Commentaries on the Religion and Political History of Charles V* (1555). As the official historian of the Schmalkaldic League, he had access to important sources and documents, and despite his Protestant faith he attempted to maintain an objective attitude. During Ascham's only visit to Strasbourg (September 1552) he and Ambassador Morison were welcomed at Sleidan's home.

Thomas Smith   (1513-1577)

Along with John Cheke, Smith was one of the acknowledged luminaries of Cambridge around midcentury, quickly rising to fame and distinction. In *The Schoolmaster* Ascham terms him and John Cheke the "two worthy stars" of Cambridge, who brought Aristotle, Plato, Cicero, and Demosthenes "to flourish as notable in Cambridge as ever they did in Greece and in Italy" (III, 237). Smith was admitted to Queens' College in 1526 at twelve years of age, a "beggarly scholar," son of a herdsman. In 1530 he received his BA, and was elected fellow of Queens'. Two or three years later he proceeded MA. In 1538 he became Public Orator for the University; in 1540 he was appointed Regius Professor of Civil Law; in 1543 or 1544 he was elected Vice-Chancellor of the University. With Cheke he introduced a reformed pronunciation of Greek, beginning in 1535. Soon they were engaged in learned debate with the older, conservative champion of the status quo, Stephen Gardiner. The issue served to focus their role as leaders of humanistic reform, and defined a cause around which promising Cambridge scholars such as Ascham rallied. Shortly after the death of Henry VIII Smith was summoned to London to become Protector Somerset's personal secretary. He rose rapidly, quickly accumulating an impressive list of offices and honors: Master of Requests, one of the two clerks of the Privy Council, Provost of Eton, and Dean of Carlisle. In April 1548 he became one of the two Principal Secretaries and member of the Privy Council. A year later he was knighted. His career turned, however, with the 1549 fall of his patron Somerset. One product of his enforced retirement was his classic account of the English commonwealth, *De republica Anglorum* (1565). In Elizabeth's reign he was again called to serve in several foreign embassies, and in 1570 he regained his position of Principal Secretary. He was also made Chancellor of the Order of the Garter. The University was the site of his greatest fame and distinction, however, and he was not particularly successful at court. Although he achieved high office there, he never acquired real power and influence within government service.

Johann (Jean) Sturm   (1507-1589)

Sturm was born in Luxembourg and educated in Liège, Louvain, and Paris, but he settled in Strasbourg, where he became that city's leader of Protestant humanism. In 1537 he was called there to teach rhetoric, and in the following year he founded his Gymnasium, which combined the city's Latin schools and theological classes into one unit. Sturm became its charismatic first rector, a post he held for 44 years. The school created a new focus of intellectual life in the city; it was dominated by classical humanists whose pedagogical reforms incorporated Erasmian ideals of learned piety. His curriculum sought to conjoin true religion and elegant Latin; "it is our position," he writes in *De literarum ludis recte aperiendis* (Strasbourg, 1538), "that the end of learning is a wise and eloquent piety" (104). He was a prolific author of a very wide range of work: editions of Classical authors, commentaries on Greek and Latin orators and rhetoricians, manuals on education and pedagogy, treatises on rhetoric and dialectic, editions of the works of contemporary educators, and books on the controversy between Lutherans and Catholics. The complete list of his publications comes to over 150 items. He was keenly interested in affairs of state and of religion; during his years in Strasbourg he worked constantly to advance the Protestant cause. His work and his influence were felt throughout Europe, particularly amongst the English, with whom he developed a variety of connections.

Most importantly, he was, in Ascham's words, "the dearest friend I have out of England" (III, 216). His influence on Ascham's views of rhetoric, imitation, and pedagogy is second to none, not even to Cheke. Sturm also corresponded with Cecil, Queen Elizabeth, and numerous others in positions of authority and influence within England. He was well known to the community of English exiles in Strasbourg during Mary's reign (e.g., Anthony Cooke, Richard Morison, John Cheke, Edmund Grindal).

Thomas Wriothesley   (1505-1550)

Within the reign of Henry VIII Wriothesley rose from humble beginnings to high and profitable office, though he never became one of the stronger or more eminent figures within the government. He studied at Cambridge, but did not take a degree, instead seeking employment at court. Thomas Cromwell employed him in a variety of capacities, including foreign embassies concerning the King's marriages. He profited handsomely from the spoils of the monasteries, and in 1540 he became one of the Principal Secretaries. He was knighted the same year. Early in 1544 he was created Baron Wriothesley, and a few months later he was named Lord Chancellor of England. In the later years of Henry's reign he was part of the conservative party at court. With Gardiner and Richard Riche, for example, he became so involved in the case of the irrepressible Protestant Anne Askew that he personally administered the torture when the horrified lieutenant flinched and could do no more. Wriothesley was one of the executors of Henry's will, and was named a member of the council to govern during Edward's minority. Within a few weeks of Edward's accession he was created Earl of Southampton. Scarcely a month later, however, he fell, forced by Protector Somerset to resign. His antipathy toward Somerset led him to join Warwick's plot against the Protector in 1549, but he soon discovered that he was merely being used; defeated, he found himself outside the sphere of authority and influence, and died soon thereafter.